"Liana's recipes make it easier to break away from those on-the-go fast 'foods' that damage our health. _10-Minute Recipes_ proves how simple it is to make something that tastes good as well as nourishes the body in a very short amount of time. Avoiding refined sugars is achievable with the raw chocolate and cookie recipes. I love eating desserts when I know what's actually in it—a key to staying on a healthy track."

— **Vani Hari,** activist and _New York Times_ best-selling author of _The Food Babe Way_

"For those who find cookbooks and eating healthy intimidating and confusing, here is your solution! In _10-Minute Recipes_, Liana shares how upgrading your diet (and life!) can be fun, easy, and oh so delicious!"

— **Jessica Ortner,** _New York Times_ best-selling author of _The Tapping Solution for Weight Loss & Body Confidence_

"If you want to nourish your body while de-fogging your brain, Liana's natural, easy, and _fast_ recipes will show you the way."

— **Dr. Mike Dow,** _New York Times_ best-selling author of _The Brain Fog Fix_

"This is a helpful book for busy people who want to live an enjoyable, pain-free life. Liana's practical tips and easy recipes make it possible, allowing you to start with just 10 minutes each day."

— **Mark Hyman, M.D.,** author of the #1 _New York Times_ bestseller _The Blood Sugar Solution 10-Day Detox Diet_

"As a personal trainer and fitness coach, I have seen people transform their lives simply by adjusting their diets and making the choice to live a healthier and cleaner lifestyle. Liana's approach to healing the body with earth's foods is remarkable and aligned with my belief. I believe food can be the cause of dis-ease and the cure as well."

— **Donovan Green,** Dr. Oz's personal trainer and health counselor

"The Earth Diet has been really impactful in my life, and I've had such dramatic changes. . . .I've never felt more energized and happier; and the truth is I feel smarter when I sit down to write and study. I feel unclogged, and it's flowing smoothly, and even my kids have noticed a difference."

— **Dr. Wayne W. Dyer,** _New York Times_ best-selling author of _I Can See Clearly Now_

10-MINUTE RECIPES

10-MINUTE RECIPES

FAST FOOD, CLEAN INGREDIENTS, NATURAL HEALTH

LIANA WERNER-GRAY

HAY HOUSE

HAY HOUSE, INC.

CARLSBAD, CALIFORNIA • NEW YORK CITY
LONDON • SYDNEY • JOHANNESBURG
VANCOUVER • NEW DELHI

Published and distributed in the United States by: Hay House, Inc.: www.hayhouse.com • **Published and distributed in Australia by:** Hay House Australia Pty. Ltd.: www.hayhouse.com.au • **Published and distributed in the United Kingdom by:** Hay House UK, Ltd.: www.hayhouse.co.uk • **Published and distributed in the Republic of South Africa by:** Hay House SA (Pty), Ltd.: www.hayhouse.co.za • **Distributed in Canada by:** Raincoast Books: www.raincoast.com • **Published in India by:** Hay House Publishers India: www.hayhouse.co.in

Project editor: Nicolette Salamanca Young
Cover design: Karla Baker • *Interior design:* Bryn Starr Best
Interior photos/illustrations used under license from Shutterstock.com except for: pg. 47, 182, 202 © Noah Loin at Rock'N Raw Photos; pg. 155, 196, 197 © Caleb and Jaron Lopez; pg. ii, iii, xv, 3, 42, 106, 152, 184, 198, 199, 204, 213, 220 © RoxxeIreland

Library of Congress Cataloging-in-Publication Data

Names: Werner-Gray, Liana, 1987- author.
Title: 10-minute recipes : fast food, clean ingredients, natural health / Liana Werner-Gray.
Other titles: Ten minute recipes
Description: 1st edition. | Carlsbad, California : Hay House, Inc., 2016. | Includes bibliographical references.
Identifiers: LCCN 2016019309 | ISBN 9781401949709 (paperback)
Subjects: LCSH: Natural foods--Therapeutic use. | Nutrition. | Quick and easy cooking. | Cooking (Natural foods) | Self-care, Health. | BISAC: HEALTH & FITNESS / Diets. | HEALTH & FITNESS / Healthy Living. | COOKING / Health & Healing / General. | LCGFT: Cookbooks.
Classification: LCC RM237.55 .W46 2016 | DDC 641.5/637--dc23 LC record available at https://lccn.loc.gov/2016019309

ISBN: 978-1-4019-4970-9

10 9 8 7 6 5 4 3 2 1

1st edition, October 2016

Printed in the United States of America

This book is for every person who wants to enjoy a simple, fulfilling, and **healthy life.** If you ever thought eating delicious, healthy foods was too time-consuming and complicated, this **is for you.**

CONTENTS

PART I:

Finding Time for Your Health

PART II:

The Recipes

PART III:

Meal Plans for Specific Goals

FOREWORD

We all deserve a life of vitality, and we have the potential to create it for ourselves! We need to remove time as the obstacle that holds us back from a healthy life. In this busy world, we forget that making time for ourselves is extremely important. When we don't prioritize health and let it slip out of balance, then other areas in our lives (like our career and relationships) also suffer. We are conditioned to work really hard, but in doing so, we compromise our health. Later, we end up having to pay a lot of money to get well again.

If you think great health is not attainable, too complicated to figure out, or too time-consuming to implement, this book can transform your perspective on how *you* can achieve your goal of a healthy lifestyle. I want you to know that a healthy lifestyle isn't about being perfect; it's about integrating it into our busy lives right now as we are, and doing the absolute best we can with what we have been given.

This is a helpful book for busy people who want to live an enjoyable, pain-free life. Liana's practical tips and easy recipes make it possible, allowing you to start with just 10 minutes each day. Something as simple as making your own salad dressings can help you avoid a lot of sugars and preservatives. Adding a cup of Ginger Tea each day can help curb cravings and reduce inflammation, which is connected to almost every known chronic disease.

You'll find recipes here to suit any mood or need. If you're stressed, go for the recipes that are high in antioxidants like the Superfood Kale Salad and Smoothie Bowls. If you're bored with your diet, add some fun in your day with recipes like the Cauliflower Rice and Hash Browns. If you're feeling guilty about having eaten the "wrong" thing, such as too many processed foods, try the Green Lemonade juice to help with digestion and ease your body back on the healthy path.

Always hungry? You'll find many recipes in this book to allow you to have fulfilling, nutrient-rich treats on hand, even if your schedule is packed with work, school, or traveling. A handful of trail mix removes the temptation to grab toxic fast foods. When we're busy, we might be tempted to reach for foods with refined sugar. However, refined sugar is an extremely addictive substance that causes suffering. The recipes in this book help steer us away from white sugar and focus on natural sugars like dates, fruits, coconut sugar, honey, and maple syrup. Chocolate can be a great on-the-go food, but it's important to eat the "real" chocolate that is dairy-free, sugar-free, soy-free, and preservative-free. There are over 30 recipes here that use cacao, so you can make your own nutrient-rich and guilt-free chocolates.

When you feel like your body needs a cleanse, check out The Detox Guide in the back of the book. However, you don't need to wait until you have a lot of spare time to do a grand detox; you can detox a little bit each day. If you'd like to drop a few pounds, know that the Weight Loss Guide contained here focuses on nourishment. I never tell my patients to lose weight. I simply help them to restore health, and the magic of biology does the rest. When we focus on nourishing foods, we don't need to worry about how much we eat, because our bodies' appetite control systems kick into gear and help us achieve balance naturally.

There is something in this book for every type of eater to fulfill every kind of craving . . . in 10 minutes or less!

— Mark Hyman, M.D.,
author of ten *New York Times* bestsellers,
including his newest book *Eat Fat, Get Thin*

When life is challenging, we can make our food choices simple.

I am probably a lot like you. I lead a fast-paced lifestyle that can get stressful, and I'm often on the go. While it can be hard to find time for myself, I make sure I treat my body with the care it deserves. Life is always a juggling act of priorities, but my health is one ball I never intend to drop!

One thing we all can agree on is that getting proper nutrition on a daily basis helps us feel better in mind, body, and spirit. That's why no matter what life throws at us and how busy we are, it's worth making the effort to eat healthy foods. For my commitment to my well-being to work with my jam-packed schedule as a health coach and natural lifestyle advocate, I've had to develop strategies for preparing food and nourishing my body quickly and easily so that I can focus on other areas of my life.

In the pages of this book, I share all of these strategies with you. You'll never have to sacrifice flavor to eat healthy because I included a variety of recipes to satisfy any craving. You'll find breakfasts, entrées, party foods, desserts, snacks, and drinks. They are sweet, savory, tangy, crunchy, salty, creamy, refreshing, and more. I'll teach you how to shop to keep your fridge and pantry properly stocked with everything you need to have on hand to make something healthy to eat or drink at a moment's notice.

I want you to see how easy it can be to prepare good fast food with clean ingredients that support you in achieving natural, vibrant health. If you have 10 minutes, you can eat well.

Fast Food

Every recipe in this book takes 10 minutes or less of hands-on cooking time. In fact, I tested each one myself so I *know* they can be prepared that quickly! Some of these recipes have been part of my life for over seven years now, and I hope that they can transform your life the way they have mine.

Bringing a pot of water to boil and preheating the oven aren't counted toward the total minutes stated in the recipes. But don't let this time go to waste; you can gather and prep ingredients while you're waiting for a pot or oven to be ready. Many of the recipes are for one or two people, so it may take you a bit longer if you decide to double (or quadruple) batches in order to cook for a family or save leftovers for later meals—but this can end up saving you time in the long run!

Clean Ingredients

Imagine standing in front of a smorgasbord of fruits and vegetables. There's probably nothing more colorful. To me, nothing smells as uplifting and alive as the aroma of freshly picked produce with a little bit of earth remaining on it.

That's why all these recipes are also part of the Earth Diet, a way of living I discovered during my personal journey to healing myself. The Earth Diet is a lifestyle that embraces everything the earth provides naturally, including fat, oil, sugar, carbs, plants, seeds, nuts, meat, and fish. Vegan, vegetarian, or meat eater, no one is left out.

The focus is not on deprivation but on nourishing the body with high-nutrient ingredients. You'll be enjoying exciting dishes with a wide variety of flavors and textures—all made from wholesome, unprocessed ingredients that are the gifts of Mother Earth.

Clean eating renews our palates. As you begin to eat less-processed foods, tastes will change for you. Eventually when you eat processed junk foods, the flavors will seem different to you and you may begin to find them distasteful. I've found that the refined sugar in foods even starts to sting my teeth! Real flavors from unprocessed ingredients change your cravings, so you begin to crave healthier foods . . . naturally.

Natural Health

Investing in your optimal health by making a nourishing drink or meal is like putting money in the bank. In this case, your body is the bank! When your body is well nourished, then your blood chemistry remains in balance and your physical systems are able to work as they should to digest and absorb nutrients, eliminate toxins, and function. Good health means that your mind is clear, your mood is even or uplifted, and when you are confronted by different types of stressors, you can manage them and rapidly restore your balance. Your taste buds will thank you if you eat wholesome natural foods.

Use your own wisdom and intuition when it comes to choosing recipes, healing, eating, and natural living. The Earth Diet principles are compatible with whatever lifestyle you lead because nothing is truly forbidden; I simply encourage you to make *better* choices for yourself wherever and whenever you can. You'll discover the easiest way of doing so with my food and lifestyle upgrades in Chapter 4.

No matter what other choices you make, the decision to add high-quality, nutrient-dense food to your life will improve your health. You may also want to follow one of the guides at the end of this book, which I created to address specific health needs. They include recipe plans and advice for weight loss, breaking addictions, and more.

With this book, you really have no more excuses for not eating well. In creating the recipes, my rule was that they had to factor in speed, convenience, pleasure, and fulfillment, as well as exceptional nourishment. If you can get these five elements in at least one meal each day, you can rest assured that you are taking good care of yourself. Live with the intention of getting full nutrition every day and you really cannot go wrong here—even in less than 10 minutes per meal.

You're going to love this. I guarantee it.

PART I

FINDING TIME FOR YOUR HEALTH

CHAPTER 1

Eating Well Can Change Your Life

"Wholesome food creates **harmony** in the body. Harmony **in the body** creates harmony in the **mind and heart.** Harmony in the mind and heart creates harmony **throughout the world.**"

When you feel sick or tired or stressed, doesn't it seem as if everything takes twice as much effort? Would you believe me if I told you that the very next meal you ate could change your life? Each food you eat is one step toward making you healthier, happier, more productive, energetic, and calmer.

Health is the foundation of a fulfilling life. To be successful and maintain happy relationships, we need to give our body what it needs so it can have the energy to do the things we love to do. Our bodies need a little physical activity, plenty of sleep, and a variety of nutrient-dense food daily.

You might imagine that eating healthy food would be impossible for a person on the go. Where does a person find the time in between work, school, kids, romantic relationships, and the many other obligations we have on our plates? Well, to give you an idea of my current schedule, I'm based in New York City but frequently travel the world, going to natural food and lifestyle events. The way I look at it, though, my health is the very thing that makes it possible for me to maintain my active, productive lifestyle. I have chosen to make "being healthy" work for me, because I want to have the energy to live a good life that I love. I don't want to rely on refined sugar snacks that give me energy for only a second and then cause me to crash; I want to feel naturally, consistently alert.

I know how hard it is to eat on the run, like in airports! I also spend a lot of time sitting at my computer (writing books and recipes, haha) and talking and texting on my phone. I've had to come up with easy recipes and strategies for quickly nourishing myself so I don't need to resort to eating junk and airport food.

It doesn't require hours of shopping, chopping, or cooking to get and stay healthy. That's why I wrote this book; no matter how old or young you are, wherever you live and whatever pressing matters fill your day, you can find quick recipes and ways to support your health.

There are so many different areas of life—lots of moving parts. If we at least take care of our health, that's one less thing we have to stress about. I know from experience how placing a low priority on my health, in favor of the more convenient choice, could have devastating effects—taking shortcuts with my health turned out not to be such a time-saver after all.

How Eating Well Changed My Life

My parents fed my sisters, brother, and me a healthy diet when we were growing up. I wasn't exposed much to junk food in my home. We lived in Alice Springs, Australia, which is a small inland city in the desert region known as the Outback. There I was immersed in the natural lifestyle of the Aborigines, who traditionally live in harmony with the land. My health was excellent until I left home and my habits changed. Then it tanked. I hit rock bottom at age 21.

As soon as I left home at the age of 17 to pursue a career in television and theater, I fell into the trap of eating so-called convenience foods. I also persuaded myself that I "needed" sugar to maintain my creative energy and handle the fast pace of auditions, rehearsals, performances, and the classes I was taking. I'd load my handbag full of chips, candy, and chocolate so I could have them with me everywhere I went. I was so controlled by

my cravings that my life felt chaotic. I'd get an impulse for a specific sweet, like gummy bears, and all I could think about was going and getting some. From morning to night, I was entirely consumed by my food cravings and obsessed with satisfying them. After indulging in junk food, however, I'd be depressed and tired. I felt guilty because I knew I wasn't feeding my body what it needed. I gained weight and felt bloated all the time.

After only a few months of living this way, I felt like a walking zombie, drained of both energy and motivation. I felt miserable and ashamed, but I wasn't able to stop. For five years, I was stuck in this unhealthy pattern and dreaded waking up in the morning. Every day, I'd promise myself that I'd change my behavior, and then I'd break that promise so I could satisfy another craving. I lost confidence in myself because I didn't have control over my habits. I was scared to move forward; what would my future look like if I continued down this path?

The situation continued getting worse and worse. I was confused and stressed and didn't know what to do to help myself. Ultimately, my catalyst for change was a lump that popped out of my neck one night while I was attending a concert. Never had I heard or imagined that a tumor could emerge so suddenly. At first I thought it was a swollen gland and ignored it. Over the next two weeks, it got harder and bigger, until I was having trouble swallowing. That's when I took myself to the hospital. The doctor I saw at the hospital did a biopsy on the spot and sent me home to wait for the results. A week later, he informed me that the test had found a tumor the size of a golf ball inside my lymphatic system. No wonder I'd been so uncomfortable!

The lymphatic system is an important part of our immune system. It functions as a kind of sewage processing plant for the body, helping us to filter toxins out of our bloodstream and eliminate them. Because of my poor health choices, I'd been overloading my lymphatic system, and this was my body's way of telling me, "Enough is enough." Fortunately for me, the tumor was precancerous and had not spread beyond my neck.

Instead of having surgery, I decided to take my health into my own hands. Wanting to save my life finally gave me the motivation to defeat my cravings and break my vicious junk food addiction. I didn't know how exactly I'd do it, but I vowed: "I will not live like this for the rest of my life. I'm done with suffering!"

I committed to doing whatever was necessary to stay healthy. I had deprived my body of nutrients and poisoned myself with junk food for five years, so now, I decided, I would rest and properly nourish my body. For accountability, I started a blog called *The Earth Diet*, where I gradually developed a readership of thousands of people with a similar interest in transforming their health through better nutrition. Out of this blog grew a global health coaching practice and a career as an author and natural lifestyle advocate.

I developed a passion for spreading hope and for helping others become healthier and happier. Eventually, I published my first book, *The Earth Diet,* based on my experiences and my nutrition philosophy.

Fast-forward several years. Today I have achieved an entirely new level of health within my body. I no longer experience cravings for junk food, which I didn't even know was possible, and I feel free around food. By this, I mean that I eat when I'm hungry and I eat what my body tells me it wants. The most important guideline I follow is that everything I eat is natural, whether it's a cookie, cake, a burger, or pasta. I never deprive myself, yet I only nourish myself with ingredients that nature provides. I've never felt more confident, grateful, and in love with my body than I am now.

After my book came out, I toured the United States, England, and Australia, spreading the word. Everywhere I went, I met people who expressed a desire for improving their health but didn't know where to start. When I asked them about their greatest obstacles to eating well, I heard again and again that a lack of time defeated them. Learning this made me feel excited, because I knew that I understood how to overcome this obstacle. Every obstacle is solvable. I approached my publisher with the idea to make a new cookbook full of easy, healthy recipes that would appeal to everyone and could be made in 10 minutes or less. You are holding that book in your hands!

How Eating Well Can Change *Your* Life

Food can heal us and make us feel good about life. People who eat nourishing food are resilient, creative, optimistic, and energetic. They have sharp minds and clear skin. They don't need to worry about their weight, because their bodies adjust until they reach a happy optimal place. I experience these things myself now, and I want them for you.

Adding more nutritious foods into your life is an incredibly simple way to reinforce good health when you're well and support your body when you're ailing. Since all the recipes in this book are based on the Earth Diet principles, you can simply choose any of them and know that you are creating something that will nourish your body and make you feel really good.

Did you know that your body is constantly being rebuilt? Blood, muscles, bones, organs—within a few years, everything is entirely replaced. Having your cells made new is a wonderful prospect for you because every meal and new decision you make is an opportunity for transformation. You are worthy of building the best body you can with the best materials, and the recipes in this book will enable you to meet your nutritional requirements every day, with minimal time and effort.

If you embrace the Earth Diet, this way of life will help you:

- Maintain or restore your body to a healthy weight
- Elevate your mood
- Strengthen your immune system
- Improve and even reverse poor health
- Reduce the chemical burden on your body
- Cleanse and detoxify your body
- Break addictive cycles

People often experience peace of mind when they experience a reduction of physical symptoms that they've been suffering with. A client of mine, Monica, was diagnosed with hypothyroidism as a teenager. She was overweight, and her doctors told her that she would never lose the weight because of the issues with her thyroid. They also led her to believe that she would need to be on medication her entire life. When she implemented the principles of the Earth Diet, within a year she lost 38 pounds and her blood results were so favorable that she was able to reduce the amount of medication she was taking. Monica felt joyful, although she was initially in disbelief that she was able to do this just by changing the way she ate. She told me that she feels like she finally has the body she always wanted and never thought it was possible to have.

If you're imagining that someone like Monica has to spend hours shopping and cooking to get results like these, you're mistaken. Monica is a busy mother and full-time teacher. She gets results because she understands her priorities and has deliberately created a plan to support healthy habits. Taking on a healthy lifestyle rubs off on everyone around us, even our kids. One day, Monica overheard her six-year-old son asking a child eating processed ice cream in the playground, "Why are you eating toxins?"

If you're ready to break free and have a totally new life, you shall. The definition of personal transformation is creating an entirely new identity. Health is not just an idea or something you do once and you're done, it's the reality of waking up and making life-sustaining choices day after day after day that are aligned with your better nature and your highest aspirations. Because I had hit rock bottom with my health, I was forced to change my lifestyle entirely or continue to suffer and potentially die much younger than I had hoped for. I made healthy living work for me, because it was a must.

Your situation may not be as extreme as mine was, but taking care of your health is just as important. There are hidden costs to poor eating habits that you can eliminate when you change your behavior. These hidden costs include low energy, reduced productivity, and less enjoyment in life. If we're sick, we spend money on doctors and medicine to heal us. We also spend it on things we believe will compensate us for our pain and suffering. As our choices become more in harmony with the balance of nature, we stop spending money excessively. We spend money the same way we eat: in a resourceful and deliberate way.

Everything becomes better when we're healthy. When we're at ease, we are more available to the people we know; we're able to be more present when we're with them. By contrast, when we're ruled by pain or addiction, we cannot be fully present and engage with them or feel the fullness of a moment.

You are not destined to suffer in your body. If you devote just 10 minutes at a time to eating well, those can be the best and most significant 10 minutes that set you up for success for the rest of your day—and life.

Take the
10-Minute Challenge

Make one recipe every day! You pick how long:
3, 4, 7, 10, 14, 30, 90, or 365 days. Share your results
with me on social media using the hashtags
#10MinuteRecipes #10Minutes

What You Can Expect to Happen

Most people who adopt the Earth Diet go through a period of detoxification. This can be a little uncomfortable. Because you're no longer relying on familiar foods, emotions that those foods have been suppressing begin rising to the surface of your consciousness. Emotions from 10 or 20 years ago may be leaving your body. If this is the case for you, the best thing to do is to rest. It won't last long. It will soon pass.

In not too long a time, a few days or a week, you'll observe that your cravings are more aligned with the healthy foods you are able to eat on the Earth Diet. You'll notice that your taste buds are more sensitive and that you enjoy smelling and tasting unprocessed foods a good deal more. You'll know that you've entirely transformed when you don't think or feel the way you used to. The cravings that motivate us to eat fat, salt, and sugar, over time can leave us feeling worse in their aftermath because such substitutions are not a helpful response to legitimate hunger. With the Earth Diet, you'll always be feeling your way forward and exploring new sources of daily fulfillment that are also healthy.

Right now, I challenge you to commit to eating a minimum of one recipe from this book per day. You might start with 3 days and

feel so good that you continue for 365! Your body will benefit so greatly from this single commitment that you may not recognize your health and life a year from now.

Conscious Eating

Rather than asking you to memorize complex instructions, the Earth Diet is actually an invitation to be more conscious and aware. It is a philosophy that guides behavior toward choices that bring you freedom, spontaneity, and great joy.

Conscious eating has become a spiritual path for me. When I am conscious, I relax because I know I can trust myself to make good choices even when I'm hungry, angry, sad, tired, or lonely. With every meal, I am given another chance to demonstrate my love for myself and the earth. That's empowering.

Have you spent years feeling embarrassed, frustrated, sad, or pissed off because of how you eat? I've coached many people who felt upset because the way they were eating seemed beyond their control. The guilt drops away quickly when you aim for simplicity and just try to make the best choice you can in the moment. When you break free of destructive patterns of mindless eating, you'll feel more confidence and experience less negative self-talk.

Try not to feel any guilt over any of your food choices. Whether you just had a bite of the most terrible meal or you slipped up and binged on junk multiple times, please don't pile on the guilt or negative thoughts about yourself. It will only make things worse! Go ahead and acknowledge the feeling and say to yourself, "It's okay. That may have happened, but I control my next choice." You live and then you learn. We all make mistakes, so be sure to forgive yourself—I do!

Even if another intense craving comes along, it is just another opportunity to explore that part of yourself. Whenever you're struck by guilt, have that conversation with yourself to release it. Remember that each meal is a fresh chance to make the better choice and renew your commitment to yourself. It's a process. Don't allow the feeling of guilt to weigh you down. Just know you are getting healthier and healthier with every choice you make.

It's spiritually liberating to realize that you are the one in control of your food choices.

Achieving Peace of Mind

Much of the world is out of balance. People everywhere are suffering physically, emotionally, and mentally from stress. Most of us work hard and feel overwhelmed, unfocused, or preoccupied. We may turn to food to soothe ourselves when we feel bad, but if we are avoiding the root issues creating our stress, we are likely to turn to the wrong types of foods: convenience foods that cannot truly fulfill us, improve our circumstances, or end our suffering.

Remember that foods that are depleted of vitamins and nutrients can stimulate us to overeat. Have you ever wondered how it is

possible to eat a burger, a package of chips, and a packet of cookies all in one sitting? This is because the food goes to the digestive system, which is where it absorbs nutrition, and since there is no nutrition in those foods, it sends a message to the brain: "Didn't get any nutrition, still hungry, send more food." And so we keep eating and eating. This pattern leaves the body feeling extremely unfulfilled. Eating healthy is the opposite: It is impossible to binge on a bowl of kale or carrots. The body feels so fulfilled.

It's impossible for junk food that's low in nutritional value and high in sugar, salt, and fat to do more than give us a temporary hit of satisfaction. We may come to associate these foods with pleasure, which makes us feel addicted to them. Yet they can never really fulfill the deeper emotional and spiritual hungers that we feel. The terrible truth is that the more nutritionally depleted we become, the worse we feel and the more we crave relief. Then, if we pile guilt on top of that—guilt for making poor choices and being seduced by temptation, guilt because we feel misaligned with our higher values—the burden can crush our self-esteem and make us feel even worse.

We need to support ourselves emotionally, not berate ourselves for "being weak" or for having the emotions that make us feel vulnerable. When we feel anxious, angry, and doubtful, we must be sure to act responsibly, rather than impulsively or reactively. You can become more conscious of your thoughts with meditation. My daily meditations for my body are the following phrases: *My body is God. God is in my body.*

Be your body's own best friend by dedicating an hour a day to the maintenance of your body. If you do not have an hour, give it 30, 20, or even 10 minutes. Commit to something manageable that is a pleasure—and if you "fall off the wagon," jump right back on. Do whatever you feel like doing: walk, stretch, lift weights, dance, or do yoga. Be present with your body as you move. You may be amazed at how honored your body feels and how well it repays you for the consideration.

Schedule in plenty of rest, relaxation, and play time. If all you are ever doing is working, you will feel out of balance. When we're tired, we crave sugars, carbs, and fats, and this is usually when we grab something quickly that is really unhealthy, which sets us up to fall into a vicious cycle of binge eating. When we are well rested, we crave foods more in harmony with our biology.

There is nothing more fundamental in our lives than what we eat. With every meal we eat, we have the opportunity to renew the balance of our body, mind, and spirit. I love taking care of my body because it takes care of me in return. When I eat healthy food, I feel as if I'm experiencing God. Source energy is love and joy. I'm experiencing those feelings when my food sustains me. I believe food is an expression of God and that the earth is the Garden of Eden.

Changing the World

When you begin to eat consciously, you'll be more in touch with your body's true hunger for certain nutrients, which will be satisfied by ripe fruits and vegetables that burst with flavor. By choosing clean, natural foods, you can also do something positive for the world and show nature the respect it deserves.

Once you see your place in nature, every decision of what to eat is simpler. Fresh ingredients that are left relatively untouched before they hit a plate or a cup are the healthi-est choices, and local ingredients harvested in season are earth friendly. When you eat from your local environment, you use fewer resources to ship food across the world through distribution and supermarkets.

Organic fruits and vegetables are becoming more affordable all the time. With planning and good shopping habits, you won't need to spend your entire paycheck to eat healthy. If you set an intention to be healthy, you'll begin to perceive solutions that you might not have been aware of previously. Growing your own foods is the ultimate in freshness and sustainability.

Environmentalists caution us to minimize the "footprint" each of us makes on the natural world as we lead our lives. We're advised to reduce our use of fossil fuel, plastic, chemicals, and leave the green spaces we visit just as we find them. We're also sometimes guided to purchase *carbon offsets* to make up for what we did "wrong." For example, after taking a trip in a car that emits noxious fumes, we can offer a donation to a farmer who will plant trees that produce oxygen in a counterbalancing quantity. That makes the air cleaner and safer for us to breathe.

In the midst of weighing the good and bad impacts of our choices and actions, it's easy to forget that none of us is separate from nature. But you are a natural being on the planet Earth. I am a natural being on the planet Earth. And our bodies—the bodies of human beings—are natural environments that deserve the same level of respect that the more enlightened among us demand on behalf of the oceans, our national parks, and endangered species.

CHAPTER 2

Quick Nutrition Basics

"If it's made in a garden, eat it. If it's made in a lab then it takes a lab to digest."

— Kris Carr

At the most basic level, the simplest way to improve your nutrition is by replacing as many processed ingredients as possible with what the earth naturally provides. As often as possible, emphasize mostly whole, raw, and plant-based foods.

Whole foods are unprocessed types of produce in their most natural state. They provide our bodies with more nutrition than processed foods, as all of their nutrients are intact. In culinary vernacular, *raw foods* are uncooked or dehydrated at temperatures below 105°F. Everyone is familiar with simple raw foods like salads, juices, and smoothies, and in this book, you'll find those familiar standbys as well as more complex recipes.

I encourage you to create your own eating plan within these few guidelines. As for myself, if I were forced to categorize my daily diet, I'd say that it's 70 percent raw vegan and 30 percent cooked vegan and meat-eating.

The 10 EARTH DIET PRINCIPLES

The following are the 10 basic principles of the Earth Diet that are most important for health. For more detailed information, I recommend picking up my first book, *The Earth Diet.*

1. Eat real "clean" food. This means organic, least-processed, and non-GMO. Eat whole foods as much as possible.

2. Eat seasonal and as local as possible.

3. Eat a majority of plant-based foods. Focus on what the earth provides naturally. Connect with nature and grow your own produce, if possible.

4. When it comes to animal products, use eggs and meat from chickens that are vegetarian-fed and free-range. If you choose to eat meat, use organic meat from free-range, grass-fed animals. Avoid nonorganic dairy products. Fish should be wild caught.

5. Drink plenty of good clean water (two to three liters daily). Get a water filter if you do not have access to pure, fresh water.

6. Avoid chemicals: pesticides, aspartame, MSG, or additives like artificial flavorings, colorings, fillers, and stabilizers. Especially avoid nonorganic soy.

7. Eat food that makes you feel happy, and express gratitude before eating.

8. Eat with intelligent awareness. Rely on your instincts to know what and how much to eat. When you have a craving, ask yourself, "How can I get this in the most natural way possible?"

9. Stay conscious. Before meals, ask yourself: "What nutrients am I getting from this?"

10. When you go off track, remember to be gentle with yourself. You can get back on track whenever you want. (When you feel you need to detox your body and aid your digestion, have a fresh vegetable juice or Lemon Water.)

The Source of Your Nutrients

I invite you to personalize your diet. How would you like to get your nutrients? Do you want to get your magnesium from Raw Three-Ingredient Chocolate Balls or Brazil nuts? Would you like to get your antioxidants (vitamins A, C, and E) from a Mini Cashew Cheesecake, from a Superfood Kale Salad, or from gluten-free Tigernut Chicken Tenders?

If you eat as naturally as possible, your body will guide you to want what it needs when it needs it. Over time, it will communicate more clearly with you about what you need to consume, and you'll be able to trust your instincts for guilt-free eating! When you make conscious food choices out of love and nourishment for yourself, you might reach for a raw organic chocolate bar, or the Cashew Cheesecake (like I'm eating right now!). Even a treat becomes something that nourishes your body along with tasting really good.

Nutrients come in abundant forms, so if you really don't like a particular food . . . skip it. Take protein, for example. While you cannot eat healthy while avoiding it altogether, your *source* of protein is your choice. There are plenty of clean proteins to alternate between, everything from organic meat to pumpkin seeds. Also, when you eat lots of fruits and vegetables, you naturally get antioxidants, which are anti-inflammatory and promote youthful vitality.

You get to decide what you want to experience on the planet as long as you're here, and it's okay to have food preferences. What one person thinks is scrumptious another thinks is yucky. We all know kids who find vegetables suspicious. I've met some adults who dislike organic chocolate. We can get attached to certain textures and flavors. There is an innate instinct to be cautious when approaching unfamiliar foods. So make the recipes that excite you the most first, and remember that it's okay to experiment from time to time. You might be surprised.

Why pH and Alkalinity Matter

A balanced pH helps set the foundation for health. The term pH stands for the power of hydrogen. When you measure the pH level in your body, you're measuring its hydrogen ion concentration. The scale goes from *acidic* (0) to *alkaline* (14). The ideal pH of the human body is close to 7.4—near neutral. (Water is neutral at a pH of 7; our bodies are 70 percent water by volume.)

With our modern world and the kinds of chemicals we are exposed to, it's easy for our bodies to veer more toward the acidic side than is healthy. Many fruits and vegetables are alkalizing, too, which supports the body in maintaining an ideal pH level. Acid-forming foods can be healthy as well; just be sure to support the health of your body by choosing an abundance of alkalizing foods and beverages whenever possible. All the raw dishes you'll find in this book are alkalizing and anti-inflammatory, and the following chart will help you make the best choices for yourself. (For more information, refer to the Alkalize Your Body Guide in Part III.)

Simple ways to alkalize your body include:

- Lemon Water: The juice of 1 lemon squeezed into a glass of water.
- pHresh Water: 1 teaspoon of the supplement pHresh Greens mixed into 1 cup water will alkalize your body instantly. (If you choose a different supergreens powder, ensure that the ingredients are alkaline.)
- Apple Cider Vinegar Water: Drink 1 teaspoon apple cider vinegar mixed into 1 cup of water. (Or add 1 teaspoon to 3 teaspoons water for an easy shot!)
- Clay Drink: Drink 1 teaspoon bentonite clay mixed into 2 cups water.
- Salt Water: Drink ½ teaspoon salt in 1 or 2 cups water. Salt is high in minerals, but it's important not to use ordinary table salt. Get "real" salt that doesn't have preservatives.

TOP ACID-FORMING SUBSTANCES & ACTIONS	TOP ALKALINE-FORMING SUBSTANCES & ACTIONS
CARBONATED BEVERAGES (SODA)	LEMON AND LIME
ASPARTAME	COLLARD GREENS
REFINED WHITE SUGAR	CELERY
WHITE FLOUR	ASPARAGUS
WHEAT	CUCUMBER
MEAT AND FISH	CARROTS
DAIRY PRODUCTS	ARTICHOKES
MICROWAVED FOODS	RED CABBAGE
ALCOHOLIC BEVERAGES	BROCCOLI
TOBACCO PRODUCTS	SEAWEEDS
CORN	ALFALFA
RICE	CAULIFLOWER
VINEGAR, EXCEPT APPLE CIDER VINEGAR	BRUSSELS SPROUTS
COFFEE AND BLACK TEA	LETTUCE
MOST NUTS	SWEET POTATOES
TABLE SALT	OLIVE OIL
VEGETABLE OIL	BLUEBERRIES
MAYONNAISE	FIGS AND DATES
LACK OF SLEEP	SLEEP
STRESS AND WORRY	MEDITATION/PARASYMPATHETIC RELAXATION

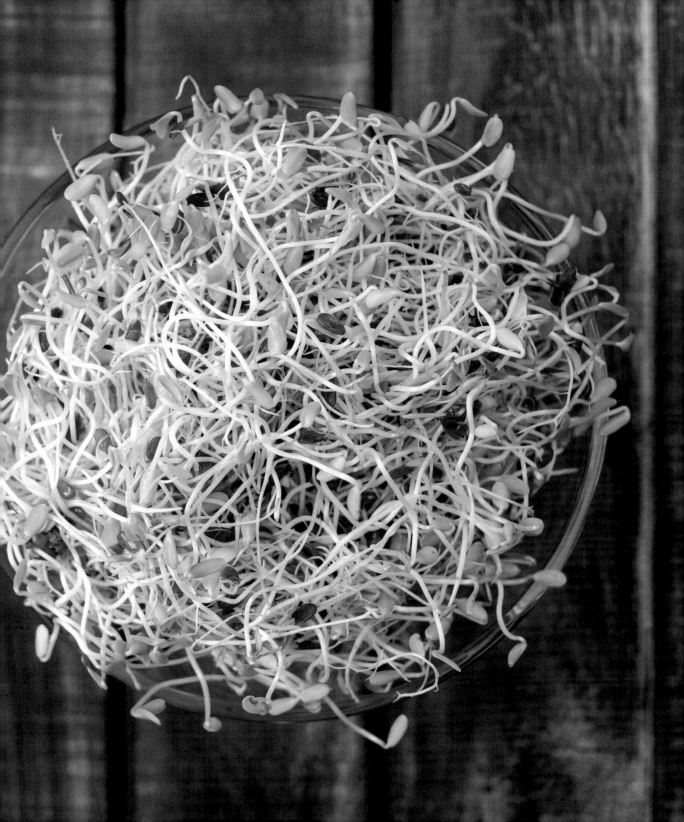

Minimum Daily Nutrition Checklist

As a health coach who cares about you, I encourage you to hold yourself accountable and reach a basic level of nutrition daily. To help you with this, I've created the following "minimum daily nutrition checklist" in three parts. Once you achieve each level in a day, consider adding items from the next.

Start by setting a daily goal of getting just these first four items. It will give you a nice amount of antioxidants, vitamins, and minerals so that your body has what it needs to stay vibrant. If you are achieving these staples, you can know that your foundation level of health is being taken care of.

☑ Lemon water (squeeze a whole lemon into a glass of water)

☑ One fresh juice (like a Super Greens or Beet Juice, for instant cellular nutrition)

☑ One piece of raw green (like a cucumber, celery stick, or asparagus)

☑ One piece of fruit (it's nature's candy and will help keep sugar cravings at bay)

One easy way to get your lemon water is to ask for lemon with your water whenever you eat out. This will alkalize your body and give you a nice dose of vitamin C for immune support.

When you're ready, the next level includes supplements. I've found bentonite clay capsules, wheatgrass capsules, and activated charcoal capsules to be the most helpful; I even keep them in my handbag. These next three basics will provide you with nutrition and even fill you up!

☑ One fresh smoothie (like a Sick Kick or Classic Green Smoothie)

☑ Bentonite clay or activated charcoal (2 to 3 capsules before bed act as detox helpers)

☑ Wheatgrass or spirulina capsules (this gives you alkalizing greens every day)

If you are able to get these seven staples daily, your body will be so well nourished and you will feel so alive. I credit these items with helping me maintain the health I have today.

When you achieve that level of nutrition, consider adding the following:

☑ One raw salad loaded with greens (think lettuce, kale, collard greens, fresh cilantro, parsley, avocado, chia seeds, hemp seeds, and a dressing of olive oil and lemon)

☑ Whole seeds as a snack (like pumpkin, hemp, or sunflower)

To stave off cravings, always have your favorite snacks on hand. Mine are raw chocolate, tigernuts, and organic gummy bears (free of corn syrup and gluten), so I always have those on hand. Make Raw Three-Ingredient Chocolate Balls and keep them in your freezer and fridge.

To encourage yourself to add items from each part of the checklist, you might make a deal with yourself. For example, "I will have some raw chocolate tonight, but first I will make sure I have a green drink." Then you can look forward to your chocolate! This keeps a nice balance of nutrition and treats, and ensures your mind stays guilt-free. Trust your body to know what it needs.

CHAPTER 3

Getting Started

"Growth is an erratic forward movement: two steps forward, one step back. Remember that and be very gentle with yourself."

— Julia Cameron

Some people are afraid to cook because they think it is really complicated, but this kind of recipe making is not! Nothing is simpler than eating whole foods from Mother Earth. *We* are the ones who complicate things! There are many recipes in this book that have as few as two ingredients. It's okay if you want to get fancy—in fact, one of the recipes you'll find in this book has a lot of herbs and spices—but within our 10-minute realm of healthy fast food, being fancy is not our first priority.

Cooking is different than it used to be. The food people want to eat these days is more whole-some and simpler in composition. Like alchemy, often the best meals are made from a few simple ingredients that have been combined with the cook's positive energy. I have friends who aren't professional chefs who nonetheless have prepared me the best meals I've ever eaten. I believe the love they put into their food is what makes it taste so great. I feel peaceful when it goes into my body. Anyone can cook a 10-minute recipe from this book—even a child (with supervision when using a flame or a blender).

TO SAVE YOURSELF TIME, CONSIDER THE FOLLOWING TIPS:

- Chop a variety of vegetables in the beginning of the week and store them in the refrigerator until you're ready to use them for a recipe.

- Buy washed and chopped organic vegetables in bags or even from your grocer's salad bar, which saves a lot of time.

- Use your hands to roughly tear leafy vegetables and herbs instead of dicing. You may be surprised by how much time this saves!

- Use the herbs you have on hand rather than rushing to the store. If a recipe calls for dried herbs and you only have fresh, just triple the quantity.

- Keep onion and garlic powder in your pantry; they provide lots of flavor while saving you some chopping time.

- Multitask: for example, while taco shells are baking, cook the filling on the stove.

- Preheat the oven or set water to boil (if the recipe calls for it) immediately, and use this time to gather ingredients so you're ready to go.

- Measure out all the ingredients you'll need for a recipe before you start so you can combine things quickly and easily.

- Limit dishes used as you prep, and clean up as you go along, to save yourself time when tidying the kitchen afterward.

- "All in at once!" For some of your favorite recipes, consider whether you can just dump all the ingredients in the pot or pan at once. When everything can cook together, it allows you to make a fresh meal in 10 minutes or less.

Set Yourself Up for Success

Get yourself in the 10-minute recipe mind-set! Embrace simplicity. A lot of the recipes use just a few ingredients, so they're easy to memorize and use for the rest of your life. There is no need to overcomplicate things; our lives are hectic enough as it is. Food can be simple and delicious. If you don't have time to prepare a dish for lunch, a meal of just avocado and sunflower seeds can be nutritious and filling.

Know that cooking a nutritious meal takes less time than we think. For example, many people assume it takes ages to boil a pot of water, but for two cups of water, it takes only *four* minutes! I also know that sometimes it can just feel like cooking is taking a long time, especially when I'm tired, but when I time myself, I'm often surprised by how quickly things come together. Once the mind grasps this, you can think, "I do have 10 minutes for myself. I can make a delicious dinner tonight."

In the beginning, it might take you a bit longer as you get used to the recipes and need to pause as you read them through. But after you've made a dish a couple times, you will know the steps offhand and be able to confidently whip it up.

Be sure to read recipes and ingredient packages carefully, as some items require special handling and extra prep time. For example, the Pad Thai can be made in 10 minutes if you have soft noodles on hand, but if you need to soak dry noodles, you'll have to follow the package instructions before starting the recipe.

Basic Equipment You'll Need

You may be surprised to discover that it's possible to make food quickly without using a microwave. None of my recipes do. The 10-minute recipes in this book are so simple that for many of them, all you need is a bowl and a spoon. In fact, you'll make and eat many of them with your hands, like the chocolate balls and protein bars.

Some recipes require a juice machine and some a blender. Some are made on the stovetop and a few are baked. But many of these recipes are for raw dishes. By nature, just mixing raw ingredients is quick and produces food that is ridiculously high in nutrients.

To make all of the recipes in this book, you'll need the following kitchen equipment.

A JUICE MACHINE to make juices. Juicers come in different price ranges, and you may also find a perfectly good one being sold on the Internet, so don't let the price stop you. Stainless-steel juice machines have proven to be the best quality. This is your greatest investment in your health and well-being. You can even use a hand juicer to juice citrus fruits for a couple of dollars. They literally work just as well as expensive machines to make orange juice, lemon juice, and grapefruit juice. They are also easier to clean.

A HIGH-SPEED BLENDER to make smoothies, raw desserts, sauces, and more. A powerful blender with a reliable motor and sharp stainless-steel blades will work. If you have a strong enough blender, you probably won't even need a food processor. The exceptions are frozen desserts and mixing dry blends. Always take care not to burn out the motor. Blenders are better for wet mixtures.

A FOOD PROCESSOR is the best machine for mixing dry ingredients. Use it to make instant ice creams, nut spreads, and more.

QUALITY COOKWARE. It's important to use quality cookware that is nonreactive to the foods you cook it in, like stainless-steel, ceramic, glass, and lead-free cookware. My personal preference is stainless steel. The pots for cooking have thick bottoms. Ultimately slow heating, as you would use when cooking on a fire or over coals, is the most natural form of cooking. Stay away from flimsy pots or nonstick pots and pans coated with Teflon and other synthetic materials. According to experts I trust, once heated these can spoil the food and become toxic. Of particular concern is what these may do to damage the thyroid gland. Make sure to have these kitchen essentials:

- A 12-inch-diameter stainless-steel skillet
- A large stainless-steel baking sheet
- A stainless-steel pot (six to eight cups)
- A stainless-steel or glass mixing bowl (six to eight cups)

UTENSILS:

You'll need:

- A large spoon
- A sharp all-purpose knife
- A bamboo or wood cutting board
- A set of measuring cups
- A set of measuring spoons

A FOOD DEHYDRATOR to make dried fruit and fruit leathers for rollups and candy. You can even dry your own herbs!

For discounts on equipment and kitchen supplies that I recommend as the healthiest and most effective, check out my website: TheEarthDiet.com/resources. Come back and visit regularly—the list of products and discounts is always evolving as I continue to search for new ways to make our lives easier, more time efficient, and healthier.

10-Minute Shopping Strategy:

Plan for the Next Four Days

If you're in a real hurry and committed to healthy eating, you'll be excited to know that there are strategic ways to shop that can save you lots of time. First, you'll want to download a free copy of the 10-Minute Shopping List from my website: TheEarthDiet.com/shoppinglist or make a copy of the one on the following pages. Hang a copy of the 10-Minute Shopping List on your refrigerator door.

Get in the habit of planning which recipes you'll make for a period of four days—the amount of time that most fresh ingredients will remain good. Once or twice a week, glance through the recipes and choose the ones that you feel pulled toward. Perhaps follow one of the guides in Part III. Review the Minimum Daily Nutrition Checklist in Chapter 2, and stock up on supplies for at least the first three.

Do your best to anticipate the fresh ingredients that you'll need to bring home. Circle these on your shopping list. Whenever you need to restock your pantry, use this to remind you of what you need to buy. (You may want to stock your pantry and freezer with staples that keep for extended periods of time, even before you need them for a particular recipe, in order to save yourself some shopping trips.)

Whether you're stocking your pantry and fridge or shopping for fresh ingredients, always choose the highest quality you can find. Study labels and opt for those products that are organic, natural, and sustainable, as well as affordable. For the names of brands I love and trust that meet these requirements, see the Resources section and the end of this book or visit TheEarthDiet.com/resources.

To save time and money, I recommend shopping for dry goods like coconut oil, olive oil, nuts, and spices in bulk. Compare prices at your local warehouse store and different online retailers. If you go to Vitacost.com, you can get discounts ranging from 25 to 60 percent if you use the code earthdiet (all lower case).

Keep the following staples on hand in your cupboard, refrigerator, and freezer, and you'll always have what you need to make something delicious to eat or drink in 10 minutes or less.

Shopping List

For the Cupboard

Flours and Baking Mixes:

- Bob's Red Mill Pancake Mix
- Organic Gemini TigerNut Flour
- Vitacost Gluten-Free Buckwheat Pancake Mix

Herbs, Seasonings, and Spices:

- Amino acids (like Bragg Liquid Aminos)
- Apple cider vinegar
- Black pepper
- Cacao powder
- Cayenne pepper
- Cilantro
- Cinnamon powder
- Cumin powder
- Earth Diet Chocolate Cups and Bars
- Fennel seeds
- Garlic powder (or minced)
- Ginger powder
- Honey
- Maple syrup
- Nutritional yeast
- Onion powder
- Oregano (or oregano essential oil)
- Parsley
- Peppercorns, ground
- Rosemary
- Sage
- Salt (Himalayan or Real Salt)
- Thyme
- Turmeric powder
- Vanilla extract or vanilla beans

Miscellaneous Dry Goods:

- Almonds, whole
- Almond butter
- Almonds, whole
- Almond butter
- Black beans, canned
- Bread (try Food for Life, Rudi's, or Udi's)
- Cashews, whole
- Chickpeas, canned (aka garbanzo beans)
- Peanut butter
- Pecans, whole
- Pizza crusts (try Ener-G, King Arthur, or Udi's)
- Tigernuts (try Organic Gemini)
- Tortillas and wraps (try Julian Bakery Paleo, Rudi's, SunFood, or Udi's)
- Walnuts, whole

Oils:

- Coconut oil, extra-virgin (try Vitacost or Nutiva)
- Olive oil, extra-virgin
- Tigernut oil (try Organic Gemini)

Pasta:

- Black bean pasta (try Explore Cuisine)
- Brown rice pasta (try Explore Cuisine or Tinkyada)
- Buckwheat noodles (try Eden Foods or King Soba)
- Chickpea pasta (try Explore Cuisine)
- Gluten-free pasta (try any from Explore Cuisine)
- Lentil pasta (try Explore Cuisine)
- Quinoa pasta
- Ramen noodles (try King Soba or Lotus foods)
- Rice noodles (try Explore Cuisine)

Seeds:

- Chia seeds (try Nutiva)
- Flaxseeds
- Hemp seeds (try Nutiva)
- Pumpkin seeds
- Sesame seeds
- Sunflower seeds

Supplements:

- Bentonite clay (Redmond Clay is my favorite) or activated charcoal capsules
- Spirulina or wheatgrass capsules
- Supergreens powder (pHresh Greens is my favorite)

Teas:

- Chamomile
- Green
- Ginseng

Fresh Foods

Buy only enough for four days ahead.

Animal Proteins:

- Eggs
- Beef, ground
- Chicken, breasts
- Chicken, ground

Produce:

- Apples
- Avocados
- Bananas
- Beets
- Blueberries
- Broccoli
- Carrots
- Cauliflower
- Celery
- Cherries
- Cilantro
- Cucumbers
- Dates
- Garlic
- Ginger
- Grapes
- Grapefruit
- Kale
- Lemons
- Lettuce
- Mangoes
- Mint
- Onions
- Oranges
- Parsley
- Potatoes
- Spinach
- Strawberries
- Tomatoes

Frozen Foods

Fruits:

- Acai Superfruit Pack (made by Sambazon)
- Blackberries
- Blueberries
- Raspberries
- Strawberries

Animal Proteins:

- Beef, ground
- Chicken, breasts
- Chicken, ground
- Salmon
- Tuna
- White fish

Entrées:

- Amy's Burritos
- Amy's Pizzas

One-Minute Solutions

Here is what we know for sure: We need adequate nutrition on a daily basis. We need to properly care for our bodies. If we always focus on the best ways to get nutrition, especially when life gets hectic or we're overwhelmed, we'll be more able to handle what life throws at us. Although we don't know with certainty if we'll ever get cancer or catch a head cold one day, we do know that if we get the vitamins, minerals, and phytonutrients we need, our immune systems will be better equipped to do the job of preserving our lives and well-being. We can't help feeling better, physically, mentally, and emotionally, when we properly nourish ourselves every day.

But when we're running out the door or ravenous or feeling lazy, how can we nourish our body well in a short amount of time? We don't want to fall back on eating quick-fix junk food even at a time like this. That's where one-minute solutions come in!

The question to ask when you only have a minute is: "What are my options to get as much nutrition as possible with what I have on hand?" You want to be assured that at least some of your nutritional needs are being met. And the fastest way to do this is to reach for a whole raw food in its natural state, like an orange, an apple, or a banana. With a piece of fruit, you know you are getting high doses of antioxidant vitamins, fiber, and hydration.

Here are some other grab-and-go fast-food solutions from nature:

- *LEMON WATER:* Squeeze a whole lemon in a glass of water. If you're eating out, ask for extra lemon slices with your water.

- *BERRIES:* A cup or two of raspberries, blueberries, blackberries, strawberries, goji berries, mulberries, and golden berries—all are superfoods, packed with antioxidant goodness.

- *RAW VEGETABLES:* Broccoli, cauliflower, cabbage, carrots, celery, tomatoes, cucumbers, bell peppers, snow peas, and tigernuts. Rip them. Slice them. Chop them. Eat them whole. It's all good.

- *WHOLE FRUITS:* In addition to the usual apples, bananas, and oranges, think of pears, pineapple, papaya, grapes, figs, mango, cantaloupe, watermelon, kiwis, and passion fruit.

- *SEEDS:* Pumpkin seeds, sunflower seeds, hemp seeds, and sesame seeds. Eat them by the spoonful or sprinkle them on your fruit.

- *NUTS:* Cashews, almonds, Brazil nuts, hazelnuts, walnuts, pecans, macadamia nuts, and peanuts (which are technically legumes).

- *FRESH GREENS:* Simply picking herbs or leafy greens (lettuce, kale, parsley, and cilantro) from the garden and chewing on them is a way to get some nutrients. You can suck the nutrients right out of them.

Want to speed up the absorption of your nutrients? Get an instant cellular infusion from juicing or blending one or more of the aforementioned foods.

The Quickest Juice and Smoothie Solutions

Aim to get at least one lemon water, juice, or smoothie every day. You can make your life easy for yourself with simple tricks like this. The Earth Diet is creative!

- Make citrus juices by hand with a citrus press (also called citrus juicers and citrus squeezers). You can find these small, portable tools for only a few dollars at grocery and kitchen stores. Stow one in your desk drawer, in the kitchen at the office, and in your handbag or knapsack. It takes only a minute to juice a lemon, orange, or grapefruit, and there's little cleanup or energy involved! You can toss the peels, rinse the tool and your hands, and still have 8 or 9 minutes left in a 10-minute break to savor your fresh juice or citrus water.

- Freeze a batch of Lemon Water in an ice cube tray. Suck on one when you're hustling around. Add some to teas, water, juices, and smoothies. Plop several into your portable water bottle in the morning before you head out.

- Make a large batch of smoothies and juices each Sunday, and freeze them in individual containers. Each day of the week, you can simply take one out of the freezer and let it defrost on your way to work or school. While fresh is always best, if you cannot make fresh juice on a particular day, then a premade juice is better than none!

The Quickest Salad Solutions

You might think it takes a long time to make a great salad because there's a lot of prep work involved: cleaning, chopping, and so on. In fact, being healthy has been made easier by farmers, distributors, and supermarket staff who prewash and package organic greens and chopped vegetables and fruits for us.

- Basic salad recipe: Quickly make a salad from a package of greens tossed with a protein (like chickpeas, pumpkin seeds, and hemp seeds) and a simple dressing made from oil, vinegar, and lemon—with any seasonings you like (salt, pepper, cumin, thyme, parsley).

- Grab-and-go salads: Mix up your favorite vegetable combinations in airtight mason jars (the kind made for canning preserves and pickles) and store them in the refrigerator. When you're ready to eat one, just dump it in a bowl and toss it with your favorite dressing. You can even eat them straight from the jar!

- Make salad dressing in bulk: At the beginning of the week, make enough dressing for several salads. Check out Chapter 11 for recipes. When it's time to eat your salad, pull one out of the fridge and dress it! Make it fancy and fashionable. By *fashionable,* I mean healthy, quick, and delicious.

TIP:

When an ingredient in a recipe is capitalized, there is a recipe for that ingredient in this book. Refer to the Recipe List on pg. 272 or the Index on pg. 279 to quickly find it. To save time, you can purchase an organic version from the store.

The Quickest Dessert Solutions

To satisfy cravings, always have your favorite healthy desserts on standby in your fridge or freezer. All of the dessert recipes in this book can be frozen! Some, like the Mini Cheesecakes are designed for single servings. Others can be divided into individual portions before freezing.

Get out a spoon and dip into a big batch of Chocolate Sauce or Instant Ice Cream. Have fun with a friend by taking turns pitching balls of Raw Melt-in-Your-Mouth Chocolate Chip Cookies straight into each other's mouths. In my fridge or freezer, you'll always find Chocolate Balls and Raw Apple Pie.

Want to know something incredible? Eating healthy desserts is how I cured myself of my self-destructive eating habits years ago. Before I knew that there were such things as healthy fast foods, I deprived myself of sweets. That made me miserable. I alternated between binging and starving myself. When I created the Earth Diet, I finally gave myself permission to eat whatever I wanted when I wanted it as long as it was sourced from the earth. A funny thing happened. Instead of spending hours eating and eating and eating —and hours more obsessing and feeling guilty—as you might imagine I would, I discovered that when we eat nutrient-dense foods, we stop eating when the nutritional needs of our bodies have been met.

The Big Batch Solution

Main dishes and soups can be doubled, tripled, or quadrupled and stored in the refrigerator or freezer (depending on how soon before you'll consume them). In the fridge, they'll keep for three or four days. In the freezer, if it's stored airtight, you can save them for a month or more. Soup in particular is a great opportunity to make a large batch so you can stock your fridge with these convenience foods.

Freeze your recipes according to the quantities in which you think you'll use them. In other words, if you're going to be eating solo, freeze single servings. If you're eating family-style, freeze a bigger batch. In either case, you can always add some fresh produce to liven up the meal once it's been reheated. Parsley, cilantro, avocado, cucumber—they're all wonderful ways to help a meal come alive again.

I find there's nothing like coming home, getting a soup out of the freezer, heating it up, adding some fresh seasonings, and kicking back on the couch with my feet up—looking at nature . . . and maybe the TV for balance (guilt-free, of course).

Once you know the tips and tricks of how to make quick recipes that you love, you'll be set for life! You'll have everything you need to be successful at staying healthy. Show your friends and family how to make quick recipes, too, and you can be surrounded by happy, healthy people. There are base recipes in this book that you can expand and improvise around, so you have no more excuses.

CHAPTER 4

Shortcuts to Upgrade Your Health

"Do the **best** you can
until you know better.
Then when **you know**
better, do better."

— Maya Angelou

- YOU HAVE A CRAVING. "How can I satisfy this in the best way possible?"
- WORST-CASE SCENARIO: low-quality, fast-food, and conventional options; GMO and nonorganic ingredients; high in refined sugars; high in trans fats; artificial colorings, flavors, and preservatives
- BETTER UPGRADE: the organic option made with clean ingredients.
- BEST UPGRADE: make your own with the highest-quality ingredients you can buy

Remove your biggest food obstacle by answering this one question: What food do you crave that holds your health back? (It might be processed candy, chocolate, cakes, chips, burgers, etc.) Replace this obstacle with a healthy alternative and watch your life change. When I switched out processed chocolate made with dairy, sugar, soy, and preservatives for raw chocolate made with real ingredients, it transformed my life.

Because I lead an active lifestyle, I had to identify ways to achieve consistent health that didn't take much time and effort. When I first broke my addiction to junk food, I did it by deliberately satisfying my cravings with healthier, whole foods. I started drinking juices, smoothies, and bentonite clay water, and inventing recipes reminiscent of my favorite junk foods. Day by day, I felt my immune system growing stronger.

Nothing is forbidden to us on the Earth Diet; we're just looking for the healthiest version of what we want. There is an endless number of simple ways to nourish yourself with high-quality, nutrient-dense food. You want to be healthy—and you want to be healthy quickly. The bottom line is that this means you don't want to spend a lot of time making decisions. You want to know which solutions to go to right away to get the job done. Great! The easiest way to improve your health is through what I call upgrades.

What Is an Upgrade?

Choosing a healthier version of what you crave is what I call an *upgrade*. I rely upon this technique to keep me from bogging down on my health and food choices. Simply take a moment to swap in a better version of something you're about to consume or put on your skin. Consider your options and ask, "How can I get these in the healthiest way possible?" You can do this for better or best. For example, you want some French fries. The worst-case scenario is buying fries at a fast-food franchise made from GMO potatoes cooked in low-quality oil, seasoned with preservative-ridden salt. What is the upgrade in this situation?

The *better* version is to get them at an organic restaurant where the cook uses non-GMO potatoes and high-quality oil.

The *best* version is to cook them at home yourself, using the 10-Minute Fries recipe, with extra-virgin coconut oil and real salt with a high mineral content, prepared in a nontoxic stainless-steel pan.

If you do opt for the worst-case scenario—perhaps because you're traveling and nowhere near an organic cafe or a kitchen—don't feel down or berate yourself for choosing that option. Instead, *upgrade the experience* by following up your meal with a Lemon Water or freshly squeezed vegetable juice to assist with digestion and elimination of toxins.

Living this way reduces guilt. When you know you're moving toward health, even by a small incremental step, you feel better and have more peace of mind. Plus, you feel way less deprived if you do the right thing. It's empowering!

Deprivation diets will only drive you crazy, leaving you feeling worse than when you started. It's important to be kind to yourself. Health is the goal—and feeling good and being at ease with yourself are indicators of good health. This is why upgrading is such a great tool. When you want chocolate, you eat chocolate. Just try to make sure it's organic. Organic cacao, which is an ingredient in chocolate, is featured in different Earth Diet recipes in this book. You can also have cheesecake, cupcakes, ice cream, mousse, burgers, burritos, fries—just upgrade them from the old familiar junk-food versions. There are recipes for all of these foods here as well.

When you upgrade, you're just making a better choice. You're not sacrificing anything —except things that are harmful, like preservatives. The result is that you're eating food that tastes amazing and provides your body with the nutrition it needs.

As far as I'm concerned, deliciousness is an essential nutrient. Having good taste and nutrition at the same time is one of the keys to the Earth Diet lifestyle.

In case you haven't noticed, I love eating dessert. If you do as well, you'll be pleased to know that you can find almost anything to cure your sweet and creamy cravings in the dessert recipe section. Just follow the rule: Upgrade it. Make sure it is as natural as possible. The quickest upgrade decision is to choose organic ingredients.

Common Food Upgrades

The following upgrades come up over and over again. If you commit these to memory, you'll save more time.

⬆ *THE SALT UPGRADE:* Any salt that has fillers and preservatives is toxic for the body. Upgrade your salt by using Real Salt, pure sea salt, or Himalayan salt.

⬆ *THE OIL UPGRADE:* Instead of using GMO vegetable oil (including plain "vegetable oil" and canola oil), use non-GMO oils from the following list: extra-virgin olive oil, extra-virgin coconut oil, avocado oil, hemp seed oil, flaxseed oil, tigernut oil, sesame oil, almond oil, and chia seed oil.

⬆ *THE DAIRY UPGRADE:* Make sure to upgrade your milk, yogurt, and cheese products to organic dairy from the milk of cows that are grass fed, free range, antibiotic-free, and growth hormone–free (rBGH-free)—as local as possible.

⬆ *THE EGG UPGRADE:* Upgrade your eggs to organic eggs from hens that are pasture raised, free range, and antibiotic-free. Buy local if possible.

⬆ *THE BREAD UPGRADE:* When you crave bread, get the highest quality freshly baked organic bread you can. If you're worried about the price difference, remind yourself that you are a high-quality person and you deserve high-quality foods! Upgrade further by baking your own bread using organic, non-GMO ingredients.

⬆ *THE SALAD DRESSING UPGRADE:* When you're having your salad, instead of using a premade, store-bought salad dressing with sugar and preservatives, choose an organic salad dressing. Upgrade further by making your own salad dressing from simple ingredients like extra-virgin olive oil and lemon, or sesame oil and vinegar. See the salad dressings in Chapter 11.

↑ *BURGER UPGRADE:* When you crave a burger, get it from an organic restaurant that uses free-range meat. Upgrade again by making your own burger at home. Try the 10-Minute Burger with Ketchup.

↑ *THE PIZZA UPGRADE:* When you're having a pizza, upgrade by buying it fresh from a pizza parlor that makes it with high-quality flour and cheese. Upgrade further by making it yourself with organic cheese and dough, topped with your favorite vegetables. Try the 10-Minute Pizza.

↑ *THE PASTA UPGRADE:* I love pasta! Basically I upgrade by using brown rice pasta, quinoa pasta, or black bean pasta, which taste amazing. All three of these types of pasta are good sources of protein and fiber, and they're also gluten-free, meaning you can eat them without getting bloated. Try the 10-Minute Mac 'n' Cheese and Black Bean Salsa Pasta.

↑ *THE FRIES UPGRADE:* When you crave French fries, get it from a café that uses high-quality oil. Upgrade further by making them at home using organic potatoes and extra-virgin coconut oil. Try the Basic French Fries.

↑ *THE CHOCOLATE UPGRADE:* When you crave chocolate, get organic chocolate that uses pure ingredients: no dairy, soy, preservatives, or refined sugar. Upgrade further by making your own raw chocolate at home. Try the Raw Three-Ingredient Chocolate Balls.

↑ *THE POTATO CHIP UPGRADE:* When you feel like chips or crisps, go for non-GMO, organic potato products. There are some excellent brands out there. Upgrade further by making Baked Kale Chips.

↑ *THE CANDY UPGRADE:* When you crave candy, get organic candy that is also free of corn syrup, gluten, gelatin, and preservatives. Upgrade further by dehydrating a fruit puree at home, which is squished into different shapes. Try one of the Fruit Leathers in Chapter 15.

↑ *THE COOKIE UPGRADE:* Buy organic, non-GMO cookies with few, simple ingredients. Upgrade further by making your own. Even more of an upgrade is eating the nutrient-dense Raw Melt-in-Your-Mouth Chocolate Chip Cookies, which give you a healthy dose of vitamins and minerals!

↑ *THE SODA UPGRADE:* Conventional soda is dangerous because it contains ridiculous amounts of GMO sugar, caffeine, preservatives, colorings, flavorings, additives, and aspartame. Upgrade with organic sodas made from non-GMO sugarcane and fruit or kombucha, which is a probiotic and aids digestion.

↑ *THE ENERGY SHOT UPGRADE:* Excessive reliance on caffeine can cause adrenal burnout. Furthermore, many of the most popular brands of energy shots contain damaging chemicals. Upgrade with the Ginger Lemon Shot. Also seek out one of the fruit-based energy shots made with yerba mate, stevia, and high levels of B vitamins (often these do also contain caffeine, so you may wish to read the labels), such as the beverages made by I Am Products.

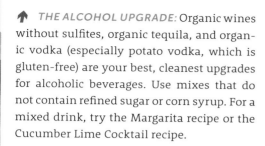

THE ALCOHOL UPGRADE: Organic wines without sulfites, organic tequila, and organic vodka (especially potato vodka, which is gluten-free) are your best, cleanest upgrades for alcoholic beverages. Use mixes that do not contain refined sugar or corn syrup. For a mixed drink, try the Margarita recipe or the Cucumber Lime Cocktail recipe.

Organic vegetables and fruits don't need upgrades. Eat plenty every day.

Common Lifestyle Upgrades

Like food, skin care and cosmetics can also be upgraded. Since the skin is the largest organ in the body and a semipermeable membrane, what you put on your skin definitely matters. For more tips, be sure to check out *The Earth Diet* and The Clear, Smooth, Radiant Skin Guide in Part III.

THE SOAP UPGRADE: Conventional soaps can be toxic for the skin because of ingredients like foaming agents (for instance, sodium lauryl sulphate), petroleum by-products, and synthetic fragrances. Worse, they are tested on animals! Upgrade to plant-based soaps made from clean carrier oils (such as jojoba oil, almond oil, sesame oil, olive oil, hemp oil) and natural fragrances from essential oils (for example, lemon, lavender, frankincense, peppermint, rose, and eucalyptus). I highly recommend Dr. Bronner's excellent biodegradable all-purpose liquid Castile soaps, which come in a variety of scents.

THE FACE CLEANSER UPGRADE: Upgrade from synthetic foaming skin cleansers. Try diluting organic apple cider vinegar in water with a drop of tea tree (*Melaleuca alternifolia*) essential oil.

THE COSMETIC UPGRADE: Buy cosmetics (blush, foundation, mascara) with fewer chemicals. Go for organic, natural, toxic-free, animal-cruelty-free cosmetics.

THE LOTION UPGRADE: Buy an all-natural skin lotion, or upgrade further by substituting whole, natural ingredients found in your kitchen cupboard, like extra-virgin coconut oil, extra-virgin olive oil, tigernut (*Cyperus esculentus*) oil, cacao butter, and aloe vera, for skin lotion. These will actually nourish your skin. Some essential oils have therapeutic properties that aid in healing skin conditions like rashes, acne, and psoriasis. Choose pure, therapeutic-grade essential oils. Lavender is soothing and antioxidant. Frankincense is antiaging, anti-wrinkle. Tea tree oil is a gentle cleanser that helps relieve acne. Citrus oils like lemon, wild orange, grapefruit, and lime are astringent and make perfect toners.

THE EXFOLIATION UPGRADE: Upgrade from an expensive packaged scrub by exfoliating your skin with a combination of salt and a clean oil, or bentonite clay and water. You can also use finely ground nuts and seeds (such as quinoa and almonds) for their rough texture. Upgrade further by gently rubbing your skin with beach sand or seaweed that floats by when you're in the ocean.

For a list of the exact food and lifestyle products I use and recommend to my friends and clients, visit www.TheEarthDiet.com/shoppinglist.

Affirmations

to Upgrade Your Life

Upgrades allow you to enjoy life even more.
The healthier you feel, the more you will be able to
live your dreams. Affirmations are a way to upgrade your *entire life*.

Affirmations are positive statements that you say to yourself to describe
your ideal reality—your vision for how you want to be and feel!

Some helpful affirmations to repeat are:

- I have plenty of time to take care of myself.

- I deserve to feel healthy every day.

- It is my God-given right to experience health! I am not here to suffer.

- I enjoy good-quality foods and beverages.

- I am a well-balanced person.

- I am so thankful for my body and my health as it is right now.

- I love my body and enjoy my health while working toward where I want to be.

- Being healthy is simple and fun.

- I am healing in every moment.

- Laughter is free medicine. Every time I eat something nourishing, have a positive thought, or laugh, I am healing.

- I am in control of what goes into my body.

- I keep the strife out of my life. I maintain a consistently healthy body and environment.

- My body naturally craves and resonates with healthy foods.

- Say or think this before every meal or drink: I am aware of how much nutrition I am receiving. I always look to make the best possible choice wherever I am and whomever I am with. My body digests everything really well.

- While cleaning your juicer or other utensils, thank yourself for making the effort, and thank the juice or food for providing so much nutrition to your cells. Simply think to yourself as you clean: Thank you, thank you, thank you.

When you really don't feel like eating something healthy or exercising, try to train your mind to think something like this:

Just do it.
Just do it.
Just do it.
Just do it!

I can do it.

I am doing it.

I did it!

PART II

THE RECIPES

CHAPTER 5

Juices

Without sufficient hydration, our cells simply won't function properly. Fresh juice is one of the quickest ways to get high amounts of nutrition straight into the cells. With juices, you can affect your antioxidant levels, blood-sugar regulation, body fat, cholesterol and lipid levels, hormonal levels, immune function, and metabolic activity. This is one of the world's best antiaging strategies.

The health improvements that come from drinking juice are remarkable. Remember you reap what you sow. If you drink a juice every single day, you *will* experience the life-changing benefits.

Super Greens

You can get all your essential greens in one drink with this recipe.

Total time: 10 minutes | Serves 1

INGREDIENTS:

1 cucumber
1 green apple or ¾ cup pineapple
3 celery stalks
½ cup kale
½ cup spinach
¼ cup parsley
¼ cup cilantro

ACTIONS:

- Juice all the ingredients in your juicer. Drink.

TIPS:

- Add dandelion greens for more intense flavor.
- Make this without the apple for a sugar-free juice. (I often do this!)

Calories: 210 | Total Fat: 1g | Carbs: 54g | Dietary Fiber: 1g | Protein: 4g

Berry Green

Drink this juice if you want greens in a sweet way.

Total time: 10 minutes | Serves 1

INGREDIENTS:

1 apple
1 cup strawberries
1 cup blueberries
1 small cucumber
1 large celery stalk
Handful of kale
Handful of fresh cilantro
¼ lemon

ACTIONS:

- Juice all the ingredients in your juicer. Drink.

TIP:

- Juice a 1-inch piece of turmeric with the other ingredients to boost its anti-inflammatory properties.

Calories: 220 | Total Fat: 1.4g | Carbs: 59g | Dietary Fiber: 13g | Protein: 4.8g

Detox Juice

This spicy detox juice has an extra kick.

Total time: 10 minutes | Serves 1

INGREDIENTS:

½ bunch celery (6 to 8 stalks)
1 lemon with rind
1-inch piece of ginger
1 yellow pepper
Dash of cayenne pepper

ACTIONS:

- Juice all the ingredients in your juicer. Drink.

Calories: 33 | Total Fat: 1g | Carbs: 11g | Dietary Fiber: 1g | Protein: 3g

Immune Booster

This juice is extremely high in vitamin C, which instantly boosts the immune system and makes you feel better.

Total time: 10 minutes | Serves 1

INGREDIENTS:

1-inch chunk of turmeric root (or ½ teaspoon turmeric powder)
1 clove garlic
1-inch chunk of ginger
3 red or green apples
¼ cup parsley
¼ cup cilantro
3 celery stalks
½ cup spinach

ACTIONS:

- Juice all the ingredients in your juicer. Drink.

Calories: 90 | Total Fat: 1.2g | Carbs: 30g | Dietary Fiber: 10g | Protein: 3.1g

Energy Juice

A morning or afternoon pick-me-up.

Total time: 10 minutes | Serves 1

INGREDIENTS:

2 large green apples
1 large cucumber
1-inch piece of ginger
½ small lemon, peeled
Dash of cayenne pepper

ACTIONS:

- Juice all ingredients in your juice machine except for the cayenne.
- Before serving, add a dash of cayenne. Drink.

Calories: 203 | Total Fat: 1g | Carbs: 53g | Dietary Fiber: 1g | Protein: 3g

Digestion Helper Juice

This delicious juice is helpful for people with issues such as constipation, bloating, and IBS.

Total time: 10 minutes | Serves 1

INGREDIENTS:

1 small beet
1½ cups pineapple
3 carrots
3 celery stalks
⅓ cup fresh parsley

ACTIONS:

- Juice all the ingredients in your juice machine. Drink.

TIP:

- If you don't have any pineapple on hand, you can substitute an equal amount of apples.

VARIATIONS:

- Spicy Digestion Helper Juice: Add one 2-inch piece of ginger.
- Vegetable Digestion Helper Juice: Replace the pineapple with more carrots or celery.

Calories: 85 | Total Fat: 1.8g | Carbs: 25g | Dietary Fiber: 10g | Protein: 4.9g

Fat Blaster

This combination is a sweet way to blast those excess fat cells.

Total time: 10 minutes | Serves 1

INGREDIENTS:

2 oranges, peeled
1 grapefruit, peeled
1 lemon, peeled

ACTIONS:

- Juice all the ingredients in your juicer. Drink.

TIPS:

- You don't need a juice machine to make this recipe. Squeeze the fruit by hand or with a citrus press, before discarding the rinds.
- For a more cleansing drink, juice the lemon without peeling. It will be a lot zestier.

VARIATIONS:

- Hot Fat Blaster: Add a dash of cayenne pepper to the finished juice.
- Immune-Boosting Fat Blaster: Add a dash of turmeric powder.

Calories: 175 | Total Fat: 1g | Carbs: 50g | Dietary Fiber: 1g | Protein: 5g

ABC Juice

This three-ingredient juice is an easy recipe for young children who are learning their ABCs to remember: apple, beet, celery!

Total time: 10 minutes | *Serves 3*

INGREDIENTS:

3 small apples
1 small beet
9 celery stalks (about one bunch)

ACTIONS:

- Juice the ingredients in your juice machine. Drink.

TIP:

- You can replace the celery stalks with 2 cucumbers or carrots.

Calories: 80 | Total Fat: 0.5g | Carbs: 20g | Dietary Fiber: 5.1g | Protein: 1.6g

Green Lemonade

A sweet and refreshing juice that kids and adults alike enjoy drinking.

Total time: 10 minutes | *Serves 1*

INGREDIENTS:

2 apples
1 large cucumber
1 large celery stalk
1 (roughly) thumb-sized piece of ginger
½ large lemon, peeled

ACTIONS:

- Juice the ingredients in your juice machine. Drink.

Calories: 131.4 | Total Fat: 0.7g | Carbs: 32.2g | Dietary Fiber: 7.2g | Protein: 2.8g

Vegetable Juice

The ingredients in this juice are non-starchy, so they don't cause the blood sugar to spike, which makes it ideal for people with diabetes or insulin resistance. It is a great way to get the vitamins and minerals your body needs.

Total time: 10 minutes | *Serves 1*

INGREDIENTS:

1 head of lettuce (any kind works well, including iceberg or red leaf) or kale
2 medium-sized tomatoes
3 carrots
1 cucumber
½ small red onion, peeled
¼ teaspoon cracked black pepper
¼ teaspoon salt

ACTIONS:

- Juice all ingredients except for the salt and pepper.
- Stir salt and pepper into the juice. Drink.

TIPS:

- Experiment with adding one or all of the following: 1 red bell pepper, 1 green bell pepper, 1 yellow bell pepper, 2 parsnips.

VARIATION:

- Spicy Vegetable Juice: Add a dash or three (or more!) of cayenne pepper to the finished juice.

Calories: 125 | Total Fat: 1g | Carbs: 25g | Dietary Fiber: 1g | Protein 9g

Kids' Paradise Juice

Kids love this colorful, 100-percent fruit juice. Filled with antioxidants, it really satisfies sweet cravings.

Total time: 10 minutes | *Serves 3*

INGREDIENTS:

1 apple
1 cup strawberries
1 cup blueberries
1 cup fresh pineapple
½ small lemon, peeled

ACTIONS:

- Juice all the ingredients in your juicer. Drink.

TIP:

- Garnish the rim of your glass with chunks of pineapple, strawberry slices, or a split grape.

VARIATION:

- Anti-inflammatory Paradise Juice: Add ¼-cup fresh cilantro and 1½-inch piece of turmeric root or ½ teaspoon turmeric powder.

Calories: 89 | Total Fat: 0.5g | Carbs: 22.7g | Dietary Fiber: 3.6g | Protein: 1g

Beet Juice

Beets are a great digestive cleanser. This juice not only detoxifies the blood and liver, it helps lift compacted waste from the bowel wall.

Total time: 10 minutes | *Serves 1*

INGREDIENTS:

1 small beet
2 red apples
3 carrots
1 thumb-sized piece of ginger
½ small lemon, peeled

ACTIONS:

- Juice all the ingredients in your juicer. Drink.

VARIATIONS:

- Beet Celery Juice: Add celery stalks to the ingredients before juicing.
- Beet Vegetable Juice: Replace the apples with carrots for sweetness.

Calories: 260 | Total Fat: 1g | Carbs: 65g | Dietary Fiber: 1g | Protein: 5g

Fun Fact:

Did you know that when you make a juice, such as carrot juice, you don't have to throw away the pulp? Feed your plants with it. Add the pulp to your compost heap, and it will create nice, lush soil that grows a great garden. Or use the pulp in a muffin or cake recipe!

Orange Carrot Ginger Juice

Carrot juice is rich in vitamins A, B, C, D, E, and K. It also contains minerals like calcium, phosphorous, and potassium, which make it great for the skin, hair, and nails. If I drink carrot juice every day for a few days, I always notice a nice glow to my skin. The addition of orange and ginger is elevating.

Total time: 10 minutes | Serves 2

INGREDIENTS:

10 carrots
2 oranges, peeled
1 thumb-sized piece of ginger
Handful of parsley

ACTIONS:

- Juice all the ingredients in your juicer. Drink.

Calories: 200 | Total Fat: 0.8g | Carbs: 48g | Dietary Fiber: 13g | Protein: 5g

Classic Fresh Orange Juice

Not just for breakfast!

Total time: 10 minutes | Serves 1

INGREDIENTS:

4 oranges, peeled

ACTIONS:

- Juice the oranges in your juice machine. Drink.

TIPS:

- You don't need a juice machine to make this recipe. Squeeze the fruit by hand or with a citrus press, before discarding the rinds.
- Add 1 lemon with rind for more zing.

Calories: 155 | Total Fat: 1g | Carbs: 36g | Dietary Fiber: 1g | Protein: 2g

Apple Juice

Skip the preservatives and added sugar of most store-bought juice brands by making your own.

Total time: 10 minutes | *Serves 1*

INGREDIENTS:

4 red or green apples

ACTIONS:

- Juice the apples in your juice machine. Drink.

TIP:

- Experiment with flavors! Add cilantro, parsley, celery, cucumber, carrot, beet, orange, and mint.

VARIATIONS:

- Apple Pie Juice: Add ½ teaspoon cinnamon to finished juice.
- Lemon Apple Juice: Add 1 lemon, peeled, to the ingredients before juicing for a vitamin C boost.

Calories: 315 | Total Fat: 1g | Carbs: 85g | Dietary Fiber: 1g | Protein: 2g

Ginger Lemon Shot

An immune-boosting energizer that is perfect for a 3 p.m. pick-me-up. Have one whenever you feel like you're getting the sniffles or feeling sluggish.

Total time: 5 minutes | *Serves 2*

INGREDIENTS:

2 lemons, peeled
2-inch piece of ginger, peeled

ACTIONS:

- Juice the lemon and ginger in a juice machine.

VARIATIONS:

- Hot Ginger Lemon Shot: Add a dash of cayenne pepper to the finished juice.
- Ginger Lemon Orange Shot: Add 1 peeled orange to the ingredients before juicing.

Calories: 19 | Total Fat: 0.2g | Carbs: 5.8g | Dietary Fiber: 1.7g | Protein: 0.7g

CHAPTER 6

Milks and Shakes

Y ou can use any raw nut or seed to make your own milk. Creamy foods are comforting and stress-reducing, especially when you know they're giving you the benefit of antioxidants, as well as calcium, iron, and magnesium.

Basic Nut and Seed Milk Formula

To save time, mix up a large batch of your favorite milk to cover your upcoming smoothie and breakfast needs for the week. Personally, I always keep Almond Milk, Sunflower Seed Milk, Coconut Milk, and Cashew Milk in my refrigerator, since I cook so much for myself and my friends. If you plan to have a smoothie every day, you'll need about a gallon of milk for the week. This milk keeps in the fridge for a week or frozen in airtight containers for a month or more.

Total time: 5 minutes | *Serves 4*

INGREDIENTS:

1 cup raw nut or seed of your choice
4 seedless dates (or 1 to 2 tablespoons raw honey or maple syrup)

ACTIONS:

- Put all ingredients in the blender with 4 cups water, and mix until a smooth consistency is achieved. Drink.

TIPS:

- Add 3 cups ice for thicker, cooler milk.
- Add a dash of salt for extra flavor.

VARIATIONS:

- Vanilla Nut or Seed Milk: Add ½ teaspoon pure vanilla extract and pinch of salt.
- Chocolate Nut or Seed Milk: Add 2 teaspoons (or more, to taste) of cacao powder.
- Strawberry Nut or Seed Milk: Add ½ cup strawberries.

Almond Milk

You can make delicious almond milk in less than five minutes. Drink as is, or use it as a base for other recipes.

Total time: 5 minutes | *Serves 4*

INGREDIENTS:

1 cup raw almonds, skins included
4 seedless dates (or 1 to 2 tablespoons raw honey or maple syrup)

ACTIONS:

- Put all ingredients and 4 cups water in the blender, and mix until a smooth consistency is achieved. Drink.

TIP:

- Keeping the skins on helps you make this very quickly, but for creamier and smoother almond milk, soak your almonds for 4 hours or until the skin is soft. Pop the almonds right out of their skins before blending.

Calories: 228 | *Total Fat: 17.6g* | *Carbs: 13.9g* | *Dietary Fiber: 5g* | *Protein: 7.7g*

Sunflower Seed Milk

Sunny and cheerful to look at, sunflowers also give us seeds that can brighten our moods. Because they combine tryptophan and carbs, as well as many other important nutrients, they raise serotonin levels and alleviate depressive symptoms naturally.

Total time: 5 minutes | *Serves 4*

INGREDIENTS:

1 cup sunflower seeds
4 seedless dates (or 1 tablespoon maple syrup or honey)

ACTIONS:

- Put all ingredients and 4 cups water in the blender, and mix until a smooth consistency is achieved. Drink.

Calories: 210 | *Total Fat: 16g* | *Carbs: 13.9g* | *Dietary Fiber: 4.2g* | *Protein: 6.4g*

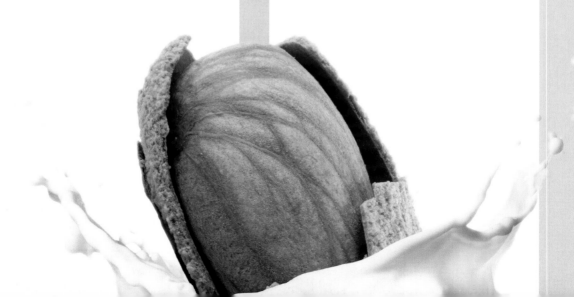

Cashew Milk

Naturally sweet and creamy, cashews make excellent, drinkable milk.

Total time: 5 minutes | Serves 4

INGREDIENTS:

1 cup cashews
2 seedless dates (or ½ tablespoon maple syrup)
Dash of salt
¼ teaspoon vanilla extract

ACTIONS:

- Put all ingredients and 4 cups water in the blender, and mix until a smooth consistency is achieved. Drink.

Calories: 220 | Total Fat: 14g | Carbs: 16.3g | Dietary Fiber: 1.7g | Protein: 5.2g

Tigernut Milk

Ancient civilizations in Africa knew about the health benefits of this incredible vegetable root. With a blender on hand, you can create a beverage that is filled with prebiotic starches, which nourish the good bacteria in our intestines that help us digest vitamins.

Total time: 5 minutes | Serves 4

INGREDIENTS:

1 cup tigernuts
4 seedless dates (or 1 to 2 tablespoons raw honey or maple syrup)

ACTIONS:

- Put all ingredients and 4 cups water in the blender, and mix until a smooth consistency is achieved. Drink.

Calories: 504 | Total Fat: 28g Carbs: 58.3g | Dietary Fiber: 40.7g | Protein: 8.2g

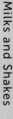

Hemp Milk

One of the properties of hemp seed that makes it a valuable immune-boosting food is that it contains 20 essential amino acids the human body needs to function optimally. The protein in hemp seed is very digestible. It has a light and deliciously nutty flavor.

Total time: 5 minutes | Serves 4

INGREDIENTS:

1 cup hemp seeds
4 seedless dates (or 1 tablespoon honey)
Dash of salt
¼ teaspoon vanilla extract

ACTIONS:

- Put all ingredients and 4 cups water in the blender, and mix until a smooth consistency is achieved. Drink.

Calories: 264 | Total Fat: 19.5g | Carbs: 10.7g | Dietary Fiber 0.7g | Protein: 15.2g

Flax Milk

Flaxseeds are high in omega-3 fatty acids and have antioxidant and anti-inflammatory benefits that make them a superfood. A subtle smoky flavor makes it a good base for Chocolate Milk and other milkshakes.

Total time: 5 minutes | Serves 4

INGREDIENTS:

1 cup flaxseeds
4 seedless dates (or 1 tablespoon honey)
Dash of salt
¼ teaspoon vanilla extract

ACTIONS:

- Put all ingredients and 4 cups water in the blender, and mix until a smooth consistency is achieved. Drink.

Calories: 269 | Total Fat: 16.9g | Carbs: 18.7g | Dietary Fiber: 12.4g | Protein: 10.8g

Protein Milk

A flavorful combination of two high-protein seeds.

Total time: 5 minutes | Serves 4

INGREDIENTS:

½ cup hemp seeds
½ cup pumpkin seeds
4 seedless dates (or 1 tablespoon honey)
Dash of salt
¼ teaspoon vanilla extract

ACTIONS:

- Put all ingredients and 4 cups water in the blender, and mix together until a smooth consistency is achieved. Drink.

Calories: 180 | Total Fat: 113g | Carbs: 12.8g | Dietary Fiber: 1.8g | Protein: 9.2g

Chocolate Hazelnut Milk

Total time: 5 minutes | Serves 2

INGREDIENTS:

¾ cup raw or roasted hazelnuts
1 tablespoon cacao powder
1 teaspoon cacao nibs
4 seedless dates (or 1 tablespoon honey)
Pinch of salt

ACTIONS:

- Put all ingredients and 3 cups water in the blender, and mix until a smooth consistency is achieved. Drink.

Calories: 349 | Total Fat: 27.1g | Carbs: 24.1g | Dietary Fiber: 5.3g | Protein: 7.6g

Oat Milk

Oats offer us 10 minerals, 15 vitamins, and tons of fiber. They help lower cholesterol levels, and doctors have been recommending them for years to heart patients. Pure oats are naturally gluten-free.

Total time: 5 minutes | Serves 4

INGREDIENTS:

¾ cup whole oats
4 seedless dates (or 1 tablespoon honey)
Dash of salt
¼ teaspoon vanilla extract

ACTIONS:

- Put all ingredients and 4 cups water in the blender, and mix together until a smooth consistency is achieved. Drink.

Calories: 80 | Total Fat: 1g | Carbs: 16.4g | Dietary Fiber: 2.2g | Protein: 2.5g

Rice Milk

An affordable, dairy-free, "alternative" milk that is high in calcium, iron, and vitamin B.

Total time: 5 minutes | Serves 4

INGREDIENTS:

¾ cup uncooked brown or white rice
4 seedless dates (or 1 tablespoon honey)
Dash of salt
¼ teaspoon vanilla extract

ACTIONS:

- Put all ingredients and 4 cups water in the blender, and mix until a smooth consistency is achieved. Drink.

Calories: 65 | Total Fat: 0.4g | Carbs: 14.7g | Dietary Fiber: 1.3g | Protein: 1.1g

Coconut Milk

Paradise in a glass! Once you learn how to do this correctly, you'll always want to make your own. It's extremely fulfilling to make fresh coconut milk at home.

Total time: 10 minutes | *Serves 1*

INGREDIENT:

1 fresh whole coconut

ACTIONS:

- Make a hole in the coconut. Here is the easiest way: On one end of every coconut, you'll see three small, dark circles. One of these holes will be softer than the others. Poke through this hole with a screwdriver or a sharp kitchen utensil, like a thin knife or a metal chopstick.
- Drain the liquid from the coconut into a blender.
- Crack the coconut open with a hammer, then scrape out the white coconut flesh inside and put this in the blender.
- Blend on high speed until a smooth, creamy consistency is achieved.

TIP:

- Add a dash of salt for flavor.

VARIATIONS:

- Vanilla Coconut Milk: Add ¼ teaspoon pure vanilla extract.
- Chocolate Coconut Milk: Add 1 teaspoon cacao powder and 1 teaspoon honey.
- Strawberry Coconut Milk: Add ½ cup strawberries.

Calories: 354 | Total Fat: 33.5g | Carbs: 15.2g | Dietary Fiber: 9g | Protein: 3.3g

Coffee Milk

Coffee beans are naturally provided by earth and can give us a lot of positive health benefits when consumed in moderation. They have antidepressant properties.

Total time: 5 minutes | *Serves 1*

INGREDIENTS:

1 cup brewed coffee
½ cup Almond Milk (or another nut milk or seed milk)
1 teaspoon honey or maple syrup to sweeten (more, if you like it sweeter)
5 large ice cubes

ACTIONS:

• In a blender or cup, mix all ingredients together.

TIP:

• Make Coffee Ice Cubes by freezing it in an ice cube tray.

Calories: 227 | *Total Fat: 16.1g* | *Carbs: 13.9g* | *Dietary Fiber: 5g* | *Protein: 7.7g*

Horchata

A traditional drink from Spain, horchata can be made from ground rice, barley, sesame seeds, or almonds. In this recipe, we use tigernuts, known as *chufas* in Spanish, which increase nutrient circulation and help us to absorb minerals.

Total time: 10 minutes | *Serves 1*

INGREDIENTS:

½ cup Tigernut Milk
¾ cup Rice Milk
1 teaspoon cinnamon powder
½ teaspoon sesame seeds
2 tablespoons honey or maple syrup
½ cup ice
Pinch of salt

ACTIONS:

• Blend all ingredients together until creamy, thick, and sweet.

Calories: 420 | *Total Fat: 15.1g* | *Carbs: 69.4g* | *Dietary Fiber: 22.5g* | *Protein: 5.4g*

Vanilla Milkshake

Total time: 5 minutes | *Serves 1*

INGREDIENTS:

1 cup Almond Milk
½ tablespoon pure vanilla extract
3 seedless dates (or 1 tablespoon raw
   honey or maple syrup)
½ cup ice

ACTIONS:

- Put all ingredients in a blender, and
  mix until well combined.

TIPS:

- To be even closer to nature, substitute
  the seeds of 1 vanilla bean for the
  vanilla extract. Scrape the seeds out of
  the vanilla bean pod and discard the
  pod before using the seeds.
- Add a pinch of salt for enhanced
  flavor.
- You can swap out the Almond Milk
  for a milk of your choice, such as
  Sunflower Seed or Tigernut Milk.

Calories: 316 | Total Fat: 17.7g | Carbs: 33.4g |
Dietary Fiber: 7g | Protein: 8.3g

Strawberry Milkshake

Total time: 5 minutes | *Serves 1*

INGREDIENTS:

1 cup Almond Milk
½ cup strawberries
3 seedless dates (or 1 tablespoon raw
   honey or maple syrup)
½ cup ice

ACTIONS:

- Put all ingredients in a blender, and
  mix until well combined.

TIPS:

- Add a pinch of salt for enhanced
  flavor.
- Use frozen fruit for enhanced texture.
- You can swap out the Almond Milk
  for a milk of your choice, such as
  Sunflower Seed or Tigernut Milk.

VARIATION:

- Strawberry Banana Shake: Add 1 to 2
  bananas.

Calories: 323 | Total Fat: 18g | Carbs: 38.4g |
Dietary Fiber: 8.9g | Protein: 8.8g

Banana Milkshake

Total time: 7 minutes | *Serves 1*

INGREDIENTS:

1 cup Almond Milk
1 banana
½ tablespoon pure vanilla extract
3 seedless dates (or 1 tablespoon raw
honey or maple syrup)
½ cup ice

ACTIONS:

- Put all ingredients in a blender, and
  mix until well combined.

TIPS:

- Add a pinch of salt for enhanced flavor.
- Use a frozen banana for enhanced texture.
- You can swap out the Almond Milk for a milk of
  your choice, such as Sunflower Seed or Tigernut
  Milk.

Calories: 426 | Total Fat: 17.7g | Carbs: 63.4g | Dietary
Fiber: 10g | Protein: 9.3g

Chocolate Shake

Total time: 5 minutes | Serves 1

INGREDIENTS:

1 cup Almond Milk
2 teaspoons cacao powder
4 seedless dates (or 1 tablespoon raw honey or maple syrup)
½ cup ice

ACTIONS:

- Put all ingredients in a blender, and mix until well combined.

TIPS:

- Add a pinch of salt for enhanced flavor.
- You can swap out the Almond Milk for a milk of your choice, such as Sunflower Seed Milk.

Calories: 361 | Total Fat: 17.7g | Carbs: 38.8g | Dietary Fiber: 7.7g | Protein: 8.5g

Cherry Chocolate Shake

Total time: 10 minutes | Serves 2

INGREDIENTS:

2 cups cherries, pitted
¼ cup cashews (or almonds or hazelnuts)
4 seedless dates (or 1 to 2 tablespoons raw honey or maple syrup)
1 tablespoon cacao powder
½ cup ice

ACTIONS:

- Put all ingredients with 1½ cups water in a blender, and mix until well combined.

Calories: 268 | Total Fat: 0.7g | Carbs: 41.7g | Dietary Fiber: 5g | Protein: 2.5g

Coffee Milkshake

Total time: 5 minutes | *Serves 1*

INGREDIENTS:

1 cup brewed coffee, cooled
½ cup Almond Milk
1 teaspoon honey or maple syrup to
    sweeten (more, if you like it sweeter)
1 cup ice

ACTIONS:

- Put all ingredients in a blender, and mix until well combined.

Calories: 133 | Total Fat: 16.1g | Carbs: 11.5g | Dietary Fiber: 2.5g | Protein: 4.2g

Hot Chocolate

Delicious on a romantic, rainy day.

Total time: 10 minutes | *Serves 1*

INGREDIENTS:

1 tablespoon cacao powder
Dash of Almond Milk or Coconut
    Milk
1 tablespoon honey or maple syrup

ACTIONS:

- Stir all ingredients and 1 cup boiling water together in a mug.

VARIATION:

- Spicy Hot Chocolate: Add a dash or 3 of cayenne pepper, to taste.

Calories: 100 | Total Fat: 2.4g | Carbs: 18.8g | Dietary Fiber: 1.5g | Protein: 1.8g

Chocolate Almond Butter Shake

Total time: 5 minutes | *Serves 1*

INGREDIENTS:

1 cup Almond Milk
2 teaspoons cacao powder
1 tablespoon almond butter
4 seedless dates (or 1 to 2
    tablespoons raw honey
    or maple syrup)
½ cup ice

ACTIONS:

- Put all ingredients in a blender, and mix until well combined.

TIPS:

- Substitute Protein Milk for Almond Milk to bump up the protein content.
- Add an Earth Diet Chocolate Almond Butter Cup for thickness and richer flavor.

VARIATION:

- Chocolate Peanut Butter Shake: Substitute 1 tablespoon peanut butter for the almond butter.

Calories: 459 | Total Fat: 26.6g | Carbs: 42.2g | Dietary Fiber: 9.3g | Protein: 10.9g

CHAPTER 7

Teas and Infused Waters

Drinking tea or infused water is an opportunity to hydrate your body in a fun and colorful way. I love teas and infusions because they're anti-inflammatory, cleansing, and nutritious as well as hydrating. Some contain ingredients, like chamomile, which are calming. Others, such as those that contain mint and cayenne pepper, are energizing.

If you're hungry, drink a glass of water or tea. Thirst often masquerades as hunger. Lots of us also run around slightly dehydrated all the time, which puts unnecessary strain on our bodies. So make a point of sipping infused water throughout the day. The infusions of fruits and vegetables give it a little nutrient and flavor kick. Always use clean, filtered water.

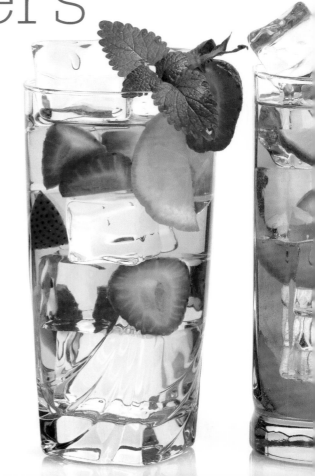

Coconut Water

Total time: 5 minutes | *Serves 1*

INGREDIENT:

1 fresh whole coconut

ACTIONS:

- Make a hole in the coconut. Here is the easiest way: On one end of every coconut, you'll see three small, dark circles. One of these holes will be softer than the others. Poke through this hole with a screwdriver or a sharp kitchen utensil, like a thin knife or a metal chopstick.

- Drain the coconut water into a glass and drink. Or place a straw in the hole and drink the Coconut Water directly from the coconut!

TIP:

- You can crack open the coconut and scoop out the flesh to use in another recipe or just eat on its own.

Calories: 91 | Total Fat: 1g | Carbs: 18g | Dietary Fiber: 5g | Protein: 3g

Lemon Water

Total time: 5 minutes | *Serves 1*

INGREDIENT:

1 lemon

ACTIONS:

- Cut lemon in half and squeeze juice into 2 cups water with a citrus press. Drink.

TIPS:

- Lemon Ice Cubes: Freeze Lemon Water in an ice cube tray, and always have them on hand! Just pop some into your water, juice, smoothie, or tea.
- If squeezing by hand, cut lemon into quarters to make it a little easier.

Calories: 12 | Total Fat: 0g | Carbs: 4g | Dietary Fiber: 0g | Protein: 0g

Fruit Water

This is a great jug to have at children's parties or dull meetings! It brightens the table, and people can't help feeling more cheerful after drinking it. The fruits add flavor to the water as well as some sweetness.

Total time: 10 minutes | Serves 8

INGREDIENTS:

1 lemon
1 orange, peeled and sliced
1 apple, sliced
1 cucumber, sliced
½ cup fresh mint leaves
½ cup strawberries, sliced
½ cup blueberries
¼ pineapple, sliced

ACTIONS:

- Add 8 cups water to a large jug, and squeeze the juice of the lemon into the water.
- Add all the fruit slices, then enjoy drinking the water with a sweet smile!

Calories: 46 | Total Fat: 0.1g | Carbs: 12g | Dietary Fiber: 2.7g | Protein: 0.6g

Hydrating Cucumber Mint Water

This water is incredibly hydrating for the cells and skin. You can make some and then keep it in the fridge. It also makes great ice cubes that you can pop into your drinks! Pat a cucumber slice under and around your eyes while you make the water, too!

Total time: 5 minutes | Serves 4

INGREDIENTS:

1 cucumber, sliced
1 cup fresh mint leaves

ACTIONS:

- Add 4 cups water to a jug along with the cucumber slices.
- Rip up the mint leaves with your hands, toss them in, then give it a quick stir. Drink.

Calories: 18 | Total Fat: 0.1g | Carbs: 5g | Dietary Fiber: 0.7g | Protein: 0.8g

Skin Cleanser Water

Total time: 5 minutes | Serves 1

INGREDIENTS:

1 lemon
1 small cucumber, thinly sliced in
    rounds
¼ cup fresh cilantro, torn with hands
Dash of cayenne pepper

ACTIONS:

- Squeeze lemon juice into 2 cups water.
  Add cucumber slices, cilantro, and
  cayenne pepper. Drink.

TIPS

- After drinking the water, you can eat
  the cucumbers or pat them on your
  face to hydrate the skin!

*Calories: 13 | Total Fat: 0g | Carbs: 20g |
Dietary Fiber: 4g | Protein: 2g*

Detox Water

Total time: 5 minutes | Serves 1

INGREDIENTS:

1 lemon
1 teaspoon apple cider vinegar
Dash of cayenne pepper
Dash of real salt
Sprinkle of black pepper

ACTIONS:

- Squeeze lemon juice into 2 cups water,
  then add the other ingredients. Stir
  and drink.

*Calories: 30 | Total Fat: 0g | Carbs: 4g |
Dietary Fiber: 0.2g | Protein: 0.2g*

Fat Flush Water

Total time: 10 minutes | Serves 2

INGREDIENTS:

1 orange
1 grapefruit
1 lemon
Dash of cayenne pepper

ACTIONS:

- Add 5 cups water to a jug. Squeeze the
  juice of the orange, grapefruit, and
  lemon into the water by hand. Stir in
  the cayenne pepper and drink.

*Calories: 75 | Total Fat: 0.2g | Carbs: 19g |
Dietary Fiber: 3.9g | Protein: 1.3g*

Beauty Water

Did you know you can actually eat rose
petals? They have healing benefits as
well as nutritional benefits!

Total time: 5 minutes | Serves 1

INGREDIENTS:

¼ cup fresh raspberries
Handful of fresh mint leaves
1 teaspoon chamomile flowers
Handful of rose petals

ACTIONS:

- Add all the ingredients into 2 cups
  water in a large cup, then stir and
  drink. Have an awareness of grace.

*Calories: 8 | Total Fat: 0g | Carbs: 2g |
Dietary Fiber: 0.5g | Protein: 0.1g*

Immune-Boosting Tea

Total time: 10 minutes | *Serves 1*

INGREDIENTS:

1-inch piece of ginger, diced
1 clove garlic, diced
¼ teaspoon turmeric powder
Dash of cayenne pepper (the beverage
    should be spicy, but comfortable to
    drink)
1 lemon
1 tablespoon raw honey (optional)

ACTIONS:

- In a saucepan, bring 2 cups water,
  ginger, garlic, turmeric, and cayenne
  pepper to a boil. Reduce the heat to
  medium and simmer for 5 minutes.
- Strain the liquid as you pour it into a
  mug.
- Squeeze in the juice of the lemon, add
  honey, if desired, and stir well. Drink
  warm.

*Calories: 87 | Total Fat: 0g | Carbs: 24g |
Dietary Fiber: 1g | Protein: 1g*

Skin Cleansing Tea

Total time: 10 minutes | *Serves 1*

INGREDIENTS:

Dash of cayenne pepper
Juice of 1 lemon
½-inch piece of ginger
1-inch piece of burdock root
Drop of tea tree (melaleuca)
    essential oil

ACTIONS:

- Add 2 cups water and all the
  ingredients to a pot, and bring to a
  boil. Reduce the heat to medium and
  simmer for 5 minutes.
- Strain the liquid as you pour it into a
  mug, then serve.

*Calories: 14 | Total Fat: 0g | Carbs: 24g |
Dietary Fiber: 4g | Protein: 2g*

Goddess Beauty Tea

Total time: 10 minutes | *Serves 2*

INGREDIENTS:

1 tablespoon lavender flowers
(or 1 drop of lavender essential oil)
1 tablespoon chamomile flowers
(or 1 drop chamomile essential oil)
1 tablespoon rose petals
(or 1 drop rose essential oil)
¼ cup fresh peppermint
(or 1 drop peppermint essential oil)

ACTIONS:

- Add 4 cups water and all the ingredients to a pot,
  and bring to a boil. Reduce the heat to medium
  and simmer for 5 minutes.
- Strain the liquid as you pour it into a mug, then
  serve.

*Calories: 0 | Total Fat: 0g | Carbs: 0g |
Dietary Fiber: 0.5g | Protein: 0g*

Weight Loss Tea

Total time: 10 minutes | *Serves 2*

INGREDIENTS:

2-inch piece of ginger, diced
Dash of cayenne pepper
½ teaspoon turmeric powder
1 lemon

ACTIONS:

- In a saucepan, bring 4 cups water, ginger, cayenne pepper, and turmeric powder to a boil. Reduce the heat to medium and simmer for 5 minutes.
- Strain the liquid as you pour it into a mug.
- Squeeze in the juice of the lemon, and stir well. Drink warm.

TIPS:

- Instead of discarding the ginger, you can eat it.
- The tea should only be as spicy as is comfortable for you to drink. Add more or less cayenne pepper, to taste.

Calories: 14 | Total Fat: 0g | Carbs: 4g | Dietary Fiber: 1g | Protein: 0g

Ginger Tea

Total time: 10 minutes | *Serves 2*

INGREDIENT:

2-inch piece of ginger, diced

ACTIONS:

- Add 4 cups water and ginger to a pot, and bring to a boil for 5 minutes.
- Strain the liquid as you pour it into a mug, then serve.

Calories: 2 | Total Fat: 0g | Carbs: 0g | Dietary Fiber: 0g | Protein: 0g

Energy Tea

Total time: 10 minutes | *Serves 2*

INGREDIENTS:

1 teaspoon fresh or dried lavender
1 teaspoon dried green tea leaves
1 teaspoon fresh or dried mint
1 teaspoon grated ginseng root or ginseng powder

ACTIONS:

- Add 4 cups water and all the ingredients to a pot, and bring to a boil for 5 minutes.
- Strain the liquid as you pour it into a mug, then serve.

Calories: 2 | Total Fat: 0g | Carbs: 0g | Dietary Fiber: 0g | Protein: 0g

Bedtime Tea

Total time: 10 minutes | *Serves 2*

INGREDIENTS:

2 tablespoons chamomile flowers
1 tablespoon lavender leaves

ACTIONS:

- Add 4 cups water and all the ingredients to a pot, and bring to a boil for 5 minutes.
- Strain the liquid as you pour it into a mug, then serve.

Calories: 3 | Total Fat: 0.1g | Carbs: 4g | Dietary Fiber: 0g | Protein: 0.2g

CHAPTER 8

Adult Beverages

People ask me what is the healthiest alcohol beverage to drink. My answer is to always try to choose things that come most naturally from the earth with the least processing and chemical additives: organic wine without sulfites, vodka, and tequila. (Home-brewed beer is another good option.) Wine is made from grapes, tequila from the agave cactus, and vodka from potatoes. Did you know that vodka can contain gluten if it was derived from wheat? Always go for vodka that comes from potatoes, as it's the cleanest upgrade.

Many of these drinks make delicious treats with or without alcohol. These recipes offer an upgrade from the common recipes made with refined sugars, dairy, gluten, corn syrup, and GMO ingredients. A lot of people wonder why they feel bloated after drinking, and it's because the ingredients in conventional drinks cause inflammation. These recipes are anti-inflammatory—a much healthier way to enjoy your favorite adult beverages.

Cucumber Lime Cocktail

Even without alcohol, this makes a wonderful nutritious juice to have anytime! This cocktail uses coconut sugar instead of the refined white sugar that often leads to inflammation and skin issues.

Total time: 10 minutes | Serves 2

INGREDIENTS:

2 cups fresh pineapple
4 celery stalks
2 cucumbers, peeled
1 lime, peeled
2 tablespoons coconut sugar, for the rim
Slices of lime, for garnish
2 to 4 ounces tequila or vodka

ACTIONS:

- Put coconut sugar on a plate. Slice a lime and wipe it around the rim of the glasses. Dip the rims of the glasses into the coconut sugar so they are coated. Set aside.
- Juice the pineapple, celery, cucumber, and lime in your juice machine.
- Pour juice into the cocktail glasses. Stir in the alcohol of your choosing.
- Garnish the rims with lime slices. Serve over ice.

TIP:

- For a party-sized pitcher of Cucumber Lime Cocktail, double the recipe.

Calories: 139.6 | Total Fat: 1.2g | Carbs: 33g | Dietary Fiber: 6.8g | Protein: 3.5g

Cosmopolitan

This beverage is high in antioxidants! The cosmopolitan you would find at a bar is usually made with cranberry cocktail juice that may contain added sugars. This version is made with pure cranberry juice. Instead of triple sec, juice your own orange and add grated orange peel.

Total time: 10 minutes | Serves 1

INGREDIENTS:

½ orange
1 small lime
1¾ ounces vodka
¼ ounce 100% cranberry juice, organic

ACTIONS:

- Squeeze the orange to get ¼ ounce of juice. Grate the orange peel until you have ½ teaspoon.
- Cut the lime in quarters, and squeeze to get ¼ ounce of juice. Save a wedge of lime for the garnish.
- Combine vodka, all juices, and orange peel in a cocktail shaker with ice. Cover and shake vigorously until chilled.
- Strain into a chilled cocktail glass and garnish with a lime wedge.

Calories: 284 | Total Fat: 0.0g | Carbs: 7.0g | Dietary Fiber: 1.2g | Protein: 0.5g

Tropical Cocktail

Many cocktails are full of refined sugars that make the beverage unhealthy and too hard to digest. This cocktail uses real fruit sugars, the kind that our bodies are designed to enjoy!

Total time: 10 minutes | *Serves 2*

INGREDIENTS:

2 passion fruits
1 mango, peeled and seeded
1 cup pineapple, cubed
1 orange, peeled
1 lime
1 (roughly) thumb-sized piece of ginger
2 to 4 ounces tequila or vodka

ACTIONS:

- Juice all the ingredients in your juicer.
- Pour juice into the cocktail glasses. Stir in the alcohol of your choosing.
- Garnish the rims with pineapple chunks, or orange or lime slices. Serve over ice.

TIP:

- For a party-sized pitcher of Tropical Cocktails, double the recipe.

Calories: 209 | *Total Fat: 0.5g* | *Carbs: 52g* | *Dietary Fiber: 9g* | *Protein: 2.2g*

Piña Colada

Total time: 7 minutes | *Serves 2*

INGREDIENTS:

1 cup Coconut Water
½ cup Coconut Milk
1 banana
1 cup pineapple, peeled
¼ cup raw cashews or almonds
1 tablespoon coconut oil
¼ teaspoon vanilla extract
1 small lime, peeled
1 to 2 ounces rum
1 cup ice

ACTIONS:

- Blend all ingredients in a blender until the mixture reaches a smooth consistency.

TIPS:

- Substitute water for Coconut Water, if necessary.
- You may use a vanilla bean instead of vanilla extract.

Calories: 180 | *Total Fat: 7g* | *Carbs: 25g* | *Dietary Fiber: 3g* | *Protein: 0.8g*

Strawberry Daiquiri

For a healthier daiquiri, we use coconut sugar instead of processed white sugar, and fresh strawberries and lime juice instead of a bottled mix that has preservatives and artificial flavorings.

Total time: 6 minutes | *Serves 1*

INGREDIENTS:

5 large strawberries
2 ounces white rum or vodka
1 tablespoon coconut sugar
½ ounce lime juice, freshly squeezed

ACTIONS:

- Blend all ingredients with ½ cup ice in a blender until the mixture reaches a smooth consistency.

Calories: 175 | Total Fat: 0.4g | Carbs: 11.6g | Dietary Fiber: 2.1g | Protein: 0.6g

Citrus and Elder-flower Cocktail

Total time: 10 minutes | *Serves 1*

INGREDIENTS:

2 ounces gin
1 ounce St. Germain elderflower liqueur
1 ounce orange juice, freshly squeezed
½ ounce lime juice, freshly squeezed
1 teaspoon coconut sugar

ACTIONS:

- Combine all ingredients in a cocktail shaker with ice.
- Cover and shake vigorously until chilled. Strain into a chilled cocktail glass.

Calories: 286 | Total Fat: 0.1g | Carbs: 20.2g | Dietary Fiber: 0.1g | Protein: 0.4g

Moscow Mule

This beverage contains vitamin C thanks to the fresh lime juice. The classic Moscow Mule is served in a copper mug.

Total time: 5 minutes | *Serves 1*

INGREDIENTS:

1½ ounces vodka
½ ounce lime juice, freshly squeezed
½ cup organic ginger beer
1 lime wedge, for garnish

ACTIONS:

- Add vodka, lime juice, and ginger beer into a copper mug or glass with ice. Stir gently to combine. Garnish with a lime wedge.

TIP:

- Grate a bit of fresh ginger into the beverage.

Calories: 149 | Total Fat: 0.0g | Carbs: 13.3g | Dietary Fiber: 0.1g | Protein: 0.1g

Tequila Kombucha Cocktail

Kombucha is a great alternative to soda. Think of it as "nature's soda." This cocktail can be great for digestive health as it's a natural probiotic! I love to use chia seed kombucha in this cocktail for a unique texture.

Total time: 5 minutes | *Serves 1*

INGREDIENTS:

16 ounces kombucha
2 ounces tequila or vodka

ACTION:

- Combine all ingredients in a cocktail shaker with ice.
- Cover and shake vigorously until chilled. Strain into a chilled cocktail glass.

Calories: 188 | Total Fat: 0.0g | Carbs: 14.0g | Dietary Fiber: 0.0g | Protein: 0.0g

Classic Bloody Mary

This is a great way to get your vegetables in while enjoying your favorite beverage. Did you know that some Bloody Marys that you purchase out there contain gluten? This recipe is free of gluten, caramel color, disodium guanylate, and yeast extract. Rather than typical processed tomato juice, you'll use juice from fresh tomatoes, which are nice and high in vitamin C.

Total time: 10 minutes | *Serves 8*

INGREDIENTS:

4 pounds of tomatoes (to make 6 cups juice)

3 tablespoons fresh juice from a lemon or lime

1 teaspoon black pepper

2 cups vodka

⅓ cup dill pickle juice

1 tablespoon organic hot pepper sauce

2 teaspoons celery salt

1¼ teaspoon garlic salt

1 teaspoon dried dill weed

¾ teaspoon Worcestershire sauce

½ teaspoon prepared horseradish

Lime wedges or pickled peppers, for garnish

ACTIONS:

- Juice the tomatoes, then add all ingredients (except garnish) to a pitcher and stir until well combined.
- Pour into eight cocktail glasses and garnish as desired.

TIP:

- Before filling each cocktail glass, dip the rim of each glass in the lemon or lime juice, then dip in black pepper.

Calories: 286 | *Total Fat: 0.1g* | *Carbs: 20.2g* | *Dietary Fiber: 0.1g* | *Protein: 0.4g*

Espresso Martini

This espresso martini is dairy-free, gluten-free, and vegan, as it uses coconut cream or Almond Milk instead of cow's milk. It also uses real vanilla extract. This is a great adult beverage for people with lactose intolerances or who choose to be dairy-free.

Total time: 8 minutes | *Serves 2*

INGREDIENTS:

1 ounce vodka
1 teaspoon vanilla extract
2 ounces coffee liqueur
1 ounce coconut cream or Almond Milk

ACTIONS:

- Combine all ingredients in a cocktail shaker with ice.
- Cover and shake until chilled. Strain into chilled martini glasses, and garnish with whole coffee beans.

TIP:

- Use vanilla-flavored vodka.

Calories: 147 | Total Fat: 0.3g | Carbs: 11.6g | Dietary Fiber: 0.1g | Protein: 0.1g

Margarita

This is one of my favorite adult beverages. It is so simple and made with clean ingredients that can be found almost anywhere.

Total time: 10 minutes | *Serves 1*

INGREDIENTS:

1 teaspoon salt
1 lime
2 tablespoons coconut sugar or agave
2 ounces tequila

ACTIONS:

- Cut the lime and use its edges to moisten the rim of a glass. Dip edges of glass in a plate of salt.
- Squeeze the lime juice into a shaker cup with ice, then add the rest of ingredients. Shake well, then serve over ice. (Alternatively, mix lime juice, coconut sugar, and tequila in a blender with ¾ cup ice until well combined.)

TIPS:

- To make a pitcher of Margaritas, quadruple all the ingredients—except for the salt.
- Add freshly squeezed orange juice for a gentler taste and to stretch out the recipe.

Calories: 168 | Total Fat: 0g | Carbs: 11g | Dietary Fiber: 0g | Protein: 0g

Mojito

This drink is quite refreshing made with fresh lime and mint.

Total time: 7 minutes | *Serves 1*

INGREDIENTS:

10 fresh mint leaves
½ lime, cut into 4 wedges
3 tablespoons coconut sugar
1½ ounces white rum or vodka
½ cup sparkling water

ACTIONS:

- Place mint leaves, coconut sugar, and 3 lime wedges into a large, sturdy glass. Use a muddler stick to crush the mint and lime (this releases the mint oils and lime juice).
- Add ice to the glass (however much you need to almost fill it to the top). Add rum, then fill the rest of the glass with sparkling water.
- Stir and taste. Add more coconut sugar, if desired. Garnish with the remaining lime wedge.

VARIATION:

- Strawberry Mojito: Muddle 7 strawberries with the mint, sugar, and lime.

Calories: 275 | Total Fat: 0.7g | Carbs: 48g | Dietary Fiber: 1.3g | Protein: 30.8

Mudslide

Enjoy a major upgrade from the conventional frozen cocktail with this dairy-free, gluten-free mudslide! This recipe is vegan and high in antioxidants.

Total time: 10 minutes | *Serves 4*

INGREDIENTS:

⅓ cup Chocolate Sauce
4 cups Instant Vanilla Ice Cream
1½ cups Irish cream liqueur
1½ cups coffee liqueur

ACTIONS:

- Lightly cover the bottom of four large sundae glasses with Chocolate Sauce.
- In a blender or large mixing bowl, blend ice cream, Irish cream, coffee liqueur, and the rest of the Chocolate Sauce. It's okay to leave lumps; you want a thick, rather than liquefied, mixture.
- Pour mixture into glasses and serve.

Calories: 998 | Total Fat: 26.3g | Carbs: 125.1g | Dietary Fiber: 9.0g | Protein: 5.6g

CHAPTER 9

Smoothies and Smoothie Bowls

Blended smoothies and smoothie bowls give you an opportunity to express yourself creatively. You can add most any ingredients to make smoothies and slushies, then drink them immediately or freeze them for ice cream pops. You can even layer them in a glass with fruit, nuts, and seeds for parfaits.

Turn any of your favorite smoothies into smoothie bowls! Just pour from the blender into a bowl and add your favorite toppings, such as nuts, seeds, and berries. Eat them with a spoon. This makes a great snack, breakfast, lunch, or dessert that is high in antioxidants!

Be creative with how you serve your smoothie bowl. If you are making your smoothie with a fruit that has a rind or a shell, like a watermelon, cantaloupe, pineapple, or coconut, you can serve it inside the rind or shell.

Classic Green Smoothie

Total time: 5 minutes | *Serves 2*

INGREDIENTS:

1½ cups Almond Milk or water
2 cups kale
2 bananas
1 cup spinach
¼ cup fresh cilantro
1 cucumber, peeled

ACTIONS:

- Blend all ingredients in the blender until the mixture reaches a smooth consistency.

TIPS:

- If you want it smoother, add water.
- For more creaminess, add 1 avocado, peeled.
- For more sweetness, add 3 seedless dates (or 1 tablespoon raw honey or maple syrup).
- For extra protein and vitamins, add 1 tablespoon spirulina.
- Reserve the cucumber skins and use them later as refreshing face wipes.

Calories: 230 | Total Fat: 10g | Carbs: 35g | Dietary Fiber: 6g | Protein: 7g

Vegetable Smoothie

Total time: 10 minutes | *Serves 2*

INGREDIENTS:

3 seedless dates (or 1 tablespoon raw honey or maple syrup)
1½ cups ice
1 tomato
¼ broccoli (roughly ¾ cups)
1 carrot
¼ cauliflower (roughly ¾ cups)
½ small beet
Dashes of salt and pepper

ACTIONS:

- Blend all ingredients with 1½ cups water in the blender until the mixture reaches a smooth consistency.

Calories: 95.7 | Total Fat: 0.3g | Carbs: 20.6g | Dietary Fiber: 5.4g | Protein: 3.3g

Tip: Freeze any smoothies to make ice cream pops. Combine any of your favorite toppings and smoothies to make a smoothie bowl.

High-Protein Smoothie

Total time: 5 minutes | *Serves 2*

INGREDIENTS:

1 cup Protein Milk

2 bananas

3 seedless dates (or 1 tablespoon raw honey or maple syrup)

¼ cup pumpkin seeds

¼ cup hemp seeds

1 tablespoon almond butter

ACTIONS:

- Blend all ingredients in the blender until the mixture reaches a smooth consistency.

VARIATION:

- Add 1 scoop Nutiva Plant Protein for a 32-gram protein smoothie.

Calories: 363 | Total Fat: 17.1g | Carbs: 45.4g | Dietary Fiber: 5.2g | Protein: 12.8g

Sick Kick Smoothie

This smoothie is packed with immune-boosting ingredients to help you kick being sick!

Total time: 7 minutes | *Serves 1*

INGREDIENTS:

2 oranges, peeled

½ lemon, peeled

½-inch piece of ginger

Dash of turmeric powder

ACTIONS:

- Blend all ingredients with ½ cup water in the blender until the mixture reaches a smooth consistency.

TIPS:

- Add 1 small clove garlic, peeled, for even more immune support.
- For spiciness, add a dash of cayenne pepper.

Calories: 120 | Total Fat: 0.2g | Carbs: 33g | Dietary Fiber: 6.4g | Protein: 2.5g

Ultimate Super-food Smoothie

You can't beat the nutritional punch of 16 superfoods in one yummy beverage.

Total time: 10 minutes | *Serves 2*

INGREDIENTS:

2 cups Almond Milk
1½ teaspoons pure vanilla extract
½ cup blueberries
½ cup kale
1 tablespoon goji berries
3 seedless dates (or 1 tablespoon raw honey or maple syrup)
2 cups ice
½ teaspoon maca powder
½ teaspoon bee pollen
½ teaspoon spirulina
¼ teaspoon cacao powder
1 teaspoon coconut oil
1 teaspoon hemp seeds
1 teaspoon chia seeds
1 teaspoon flaxseeds
¼ teaspoon turmeric powder

ACTIONS:

- Blend all ingredients in the blender until the mixture reaches a smooth consistency.

Calories: 244 | Total Fat: 8.8g | Carbs: 24.4g | Dietary Fiber: 6.7g | Protein: 6g

Antioxidant Vitamin Blast Smoothie

Total time: 5 minutes | *Serves 1 to 2*

INGREDIENTS:

1 cup orange juice, freshly squeezed (3 to 5 oranges)
2 cups berries of your choice (blueberries, strawberries, and/or raspberries)
Wedge of lemon (optional)

ACTIONS:

- Put the juice and berries in the blender and squeeze in lemon juice, if desired. Blend until the mixture reaches a smooth consistency.

TIPS:

- If the mixture is too thick for your liking, add more liquid—either more orange juice or some water.
- Substitute grapefruit juice for the orange juice.
- For a cooler smoothie, use frozen berries.
- Add honey, dates, or maple syrup if it is not sweet enough for you.

VARIATION:

- Superfood Mixed-Antioxidant Smoothie: Add ⅓ cup blackberries, ⅓ cup mulberries, ⅓ cup goji berries, and ¼ cup water.

Calories: 223 | Total Fat: 1g | Carbs: 53g | Dietary Fiber: 9g | Protein: 4g

Acai Berry Smoothie

Total time: 5 minutes | *Serves 1*

INGREDIENTS:

1 Acai Superfruit Pack (Sambazon) or 1 teaspoon acai powder
⅓ cup blueberries
⅓ cup strawberries
1 cup liquid of your choice (water, Coconut Water, Almond Milk, Apple Juice)
Dash of honey or maple syrup

ACTIONS:

- Blend all ingredients in the blender until the mixture reaches a smooth consistency.

VARIATION:

- Acai Banana Smoothie: Replace berries with 1 banana.

Calories: 154 | *Total Fat: 5g* | *Carbs: 17g* | *Dietary Fiber: 6g* | *Protein: 1.6g*

Chocolate Nut Berry Smoothie

My personal favorite smoothie.

Total time: 10 minutes | *Serves 1*

INGREDIENTS:

2 cups berries of your choice (strawberries, raspberries, and/or blueberries)
3 tablespoons almond butter
1 tablespoon cacao powder or more, to taste
1 tablespoon raw honey

ACTIONS:

- Blend all ingredients with 1 cup water in the blender until the mixture reaches a smooth consistency.

TIP:

- Add bee pollen and hemp seeds, for additional health benefits.

VARIATION:

- For more protein, substitute Almond Milk for the water.

Calories: 236 | *Total Fat: 12.3g* | *Carbs: 30.2g* | *Dietary Fiber: 7.5g* | *Protein: 7.8g*

Chocolate Acai Smoothie

Total time: 5 minutes | *Serves 1*

INGREDIENTS:

1 Acai Superfruit Pack (Sambazon) or 1 teaspoon acai powder
1 banana
1 cup liquid of your choice (water, Coconut Water, Almond Milk, Apple Juice)
1 teaspoon honey or maple syrup
1 teaspoon cacao powder (or more if you like it really chocolaty)

ACTIONS:

- Blend all ingredients in the blender until the mixture reaches a smooth consistency.

Calories: 180 | *Total Fat: 6g* | *Carbs: 28g* | *Dietary Fiber: 5g* | *Protein: 3g*

Chocolate Smoothie

Total time: 10 minutes | *Serves 1 to 2*

INGREDIENTS:

1 cup Almond Milk or Sunflower Seed Milk

2 teaspoons cacao powder

1 teaspoon cacao nibs

7 seedless dates (or 2 to 3 tablespoons raw honey or maple syrup)

2½ cups ice

1 teaspoon pure vanilla extract

¼ teaspoon salt

ACTIONS:

- Blend all ingredients in the blender until the mixture reaches a smooth consistency.

VARIATIONS:

- Chocolate Coconut Smoothie: Add 1 tablespoon coconut oil and 1 tablespoon coconut flakes or shavings.
- Chocolate Coffee Smoothie: Add 2 teaspoons organic coffee beans, freshly ground.

Calories: 338 | Total Fat: 13.4g | Carbs: 47.1g | Dietary Fiber: 8.6g | Protein: 6.8g

Chocolate Peanut Butter Smoothie

Total time: 7 minutes | *Serves 1*

INGREDIENTS:

1½ cups Almond Milk or Sunflower Seed Milk

2 to 3 tablespoons peanut butter

2 teaspoons cacao powder

2 frozen bananas

1 tablespoon maple syrup or honey (or 3 seedless dates)

ACTIONS:

- Blend all ingredients in the blender until the mixture reaches a smooth consistency.

TIPS:

- If you prefer a darker, richer chocolate flavor, add more cacao powder.
- Add 1 tablespoon whole chia seeds, for extra thickness and additional health benefits.

VARIATIONS:

- Peanut Butter Cup Smoothie: Add 1 or 2 Earth Diet Chocolate Peanut Butter Cups for thickness and richer flavor.
- Chocolate Almond Butter Smoothie: Replace the peanut butter with almond butter.
- Almond Butter Cup Smoothie: Replace the peanut butter with almond butter and add 1 or 2 Earth Diet Chocolate Almond Butter Cups.

Calories: 180 | Total Fat: 18g | Carbs: 60g | Dietary Fiber: 6g | Protein: 13g

Banana Smoothie

Total time: 5 minutes | *Serves 2*

INGREDIENTS:

1 cup **Almond Milk**

2 **bananas**

3 **seedless dates** (or 1 tablespoon raw honey or maple syrup)

ACTIONS:

- Blend all ingredients in the blender until the mixture reaches a smooth consistency.

TIPS:

- For more flavor, add a pinch of salt. For thicker consistency, add ½ cup ice or use frozen bananas.
- To enhance the flavor, add ½ teaspoon pure vanilla extract.

VARIATIONS:

- Chocolate Banana Smoothie: Add 1½ teaspoons cacao powder.
- Chocolate Peanut Butter Banana Smoothie: Add 1½ teaspoons cacao powder and 2 tablespoons peanut butter.
- Banana Berry Smoothie: Add ¾ cup berries.
- Chocolate Banana Berry Smoothie: Add ¾ cup berries and 2 teaspoons cacao powder.

Calories: 160 | *Total Fat: 1.5g* | *Carbs: 37.3g* | *Dietary Fiber: 4.5g* | *Protein: 1.8g*

Strawberry Slushy

Fruit is so perfectly sweet that it makes incredible slushies.

Total time: 7 minutes | *Serves 1*

INGREDIENTS:

½ cup **crushed ice**

1 cup **strawberries**

2 **red apples**

ACTIONS:

- Core the apples and cut into pieces suitable for blending.
- Blend all ingredients in the blender until the mixture reaches a slushy consistency.

TIPS:

- Use frozen berries for an ice-cold slushy.
- If you prefer a thinner consistency, add water.
- Freeze the slushy in an ice cube tray, and add these to 1 cup juice or water whenever you feel like it!

VARIATION:

- Watermelon Slushy: Substitute 1 cup watermelon for the strawberries.

Calories: 235 | *Total Fat: 1g* | *Carbs: 61g* | *Dietary Fiber: 12g* | *Protein: 2g*

Strawberry Smoothie

Total time: 5 minutes | Serves 1

INGREDIENTS:

1 cup Almond Milk
1 cup strawberries
3 seedless dates (or 1 tablespoon raw honey or maple syrup)
¼ cup ice

ACTIONS:

- Blend all ingredients in the blender until the mixture reaches a smooth consistency.

TIPS:

- Any kind of nut or seed milk, or water, may be substituted for the Almond Milk.
- For more protein, add 1 tablespoon (or more, to taste) almond butter or Super Protein Powder.
- For a colder smoothie, use frozen strawberries.

Calories: 518 | Total Fat: 18g | Carbs: 91g | Dietary Fiber: 14g | Protein: 10g

Strawberries and Cream Smoothie

Total time: 10 minutes | Serves 1

INGREDIENTS:

1 cup Cashew Milk
1 cup frozen strawberries
3 seedless dates (or 1 tablespoon raw honey or maple syrup)
½ teaspoon honey or maple syrup
¼ teaspoon vanilla extract
Dash of salt

ACTIONS:

- Blend all ingredients in the blender until the mixture reaches a smooth consistency.

Calories: 530 | Total Fat: 19g | Carbs: 93g | Dietary Fiber: 14g | Protein: 10g

Vanilla Smoothie

Total time: 5 minutes | Serves 1

INGREDIENTS:

1 cup Almond Milk
1½ teaspoons pure vanilla extract
3 seedless dates (or 1 tablespoon raw honey or maple syrup)
2 cups ice

ACTIONS:

- Blend all ingredients in the blender until the mixture reaches a smooth consistency.

Calories: 489 | Total Fat: 18g | Carbs: 80g | Dietary Fiber: 11g | Protein: 9g

Avocado Smoothie

Get your daily greens in one delicious drink.

Total time: 5 minutes | Serves 2

INGREDIENTS:

1½ cups Almond Milk or water
1 avocado, peeled and seeded
1 cup kale
2 bananas
1 cup spinach

ACTIONS:

- Blend all ingredients in the blender until the mixture reaches a smooth consistency.

TIP:

- For more flavor, add a dash of cinnamon.

Calories: 282 | Total Fat: 13.8g | Carbs: 40.2g | Dietary Fiber: 7.9g | Protein: 5.9g

Mango Smoothie

Total time: 10 minutes | Serves 1

INGREDIENTS:

2 mangoes, peeled and seeded
¾ cup Coconut Milk

ACTIONS:

- Blend all ingredients in the blender until the mixture reaches a smooth consistency.

TIP:

- For more sweetness, add 3 dates or 1 tablespoon honey.

Calories: 197 | Total Fat: 10g | Carbs: 43.5g | Dietary Fiber: 4.6g | Protein: 3.3g

Pineapple Papaya Smoothie

Total time: 10 minutes | Serves 1

INGREDIENTS:

1 papaya, peeled and cut in chunks
1 pineapple, peeled and cut in chunks
¾ cup ice

ACTIONS:

- Blend all ingredients in the blender until the mixture reaches a smooth consistency.

Calories: 349 | Total Fat: 2.1g | Carbs: 58.5g | Dietary Fiber: 10.8g | Protein: 3.8g

Beginners' Breakfast Bowl

If you've never had a breakfast bowl before, begin with this basic recipe. You'll catch on quickly!

Total time: 6 minutes | Serves 2

INGREDIENTS:

Smoothie:
¾ cup Almond Milk
2 frozen bananas
3 seedless dates (or 1 tablespoon raw honey or maple syrup)
Toppings:
¼ cup walnuts or almonds
¼ cup strawberries, sliced

ACTIONS:

• Blend all smoothie ingredients together in a blender, then pour into 2 bowls. Add toppings.

Calories: 259 | Total Fat: 11.3g | Carbs: 40.6g | Dietary Fiber: 5.9g | Protein: 4.1g

Kids' Happy Face Breakfast Bowl

Total time: 10 minutes | Serves 2

INGREDIENTS:

Smoothie:
¾ cup Almond Milk
2 frozen bananas
3 seedless dates (or 1 tablespoon raw honey or maple syrup)
Toppings:
2 tablespoons walnuts
¼ cup strawberries, sliced
2 tablespoons fresh blackberries
1 orange, quartered
1 kiwifruit, sliced
2 grapes, cut in half

ACTIONS:

• Blend all smoothie ingredients together in a blender, then pour into 2 bowls.
• Arrange the fruit to make a face on each bowl: sliced strawberries as the smile, sliced kiwifruit as the eyes, grapes as the eyeballs, blackberries and walnuts as the hair, and sliced oranges as the ears!

Calories: 263.3 | Total Fat: 6.4g | Carbs: 52.4g | Dietary Fiber: 7.7g | Protein: 3.8g

Liana's Favorite Smoothie Bowl

Total time: 10 minutes | *Serves 2*

INGREDIENTS:

Smoothie:

2 cups frozen berries (strawberries, raspberries, and blueberries)

3 tablespoons almond butter

1 tablespoon cacao powder

1 tablespoon raw honey

Toppings:

1 teaspoon bee pollen

2 teaspoons hemp seeds

1 tablespoon roasted almonds, chopped

½ tablespoon roasted hazelnuts, chopped

1 tablespoon fresh blueberries

4 strawberries, sliced

Sprinkle of blue-green algae

ACTIONS:

- Blend ¾ cup water and all smoothie ingredients in a blender until smooth. Pour into 2 bowls, then add the toppings.

Calories: 400 | Total Fat: 21.6g | Carbs: 43.4g | Dietary Fiber: 12.8g | Protein: 13.5g

Banana Berry Smoothie Bowl

Total time: 10 minutes | *Serves 2*

INGREDIENTS:

Smoothie:

1 cup Almond Milk

2 frozen bananas

3 seedless dates (or 1 tablespoon raw honey or maple syrup)

¾ cup frozen berries

Toppings:

¼ cup fresh blueberries

¼ cup fresh strawberries, sliced

ACTIONS:

- Blend all smoothie ingredients together in a blender, then pour into 2 bowls. Top with the fresh berries.

TIP:

- Serve with Almond Granola or chopped almonds and walnuts.

Calories: 211.5 | Total Fat: 1.9g | Carbs: 49.9g | Dietary Fiber: 8.5g | Protein: 2.6g

Superloaded Superfood Smoothie Bowl

Total time: 10 minutes | *Serves 2*

INGREDIENTS:

Smoothie:
1 cup Almond Milk
2 frozen bananas
3 seedless dates (or 1 tablespoon raw
   honey or maple syrup)
1 teaspoon chia seeds
¾ cup frozen berries
Toppings:
¼ cup fresh blueberries
¼ cup fresh strawberries, sliced
1 tablespoon hemp seeds
2 teaspoons pumpkin seeds
1 teaspoon cacao nibs

ACTIONS

- Blend all smoothie ingredients
  together in a blender, then pour into 2
  bowls. Add the toppings.

TIP:

- Serve with Almond Granola or
  chopped almonds and walnuts.

*Calories: 274.5 | Total Fat: 5.7g | Carbs: 53.6g |
Dietary Fiber: 9.4g | Protein: 6.1g*

Chocolate Smoothie Bowl

This is good for breakfast, and also
makes an excellent dessert.

Total time: 7 minutes | *Serves 2*

INGREDIENTS:

Smoothie:
1½ cups Almond Milk or Sunflower
   Seed Milk
2 teaspoons cacao powder
2 frozen bananas
1 tablespoon maple syrup or honey
Toppings:
2 tablespoons almonds, chopped
2 teaspoons cacao nibs
½ teaspoon cacao powder

ACTIONS:

- Blend all smoothie ingredients
  together in a blender, then pour into 2
  bowls. Add the toppings.

*Calories: 247 | Total Fat: 7.4g | Carbs: 37.5g |
Dietary Fiber: 5.2g | Protein: 3.6g*

Chocolate Peanut Butter Smoothie Bowl

Total time: 7 minutes | *Serves 2*

INGREDIENTS:

Smoothie:

1¼ cup Almond Milk or Sunflower Seed Milk

2 tablespoons peanut butter

2 teaspoons cacao powder

2 frozen bananas

1 tablespoon maple syrup or honey

1 tablespoon peanut butter

Toppings:

1 tablespoon roasted peanuts

2 teaspoons cacao nibs

ACTIONS:

- Blend all smoothie ingredients together in a blender, then pour into 2 bowls. Add the toppings.

VARIATION:

- Chocolate Almond Butter Smoothie Bowl: Substitute almond butter for the peanut butter and garnish with almonds.

Calories: 423 | *Total Fat: 19g* | *Carbs: 41.1g* | *Dietary Fiber: 5.7g* | *Protein: 7.2g*

Acai Banana Bowl

If you love smooth and crunchy textures together, you'll love the roasted almonds on the Acai Banana Bowl.

Total time: 8 minutes | *Serves 1*

INGREDIENTS:

Smoothie:

2 Acai Superfruit Pack (Sambazon)

1 banana

¼ cup liquid of your choice (water, Coconut Water, Almond Milk, Apple Juice)

Your choice of toppings:

Roasted nuts like almonds, raw nuts, chopped fruit like banana, apple, strawberries, peaches, cacao nibs, golden berries, goji berries, granola, oats, or coconut shavings.

ACTIONS:

- Blend all smoothie ingredients together in a blender. Pour into a bowl, then add the toppings.

TIP:

- You can use a frozen banana. To freeze a banana, peel it and then wrap it in plastic wrap and place it in the freezer. This makes it easier when you are ready to make smoothies or instant ice cream; you can just grab them out of the freezer, unwrap, and blend!

VARIATION:

- Acai Blueberry Bowl: Substitute ½ cup frozen blueberries for the banana.

Calories: 185 | *Total Fat: 5g* | *Carbs: 33g* | *Dietary Fiber: 5g* | *Protein: 2g*

Chocolate Acai Bowl

Total time: 6 minutes | *Serves 1*

INGREDIENTS:

Smoothie:
2 Acai Superfruit Packs (Sambazon)
1 banana
¼ cup Almond Milk or Chocolate Milk
2 teaspoons cacao powder
Topping:
1 teaspoon cacao nibs

ACTIONS:

- Blend all smoothie ingredients together in a blender, then pour into a bowl. Add the toppings.

TIP:

- Add walnuts or almonds for extra crunch! You can also add chopped bananas.

VARIATION:

- Chocolate Coconut Acai Bowl: Add 1 teaspoon coconut oil and ¼ cup coconut water to the smoothie mixture. Top with coconut flakes or shavings, if desired.

Calories: 310 | Total Fat: 12.3g | Carbs: 37.5g | Dietary Fiber: 8.8g | Protein: 3.8g

Ice Cream Sundae Smoothie Bowl

Total time: 10 minutes | *Serves 2*

INGREDIENTS:

Smoothie:
2 cups Almond Milk
1 tablespoon pure vanilla extract
3 seedless dates (or 1 tablespoon raw honey or maple syrup)
2 teaspoons honey or maple syrup
2 cups ice
Toppings:
2 tablespoons Chocolate Sauce
1 tablespoon almonds or hazelnuts, chopped
1 banana, sliced

ACTIONS:

- Blend all smoothie ingredients together in a blender, then pour into 2 bowls.
- Drizzle each bowl with Chocolate Sauce, and top with chopped nuts and banana slices.

TIP:

- For added fun, serve with cherries or berries on top!

Calories: 283 | Total Fat: 10.7g | Carbs: 44.3g | Dietary Fiber: 6g | Protein: 5.3g

CHAPTER 10

Breakfasts

Even if you're in a hurry, it's important to start the day off right. There's a lot you can do in the morning with 10 minutes. In this chapter, you'll find recipes for fresh cereals and granolas, pancakes, smoothie bowls, and eggs. If you really want to save time and effort, make a bigger batch by doubling, tripling, or quadrupling one of the baked granola recipes—as it keeps for up to 10 days in an airtight container. It's good as a cereal, a topping on a smoothie bowl, mixed in yogurt, or in a fruit parfait. Fresh muesli can be made in bulk also, and used in similar ways, but it needs to be stored in the refrigerator.

Another way to shorten your prep time when you're planning for the week ahead is to cut some fruits into bite-sized chunks and keep those in the fridge. Squeeze fresh lemon juice over the fruits to prevent them from browning and seal in airtight containers.

It's vital to nourish your body with breakfast as it sets the foundation for the day.

Breakfast Cereal

This vibrant, fulfilling cereal has a lot of different textures because of the crunchy nuts, sweet fruits, and savory oats.

Total time: 10 minutes | Serves 3

INGREDIENTS:

½ cup gluten-free rolled oats

½ cup raw macadamia nuts
(or walnuts, tigernuts, or pecans)

½ cup blueberries

½ cup almond meal

1 apple, cored

1 teaspoon cinnamon
(or more, to taste)

¼ cup raw walnuts

1 teaspoon raw honey
or maple syrup

1 to 2 cups Almond Milk

Additional honey or maple syrup
(optional)

ACTIONS:

- In a bowl, toss together the rolled oats, macadamia nuts, blueberries, and almond meal. Set aside.
- In a food processor, blend the apple, cinnamon, walnuts, and honey until the mixture reaches a crumbly consistency. If the mixture does not begin sticking together in clumps, add a bit more honey.
- Take the mixture from the food processor, and roll it into loose balls about 1 inch in diameter. Add these to the bowl with the rolled oats mixture to complete your breakfast cereal.
- Pour Almond Milk over your cereal.
- For more sweetness, add additional honey or maple syrup, to taste.

TIPS:

- Add any raw nuts and chopped fruits of your choice.
- Sprinkle 1 tablespoon psyllium husks over the cereal for added health benefits.
- Sprinkle 1 tablespoon flaxseeds over cereal for added health benefits.

Calories: 502 | Total Fat: 37g | Carbs: 40g | Dietary Fiber: 10g | Protein: 11g

Chia Seed Cereal

Total time: 10 minutes | *Serves 1*

INGREDIENTS:

3 tablespoons chia seeds

½ cup water, nut milk, or Sunflower Seed Milk

Chopped fruit of your choice: one apple, banana, peach, pear, nectarine, or ½ cup berries

ACTIONS:

- Place the chia seeds and liquid into a cereal bowl. Soak for 5 minutes.
- Add the fruit and eat!

TIP:

- Add 1 teaspoon raw honey, maple syrup, or chopped dates, if you want it sweeter.

VARIATIONS:

- Chia Hemp Seed Cereal: Add 1 tablespoon hemp seeds.
- Oatmeal Chia Seed Cereal: Add 1 tablespoon oats.

Calories: 87 | Total Fat: 8g | Carbs: 9g | Dietary Fiber: 8g | Protein: 5g

Almond Granola

Total time: 10 minutes | *Serves 4 to 6*

INGREDIENTS:

¼ cup almond butter

1 tablespoon almonds

2 tablespoons honey or maple syrup

½ teaspoon cinnamon

½ teaspoon vanilla extract

½ tablespoon flaxseeds

½ tablespoon chia seeds

1 cup rolled oats

ACTIONS:

- Preheat the oven to 400°F.
- Add all ingredients to a bowl, and mix until well combined.
- Line a baking sheet with parchment paper or smooth over with coconut oil. Spread the oat mixture over the baking sheet.
- Bake for 9 minutes. If you like it crunchier, bake for an additional 5 minutes. Eat as a snack on its own, in cereal, or as a topping on an Acai Bowl or a dish of Instant Ice Cream.

Calories: 152 | Total Fat: 8g | Carbs: 18g | Dietary Fiber: 3g | Protein: 4g

Granola Cereal

Total time: 10 minutes | *Serves 4*

INGREDIENTS:

1 batch of granola (like Almond Granola, High-Protein Granola, or Peanut Butter Granola)

4 cups nut or seed milk

Fresh or dried fruit of your choice: chopped bananas, apples, apricots, blueberries

ACTIONS:

- Add 1 cup milk to each bowl, then granola, then the toppings.

Calories: 192 | Total Fat: 11g | Carbs: 20g | Dietary Fiber: 4g | Protein: 5g

Raw Tigernut Granola Cereal

Most granolas are baked, but this recipe is for a raw granola cereal!

Total time: 6 minutes | Serves 1 to 2

INGREDIENTS:

½ cup Tigernut Milk
¼ cup oats
¼ cup nuts and seeds, any kind
Pinch or two of cinnamon
1 teaspoon maple syrup
¼ teaspoon vanilla extract
Pinch of coconut sugar
7 tigernuts
¼ cup your choice of fruit, like
   blueberries or chopped bananas
1 teaspoon hemp seeds
1 teaspoon chia seeds

ACTIONS:

- Add all ingredients to a bowl, and mix until well combined. Enjoy.

TIP:

- If you have more time to spend on preparing this dish, layer your granola cereal. For example, add the milk to the bowl first, then the oats and tigernuts. Next add the vanilla and maple syrup. Sprinkle cinnamon, coconut sugar, hemp seeds, and chia seeds on top. Then layer with fresh fruit.

Calories: 300 | Total Fat: 17g | Carbs: 35g | Dietary Fiber: 16g | Protein: 10g

Peanut Butter Granola

Total time: 10 minutes | Serves 4 to 6

INGREDIENTS:

¼ cup peanut butter
¼ cup roasted or raw peanuts
2 tablespoons honey or maple syrup
½ teaspoon cinnamon
½ teaspoon vanilla extract
½ tablespoon flaxseeds
½ tablespoon chia seeds
1 cup rolled oats

ACTIONS:

- Preheat the oven to 400°F.
- Add all ingredients to a bowl, and mix until well combined.
- Line a baking sheet with parchment paper or smooth over with coconut oil. Spread the oat mixture over the baking sheet.
- Bake for 9 minutes. If you like it crunchier, bake for an additional 5 minutes. Eat as a snack on its own, in cereal, or as a topping on an Acai Bowl or a dish of Instant Ice Cream.

Calories: 175 | Total Fat: 10g | Carbs: 19g | Dietary Fiber: 3g | Protein: 6g

High-Protein Granola

This is super high in protein because of the pumpkin seeds, hemp seeds, and almond butter.

Total time: 10 minutes | Serves 4 to 6

INGREDIENTS:

¼ cup almond butter
½ cup pumpkin seeds
¼ cup chia seeds
3 tablespoons honey or maple syrup
½ teaspoon cinnamon
½ teaspoon vanilla extract
½ tablespoon flaxseeds
½ tablespoon chia seeds
1 cup rolled oats

ACTIONS:

- Preheat the oven to 400°F.
- Add all ingredients to a bowl, and mix until well combined.
- Line a baking sheet with parchment paper or smooth over with coconut oil. Spread the oat mixture over the baking sheet.
- Bake for 9 minutes. If you like it crunchier, bake for an additional 5 minutes. Eat as a snack on its own, in cereal, or as a topping on an Acai Bowl or a dish of Instant Ice Cream.

Calories: 204 | Total Fat: 8g | Carbs: 25g | Dietary Fiber: 4.8g | Protein: 9g

Tigernut Granola

Total time: 10 minutes | Serves 4 to 6

INGREDIENTS:

¼ cup almond butter
1 tablespoon tigernuts
2 tablespoons honey or maple syrup
½ teaspoon cinnamon
½ teaspoon vanilla extract
1 tablespoon sesame seeds
½ cup rolled oats
½ cup tigernut flour

ACTIONS:

- Preheat the oven to 400°F.
- Add all ingredients to a bowl, and mix until well combined.
- Line a baking sheet with parchment paper or smooth over with coconut oil. Spread the oat mixture over the baking sheet.
- Bake for 9 minutes. If you like it crunchier, bake for an additional 5 minutes. Eat as a snack on its own, in cereal, or as a topping on an Acai Bowl or a dish of Instant Ice Cream.

Calories: 142 | Total Fat: 6g | Carbs: 58g | Dietary Fiber: 16g | Protein: 4g

Fresh Muesli

Total time: 10 minutes | Serves 2

INGREDIENTS:

1 apple, diced
1 peach, diced
1 banana, sliced
1 tablespoon raisins
¼ cup walnuts
½ cup oats
1 tablespoon sunflower seeds
2 cups nut or seed milk

ACTIONS:

- Combine all the ingredients, and divide into 2 bowls. Pour milk over them, and enjoy.

TIP:

- If you want it sweeter, drizzle with maple syrup or honey, or sprinkle coconut sugar on it.

Calories: 360.6 | Total Fat: 17.1g | Carbs: 50.3g | Dietary Fiber: 7.9g | Protein: 7.4g

High-Protein Muesli

Total time: 10 minutes | Serves 2

INGREDIENTS:

1 apple, diced
1 peach, diced
1 banana, sliced
¼ cup pumpkin seeds
1 tablespoon sesame seeds
1 tablespoon flaxseeds
¼ cup hemp seeds
¼ cup walnuts
1 tablespoon sunflower seeds
1 cup nut or seed milk

ACTIONS:

- Combine all the ingredients, and divide into 2 bowls. Pour milk over them, and enjoy.

TIP:

- If you want it sweeter, drizzle with maple syrup or honey, or sprinkle coconut sugar on it.

Calories: 458.8 | Total Fat: 29.1g | Carbs: 41.3g | Dietary Fiber: 8.8g | Protein: 15.2g

Vegan Yogurt

Although this is ready to serve as soon as it is blended, it will keep in the fridge for up to four days.

Total time: 6 minutes | Serves 4

INGREDIENTS:

½ cup almonds
½ cup cashews
½ cup coconut water
1 tablespoon lemon juice (approximately ½ a lemon)
¼ teaspoon vanilla extract

ACTIONS:

- Blend ½ cup water and all ingredients in a blender on high until completely smooth.

TIP:

- Add your favorite toppings, such as granola, fruit, and chopped nuts!

Calories: 259.2 | Total Fat: 11.3g | Carbs: 40.6g | Dietary Fiber: 5.9g | Protein: 4.1g

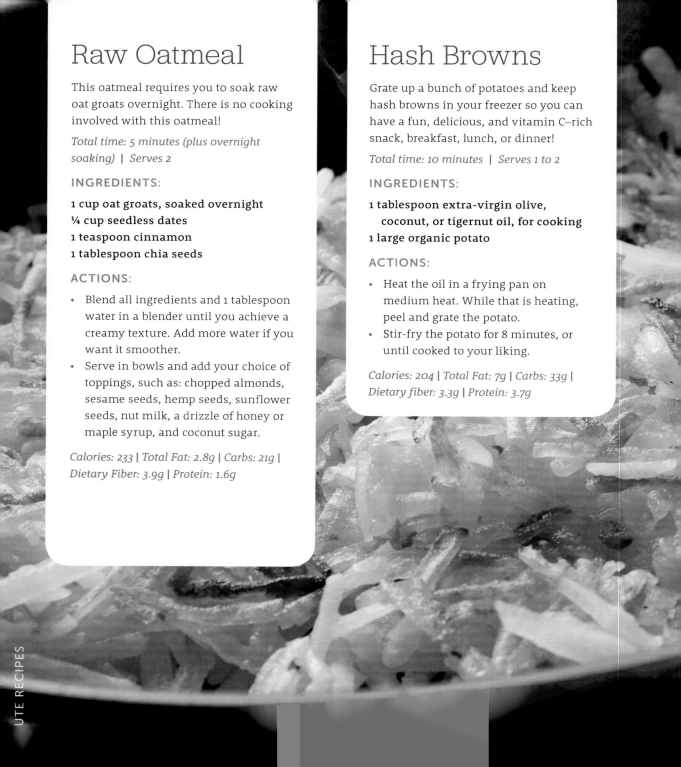

Raw Oatmeal

This oatmeal requires you to soak raw oat groats overnight. There is no cooking involved with this oatmeal!

Total time: 5 minutes (plus overnight soaking) | *Serves 2*

INGREDIENTS:

1 cup oat groats, soaked overnight
¼ cup seedless dates
1 teaspoon cinnamon
1 tablespoon chia seeds

ACTIONS:

• Blend all ingredients and 1 tablespoon water in a blender until you achieve a creamy texture. Add more water if you want it smoother.
• Serve in bowls and add your choice of toppings, such as: chopped almonds, sesame seeds, hemp seeds, sunflower seeds, nut milk, a drizzle of honey or maple syrup, and coconut sugar.

Calories: 233 | Total Fat: 2.8g | Carbs: 21g | Dietary Fiber: 3.9g | Protein: 1.6g

Hash Browns

Grate up a bunch of potatoes and keep hash browns in your freezer so you can have a fun, delicious, and vitamin C–rich snack, breakfast, lunch, or dinner!

Total time: 10 minutes | *Serves 1 to 2*

INGREDIENTS:

1 tablespoon extra-virgin olive, coconut, or tigernut oil, for cooking
1 large organic potato

ACTIONS:

• Heat the oil in a frying pan on medium heat. While that is heating, peel and grate the potato.
• Stir-fry the potato for 8 minutes, or until cooked to your liking.

Calories: 204 | Total Fat: 7g | Carbs: 33g | Dietary fiber: 3.3g | Protein: 3.7g

Perfect Porridge

This is the ideal breakfast when you're craving something warm and comforting. Have fun with all the different textures and flavors! Adding nutrient-rich raw toppings, such as berries, make this a hybrid of raw and cooked. I often enjoy mine simply drizzled with maple syrup.

Total time: 10 minutes | *Serves 2 to 4*

INGREDIENTS:

Porridge::

1 cup organic oats (go for gluten-free)

Choose Your Toppings:

Almond butter

Almond Milk

Apples

Bananas

Cacao nibs

Cacao powder

Chia seeds

Cinnamon

Coconut sugar

Flaxseeds

Flaxseed meal

Honey

Maple syrup

Nuts (such as almonds, pecans, walnuts, and Brazil nuts)

Raisins

Sesame seeds

Sunflower Seed Milk

Tigernut Milk

Vanilla extract or powder

ACTIONS:

- In a pot, add oats to 2 cups of water brought to a boil. Cook for 9 minutes, or until desired consistency.
- Serve the oats in bowls, then add your choice of toppings to make it your style!

Calories: 280 | Total Fat: 5g | Carbs: 50g | Dietary Fiber: 8g | Protein: 12g

Gluten-Free Vegan Pancakes

The buckwheat and rice flours make these pancakes gluten-free, and the flaxseed meal replaces the egg in this vegan recipe.

Total time: 10 minutes | *Serves 2 (makes 4 large pancakes)*

INGREDIENTS:

Coconut oil, for cooking

⅓ cup rice flour

⅓ cup buckwheat flour

1 teaspoon flaxseed meal

¼ teaspoon salt

½ teaspoon baking soda

½ tablespoon olive oil

1 tablespoon maple syrup

ACTIONS:

- Heat a griddle on medium with oil. Sift the flours, flaxseed, salt, and baking soda into a bowl and form a well. Pour ½ cup water and olive oil into the well, then mix until smooth. Add the maple syrup and stir.
- Pour pancake batter onto the griddle, and flip when the tops are bubbly. Cook until both sides are golden brown.

TIPS:

- Add more flour or 1 tablespoon water to alter the consistency of your pancakes.
- Serve with your choice of toppings such as fresh berries, chopped nuts, Instant Ice Cream, Chocolate Sauce, and maple syrup.

Calories: 137.1 | Total Fat: 5.9g | Carbs: 19.1g | Dietary Fiber: 2.0g | Protein: 2.2g

Bob's Gluten-Free Pancakes

Total time: 10 minutes | Serves 2 (makes 4 large pancakes)

INGREDIENTS:

Oil for the griddle (approximately a teaspoon per pancake)
¾ cup Bob's Red Mill Gluten Free Pancake Mix
1 large egg
¾ cup nut milk or water
1 tablespoon coconut oil or olive oil

ACTIONS:

- Heat a griddle on medium-high with oil. Combine the pancake mix with the egg, nut milk, and oil.
- Pour pancake batter onto the griddle, and flip when the tops are bubbly. Cook until both sides are golden brown.

TIP:

- Serve with Vegan Butter, Chocolate Sauce, maple syrup, and toppings like fresh fruit and nuts.

VARIATION:

- Blueberry Pancakes: Scatter blueberries onto the pancake batter on the griddle, then flip as usual.

Calories: 366 | Total Fat: 16.5g | Carbs: 32g | Dietary Fiber: 2g | Protein: 4g

Buckwheat Pancakes

Did you know? Buckwheat is not actually wheat and so it is gluten-free.

Total time: 10 minutes | Serves 4 (makes 8 pancakes)

INGREDIENTS:

2 tablespoons extra-virgin coconut oil or Nutiva Shortening, for cooking
2 cups Vitacost Gluten-Free Buckwheat Pancake Mix
2 large eggs
1 tablespoon extra-virgin olive oil

ACTIONS:

- Heat a griddle on medium with coconut oil. Combine pancake mix, eggs, ¾ cup water, and oil.
- Pour pancake batter onto the griddle, and flip when the tops are bubbly. Cook until both sides are golden brown.

TIP:

- Serve with your choice of toppings such as maple syrup, honey, coconut sugar, Nutiva Shortening, and fresh berries.

Calories: 349.4 | Total Fat: 2.1g | Carbs: 58.5g | Dietary Fiber: 10.8g | Protein: 3.8g

French Toast

Total time: 10 minutes | Serves 2

INGREDIENTS:

1 tablespoon coconut oil, for cooking
1 large egg
¼ cup Almond Milk
¼ teaspoon vanilla extract
Dash of cinnamon
Dash of nutmeg
Dash of salt
2 pieces of thick organic bread

ACTIONS:

- Heat a griddle over medium-high with oil. Beat together the egg, milk, vanilla, spices, and salt.
- Dunk the bread into the egg mixture, soaking both sides. Cook each side of the bread on the griddle until golden brown.

TIP:

- Serve with your choice of toppings such as fresh berries, maple syrup, chopped nuts, Instant Ice Cream, and Chocolate Sauce.

Calories: 241 | Total Fat: 10.2g | Carbs: 29g | Dietary Fiber: 0.2g | Protein: 9.1g

Tigernut French Toast

The tigernut flour in this recipe gives the French Toast the taste of caramel!

Total time: 10 minutes | Serves 2

INGREDIENTS:

1 tablespoon coconut oil, for cooking
1 large egg
2 pieces of organic bread
½ cup tigernut flour
1 tablespoon coconut sugar or maple syrup (optional)

ACTIONS:

- Heat a griddle on medium-high with coconut oil. Whisk the egg in a bowl, and dip the bread into the bowl, making sure both sides are well coated. Dust with tigernut flour, then drop onto the griddle.
- Cook for a few minutes on each side until golden brown.
- Serve on plates and sprinkle with coconut sugar or drizzle with maple syrup as desired.

Calories: 408 | Total Fat: 24g | Carbs: 40g | Dietary Fiber: 22g | Protein: 9.5g

Eggs in a Hole

Total time: 10 minutes | *Serves 2*

INGREDIENTS:

2 tablespoons coconut oil, for cooking
2 pieces of organic bread
2 large eggs
Salt and pepper, to taste

ACTIONS:

- Heat the oil in a frying pan on medium-high. Toast two pieces of bread, but just a little, not golden brown. Then cut two holes into each piece of toast; you can use a small glass to do this.
- Place the toast in the frying pan, and crack one egg into each hole. If you don't want runny yolks, then poke a fork in the yolks. Flip once. Serve with salt and pepper to taste.

TIP:

- Avocado goes great with this!

VARIATION:

- Cheesy Eggs in a Hole: Sprinkle 1½ tablespoons nutritional yeast over each egg.

Calories: 287 | Total Fat: 20.1g | Carbs: 15g | Dietary Fiber: 4g | Protein: 13g

Humpty Dumpty

This is a fun, high-protein meal for adults and children. Serve it on toast or with Gluten-Free Tortillas to dunk into the runny yolk.

Total time: 10 minutes | *Serves 2*

INGREDIENTS:

2 large eggs
2 pieces of bread or Gluten-Free Tortillas

ACTIONS:

- Place the eggs in a saucepan. Cover with water so a tiny portion of each egg is uncovered.
- Bring the water to a boil, and then lower the heat, simmering the eggs for another 6 to 7 minutes. While the eggs are cooking, pop the bread in the toaster.
- After cooking, serve in egg cups. Slice the top off, and then dunk your toast or Gluten-Free Tortillas in the yolk before scooping out the whites.

TIP:

- When the tips of the eggs are dry to the touch, they are done!

Calories: 170 | Total Fat: 6.5g | Carbs: 15g | Dietary Fiber: 4g | Protein: 13g

Basic Omelet Formula

An omelet is delicious, quick, and high in protein. With vegetables added, it also provides the body with high amounts of antioxidants. Omelets make great breakfasts, lunches, and dinners.

The basic concept of an omelet is heating up some oil in a pan, whisking eggs with the spices of your choice in a bowl, then pouring the batter into the hot pan. Add toppings of your choice into the egg mixture, then fold and cook until done. You can use plain eggs, or add 1 tablespoon milk or water per egg to the mixture.

CHOOSE YOUR OIL:

Extra-virgin coconut oil
Extra-virgin olive oil
Tigernut oil

CHOOSE YOUR TOPPINGS:

Salt
Pepper
Nutritional yeast
Organic cheese
Basil
Cilantro
Parsley
Turmeric
Cumin
Tomatoes
Zucchini
Spinach
Kale
Artichoke

Omelet

Total time: 10 minutes | Serves 2

INGREDIENTS:

3 tablespoons extra-virgin coconut oil, for cooking
5 large eggs
Black pepper and salt, to taste

ACTIONS:

- Heat the coconut oil in a frying pan over medium heat. Crack the eggs into a bowl and whisk with a fork, then pour into the pan.
- Cook until the top begins to firm, then flip. Continue cooking until desired doneness is achieved.

TIP:

- Serve with avocado slices.

VARIATIONS:

- Spicy Eggs: Whisk ½ teaspoon cayenne pepper with eggs.
- Cheesy Eggs: Add 2 tablespoons nutritional yeast to eggs in the pan.
- Eggs with Greens: Add 2 tablespoons chopped green onions and 2 tablespoons fresh cilantro to eggs in the pan.
- Egg Wraps: Serve on Gluten-Free Tortillas.

Calories: 393 | Total Fat: 38g | Carbs: 1g | Dietary Fiber: 0g | Protein: 14g

Mediterranean Omelet

INGREDIENTS:

2 tablespoons extra-virgin olive oil
8 large eggs
¼ cup olives, sliced
1 cup spinach
1 small tomato, sliced
Small handful of fresh parsley
1 teaspoon garlic, minced
Handful of organic cheese or
    nutritional yeast

Turkey Omelet

INGREDIENTS:

2 tablespoons extra-virgin
    coconut oil
8 large eggs
Small handful of fresh parsley
¼ teaspoon onion powder
1 teaspoon garlic, minced
8 slices turkey
1 small tomato, sliced

Artichoke Omelet

INGREDIENTS:

1 tablespoon extra-virgin coconut oil 4
    large eggs
½ cup artichoke hearts
½ teaspoon garlic, minced
1 scallion, sliced in circles
Salt, to taste

CHAPTER 11

Salads
and
Salad Dressings

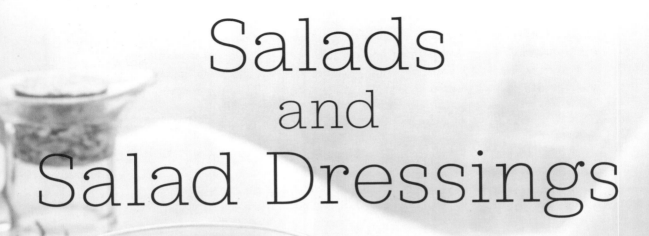

A hearty salad, easily made in less than 10 minutes, can be a full dinner. Your salad should excite you. If it doesn't excite you, you haven't met your soul salad yet.

My definition of a salad is a dish built on a base of greens (kale, spinach, lettuce, and so on). It is composed with a variety of toppings and dressings, everything from herbs and spices to nuts and seeds. Be creative with your choice of vegetables, fruits, and proteins. I always found salads boring until I took matters into my hands and designed my own by experimenting with different combinations of taste and texture. The Superfood Kale Salad is what finally converted me into a proper salad lover. That's my personal soul salad.

Mason Jar Salads

Have fun with these salad jar suggestions. Experiment with colors and ingredients to create vibrant layers and textures. Inspire others with your art. Post a picture on Instagram or Pinterest and tag it: #10MinuteRecipes #10Minutes #10MinuteChallenge #saladinajar #masonjarsalad #saladselfie.

Salad keeps fresh in a mason jar, so you can make up to seven of these once a week and then grab one from the fridge each day as you leave for work or school.

Salad in a Jar 101

HOW TO BUILD A MASON JAR SALAD:
To keep your salad from getting soggy, put your salad dressing in the jar first.

NEXT ADD YOUR "WET" INGREDIENTS, like cucumbers, tomatoes, or strawberries.

LAYER IN THE HEAVIER INGREDIENTS: vegetables like carrots, broccoli, snap peas, beans, or cauliflower.

ADD YOUR DRY INGREDIENTS: any nuts and seeds, then your protein like pasta, meat, chicken, or egg.

FINALLY ADD YOUR LIGHTEST INGREDIENTS, such as leafy greens and fresh herbs.

WHEN YOU ARE READY TO EAT, just shake up your salad in the jar! You can either dump it into a bowl or eat it straight from the jar.

Fruit Jar Salad

Layer 1: Lemon juice (for dressing) and watermelon

Layer 2: Strawberries, blueberries, and grapes

Layer 3: Cantaloupe

Layer 4: Sunflower seeds, pumpkin seeds, hemp seeds, chia seeds, and flaxseeds

Mediterranean Jar Salad

Layer 1: Balsamic vinegar

Layer 2: Artichokes, black olives, tomatoes, cucumber, and white cannellini beans

Layer 3: Nutritional yeast, organic feta (or the cheese of your choice), and pine nuts

Layer 4: Mixed greens and a sprinkle of oregano and thyme

High-Protein Jar Salad

Layer 1: Lemon and olive oil dressing

Layer 2: Chickpeas and broccoli

Layer 3: Cooked quinoa, cooked chicken, hemp seeds, pumpkin seeds

Layer 4: Spinach

Detox Jar Salad

Layer 1: Lemon, garlic, ginger, and olive oil dressing

Layer 2: Pineapple, blueberries, and strawberries

Layer 3: Cooked quinoa

Layer 4: Sprouts, kale, and dandelion greens

Fruit and Vegetable Jar Salad

Layer 1: Dressing of olive oil, flax oil, and lemon juice

Layer 2: Strawberries and cantaloupe

Layer 3: Carrots

Layer 4: Walnuts and almonds

Layer 5: Spinach and lettuce

Four-Ingredient Green Salad

This salad is quite surprising as it is built on a foundation of herbs, and it is so simple yet really flavorful and refreshing.

Total time: 10 minutes | Serves 1

INGREDIENTS:

1 avocado, cubed
1 cup fresh parsley leaves
1 cup fresh cilantro leaves
1 lemon
Salt and pepper, to taste

ACTIONS:

- Place the avocado, parsley, and cilantro in a bowl.
- Squeeze lemon juice over the salad. Season with salt and pepper, to taste.

TIP:

- Include the stems from the parsley and cilantro, for added nutrients.

VARIATION:

- Five-Ingredient Green Salad: Add 1 chopped cucumber.

Calories: 332 | Total Fat: 27g | Carbs: 23g | Dietary Fiber: 16g | Protein: 7g

Superfood Kale Salad

This is the salad that converted me to loving salads.

Total time: 10 minutes | Serves 3

INGREDIENTS:

1 bunch kale, center ribs and stems removed (reserve these for juicing or eating later)
1 avocado
1 tablespoon apple cider vinegar
1½ tablespoons flaxseed oil
¾ teaspoon salt
¼ cup nutritional yeast
5 tablespoons sunflower seeds

ACTIONS:

- Tear the kale leaves into small pieces, and place in a large bowl.
- Massage the avocado into the pieces of kale with your fingers, covering the kale with avocado.
- Add remaining ingredients to the bowl and stir, or continue to massage the mixture with your fingers, until everything is well combined.

TIPS:

- For a cheesier flavor, increase the amount of nutritional yeast.
- For more protein, add pumpkin seeds.

VARIATIONS:

- Garlic Kale Salad: Add 2 teaspoons garlic powder or minced garlic.
- Kale Wraps: Wrap salad in a brown rice wrapper for portability.

Calories: 426 | Total Fat: 24g | Carbs: 35g | Dietary Fiber: 17g | Protein: 29g

Taco Salad

Total time: 10 minutes | *Serves 4*

INGREDIENTS:

8 cups mixed greens, such as kale,
   spinach, lettuce
1 avocado, sliced
1 tablespoon nutritional yeast
Taco Filling:
1½ cups walnuts
1 cup sun-dried tomatoes
2 tablespoons extra-virgin olive oil
1 teaspoon sage
1 teaspoon cumin
1 teaspoon fennel seeds
1 teaspoon thyme
1 teaspoon rosemary
1 teaspoon oregano
Pinch black pepper
Pinch cayenne pepper
Pinch salt

ACTIONS:

- In a blender, mix the ingredients for
  the taco filling until well combined.
- Add salad greens to 4 bowls, then
  spoon the filling on top. Finish with
  avocado slices and nutritional yeast.

TIPS:

- Serve with Vegan Sour Cream.
- Drizzle olive oil and lemon over each
  salad, or use one of the dressings at
  the end of this chapter.

*Calories: 468.3 | Total Fat: 43.1g | Carbs:
20.5g | Dietary Fiber: 13.1g | Protein: 11.7g*

Mango Avocado Salad

Total time: 10 minutes | *Serves 4*

INGREDIENTS:

Salad:
4 cups mixed greens (best is a
   combination of arugula, rocket,
   spinach, and kale)
1 ripe mango, cubed
1 avocado, cubed
Pepper, to taste
1 tablespoon black or white sesame
   seeds
Dressing:
3 tablespoons olive oil
Juice of 1 lime
½ small red onion, chopped
¼ teaspoon salt

ACTIONS:

- Place the greens in 4 bowls. Mix the
  dressing ingredients well in a separate
  bowl. Pour ¾ of the dressing on the
  salad and toss until well coated.
- Arrange the avocado and mango
  on top. Drizzle with the remaining
  dressing, and finish with pepper and
  sesame seeds.

TIP:

- Serve with Vegan Yogurt.

*Calories: 224.1 | Total Fat: 41.2g | Carbs:
11.6g | Dietary Fiber: 3.4g | Protein: 2.5g*

Avocado Sesame Seed Salad

Total time: 10 minutes | *Serves 2*

INGREDIENTS:

Salad:

1 orange, peeled and sliced

2 cups arugula, torn into pieces

1 slice of red onion

1 avocado, peeled and sliced

¾ cup snap peas

1 tablespoon black or roasted sesame seeds

Fresh parsley and cilantro, for garnish

Dressing:

1 teaspoon sesame seed oil

2 teaspoons olive oil

Dash of salt and pepper

Juice of ½ lemon

1 tablespoon orange juice

ACTIONS:

- Layer your plate, starting with the orange slices. Then add the arugula, followed by the onion, and then the avocado and snap peas.
- Mix the dressing ingredients well in a separate bowl. Pour on the salad and toss until well coated.
- Finish by sprinkling the salad with sesame seeds and fresh herbs.

Calories: 273.7 | Total Fat: 20.8g | Carbs: 22.6g | Dietary Fiber: 6.3g | Protein: 5.8g

Ultimate Nourishing Detox Salad

Total time: 10 minutes | *Serves 4*

INGREDIENTS:

Salad:

1 head of lettuce, torn into pieces

½ bunch kale, in pieces

¼ cup fresh fennel, chopped or sliced (optional) or 1 teaspoon fennel seeds

8 asparagus stalks

1 avocado, cubed

1 grapefruit, peeled and sliced

1 cucumber, chopped

1 small red onion, sliced

1 cup alfalfa sprouts

1 large radish, sliced

1 celery stalk, cut

Dressing:

2 teaspoons garlic, minced

2 inches ginger, grated

Juice of 1 lemon

3 tablespoons olive oil

ACTIONS:

- Combine all salad ingredients in a bowl and toss.
- Mix the dressing ingredients well in a separate bowl. Pour on the salad and toss until well coated.

Calories: 239.3 | Total Fat: 16.7g | Carbs: 23.9g | Dietary Fiber: 8.2g | Protein: 5.3g

Grated Beet and Carrot Salad

Total time: 10 minutes | *Serves 2*

INGREDIENTS:

Salad:

4 carrots

1 small beet

1 tablespoon fresh basil, diced

Dressing:

1 tablespoon apple cider vinegar

1 tablespoon balsamic vinegar

1 teaspoon honey

ACTIONS:

- Grate the carrots and beet. Add to a bowl along with the basil.
- Mix the dressing ingredients well in a separate bowl. Pour on the salad and toss until well coated.

Calories: 79.6 | Total Fat: 0.3g | Carbs: 18.6g | Dietary Fiber: 4.6g | Protein: 1.9g

Asian Cabbage Salad

Total time: 10 minutes | *Serves 4*

INGREDIENTS:

Salad:

4 cups cabbage, shredded

2 carrots, grated or shredded

Dressing:

¼ cup olive oil

½ teaspoon sesame oil

1 tablespoon rice vinegar

2 tablespoons coconut sugar or maple syrup

2 tablespoons roasted sesame seeds

½ teaspoon salt

¼ teaspoon black pepper

1 teaspoon amino acids, like Bragg Liquid Aminos or soy sauce (optional)

ACTIONS:

- Mix the cabbage and carrots in a large bowl and toss.
- Mix the dressing ingredients well in a separate bowl. Pour on the salad and toss until well coated.

Calories: 199.9 | Total Fat: 16.1g | Carbs: 14.5g | Dietary Fiber: 2.8g | Protein: 2.2g

Thai Salad

This recipe is great with or without shrimp.

Total time: 10 minutes | Serves 4

INGREDIENTS:

Salad:

1 tablespoon coconut oil (for cooking shrimp)

1 pound shrimp, peeled and deveined (optional)

4 cups mixed greens

½ cup fresh bean sprouts

1 slice of red onion

1 tablespoon fresh mint leaves

2 tablespoons fresh cilantro leaves

4 cherry tomatoes, quartered

4 teaspoons dry roasted peanuts

1 lime

Dressing:

2 tablespoons rice vinegar

1 tablespoon green onions, chopped

1 tablespoon peanut butter

1 tablespoon amino acids, like Bragg Liquid Aminos or soy sauce

1 teaspoon ginger, peeled and grated

Dash of cayenne pepper

1 teaspoon sesame oil

ACTIONS:

- If you are including shrimp in this dish, heat oil in a pan on high and cook shrimp for 6 minutes, stirring occasionally, or until the shrimp are no longer transparent. While the shrimp are cooking, prepare the rest of the salad.
- Add mixed greens, bean sprouts, red onion, mint, cilantro, and tomatoes to 4 serving bowls.
- Mix the dressing ingredients well in a separate bowl. Pour on the salad and toss until well coated.
- Top with the cooked shrimp and peanuts. Squeeze lime juice over the entire salad.

Calories: 245.3 | Total Fat: 11.2g | Carbs: 10.6g | Dietary Fiber: 2.5g | Protein: 27.8g

Chickpea Cucumber Cumin Salad

You can use chickpeas from a can or Chickpea Fries.

Total time: 5 minutes | Serves 4

INGREDIENTS:

Salad:

1 cup kale, chopped
½ cup spinach
1 large cucumber, cubed
One 14-ounce can organic BPA-free chickpeas, drained

Dressing:

Juice of 1 lemon
2 tablespoons olive oil
1 teaspoon cumin
¼ teaspoon salt
Cracked black pepper to taste

ACTIONS:

- Place kale, spinach, cucumber, and chickpeas in 4 salad bowls.
- Mix the dressing ingredients well in a separate bowl. Pour on the salad and toss until well coated.

Calories: 136.5 | Total Fat: 7.8g | Carbs: 14.1g | Dietary Fiber: 2.8g | Protein: 3.7g

Protein Salad

Using precut chicken tenders will save you time in the kitchen. You can also make this without the chicken, and it will still be high in protein!

Total time: 10 minutes | Serves 4

INGREDIENTS:

Salad:

1 tablespoon coconut oil (optional, for cooking the chicken)
1 pound chicken tenders (optional)
8 cups mixed greens including kale, lettuce, and spinach
½ cup chickpeas
2 tablespoons hemp seeds
2 tablespoons sunflower seeds
2 tablespoons pumpkin seeds
Fresh parsley, thyme, and/or dill (optional)

Dressing:

1 lemon
2 tablespoons extra-virgin olive oil

ACTIONS:

- Heat the oil in a pan and sauté chicken on medium-high heat for 8 minutes or until done. While the chicken is cooking, prepare the rest of the salad.
- Add the mixed greens and chickpeas to 4 salad bowls. Top with seeds.
- Mix the dressing ingredients well in a separate bowl. Pour on the salad and toss until well coated.
- Add cooked chicken, then garnish with fresh parsley, thyme, and/or dill, if desired.

Calories: 466.7 | Total Fat: 16.9g | Carbs: 29.5g | Dietary Fiber: 14.5g | Protein: 41.9g

Kelp Noodle Salad with Peanut Sauce

You should be able to find kelp noodles in the Asian food aisle of your local supermarket.

Total time: 10 minutes | *Serves 4*

INGREDIENTS:

One (12-ounce) packet kelp noodles
¼ cup peanut butter
2 tablespoons apple cider vinegar
1 tablespoon maple syrup
1 teaspoon garlic, minced
¼ cup fresh cilantro, diced
1 green onion, diced

ACTIONS:

- Wash the kelp noodles, as instructed on the packet.
- Make the peanut sauce by adding peanut butter, apple cider vinegar, maple syrup, and garlic in a bowl. Mix until well combined.
- Massage the peanut sauce into the kelp noodles.
- Garnish with fresh cilantro and green onions.

TIPS:

- Add other flavors and variations by garnishing with crushed red pepper flakes, cayenne pepper, sesame seeds, or 1 inch grated ginger.
- Make it into a larger salad by dicing ½ small lettuce and grating 2 carrots and 1 small beet into it. Massage it all together.

Calories: 116.6 | *Total Fat: 8.1g* | *Carbs: 8.4g* | *Dietary Fiber: 1.1g* | *Protein: 4.9g*

Seaweed Salad

This salad is just like the salad you would order at a sushi restaurant. It is really important to get the right seaweed because this can make or break this recipe.

Total time: 10 minutes | *Serves 4*

INGREDIENTS:

¾ ounce dried wakame seaweed (whole or cut)
3 tablespoons rice vinegar
3 tablespoons amino acids (like Bragg Liquid Aminos or soy sauce) or 1 teaspoon salt and 2 teaspoons water
1 tablespoon sesame oil
¼ cup coconut sugar
¼ cup carrot, shredded
2 scallions, thinly sliced
2 tablespoons fresh cilantro, chopped
1 tablespoon sesame seeds, toasted

ACTIONS:

- Add the seaweed to a bowl, cover in warm water, and soak for 5 minutes. Drain, rinse, and then squeeze out excess water. Cut the wakame into ½-inch-wide strips, unless it's already precut.
- In a large bowl, stir together vinegar, amino acids (or salt water), sesame oil, and coconut sugar.
- Add the seaweed, carrots, scallions, and cilantro, and toss to combine. Finish by sprinkling sesame seeds.

TIPS:

- Add ½ teaspoon minced garlic and 1 teaspoon grated ginger for additional flavor.
- Sprinkle with red chili flakes, if desired.

Calories: 87.2 | *Total Fat: 4.7g* | *Carbs: 12.5g* | *Dietary Fiber: 0.8g* | *Protein: 2.9g*

Ultimate Base Dressing

Total time: 3 minutes | Serves 4

INGREDIENTS:

⅓ cup olive oil

Juice of 1 lemon

ACTIONS:

- Mix all ingredients in a bowl until well combined.

Calories: 162 | Total Fat: 18.0g | Carbs: 1.0g | Dietary Fiber: 0.1g | Protein: 0.1g

Salad Dressing Formula

The ultimate base for salad dressing is the juice of a lemon mixed with olive oil. Then you can add other spices and herbs to make different flavors. Refrigerated in an airtight container or jar, salad dressing generally lasts for up to two months.

Tigernut Oil Salad Dressing

Total time: 3 minutes | Serves 4

INGREDIENTS:

⅓ cup Organic Gemini TigerNut Oil

Juice of 1 lemon

Salt and pepper to taste

ACTIONS:

- Mix all ingredients in a bowl until well combined.

Calories: 162.9 | Total Fat: 9.3g | Carbs: 18.3g | Dietary Fiber: 13.4g | Protein: 2.8g

Salt and Pepper Dressing

Total time: 4 minutes | Serves 4

INGREDIENTS:

⅓ cup olive oil

Juice of 1 lemon

¼ teaspoon salt

¼ teaspoon cracked black pepper

ACTIONS:

- Mix all ingredients in a bowl until well combined.

Calories: 162.6 | Total Fat: 18.0g | Carbs: 1.2g | Dietary Fiber: 0.1g | Protein: 0.1g

Sweet Salad Dressing

Total time: 3 minutes | Serves 4

INGREDIENTS:

⅓ cup olive oil
Juice of 1 lemon
1 to 2 tablespoons maple syrup, honey, or coconut sugar

ACTIONS:

- Mix all ingredients in a bowl until well combined.

Calories: 188.1 | Total Fat: 18.0g | Carbs: 7.7g | Dietary Fiber: 0.1g | Protein: 0.1g

Hot Chipotle Dressing

Total time: 3 minutes | Serves 4

INGREDIENTS:

⅓ cup olive oil
Juice of 1 lemon
1 large hot chipotle pepper, chopped
Dash of cayenne pepper

ACTIONS:

- Mix all ingredients in a bowl until well combined.

Calories: 162.1 | Total Fat: 18.0g | Carbs: 1.1g | Dietary Fiber: 0.1g | Protein: 0.1g

Sweet and Spicy Salad Dressing

Total time: 5 minutes | Serves 4

INGREDIENTS:

⅓ cup olive oil
Juice of 1 lemon
2 tablespoons maple syrup or honey
1 small hot chili, diced

ACTIONS:

- Mix all ingredients in a bowl until well combined.

Calories: 192.6 | Total Fat: 18.0g | Carbs: 8.8g | Dietary Fiber: 0.2g | Protein: 0.3g

Tangy Ginger Garlic Dressing

Total time: 5 minutes | Serves 4

INGREDIENTS:

⅓ cup olive oil
Juice of 1 lemon
2 teaspoons garlic, minced
1-inch piece of ginger, minced

ACTIONS:

- Mix all ingredients in a bowl until well combined.

Calories: 100 | Total Fat: 11g | Carbs: 1g | Dietary Fiber: 0g | Protein: 0g

Turmeric Salad Dressing

Total time: 3 minutes | *Serves 4*

INGREDIENTS:

⅓ cup olive oil
Juice of 1 lemon
1 teaspoon turmeric powder

ACTIONS:

- Mix all ingredients in a bowl until well combined.

Calories: 162 | Total Fat: 18.0g | Carbs: 1.0g | Dietary Fiber: 0.1g | Protein: 0.1g

Hummus Salad Dressing

Total time: 3 minutes | *Serves 4*

INGREDIENTS:

⅓ cup olive oil
Juice of 1 lemon
2 to 3 tablespoons Hummus

ACTIONS:

- Mix all ingredients in a bowl until well combined.

Calories: 224 | Total Fat: 20.0g | Carbs: 9.0g | Dietary Fiber: 2.6g | Protein: 2.9g

Cheesy Salad Dressing

Total time: 3 minutes | *Serves 4*

INGREDIENTS:

⅓ cup olive oil
Juice of 1 lemon
1 to 2 tablespoons nutritional yeast
½ teaspoon salt

ACTIONS:

- Mix all ingredients in a bowl until well combined.

Calories: 177 | Total Fat: 18.2g | Carbs: 2.3g | Dietary Fiber: 1.1g | Protein: 2.1g

Tahini Salad Dressing

Total time: 3 minutes | *Serves 4*

INGREDIENTS:

⅓ cup olive oil
Juice of 1 lemon
2 to 3 tablespoons Tahini

ACTIONS:

- Mix all ingredients in a bowl until well combined.

Calories: 182.3 | Total Fat: 20.1g | Carbs: 1.7g | Dietary Fiber: 0.4g | Protein: 0.6g

Creamy Avocado Salad Dressing

Total time: 4 minutes | Serves 4

INGREDIENTS:

⅓ cup extra-virgin olive oil
Juice of 1 lemon
1 avocado, seeded and peeled

ACTIONS:

- Mix all ingredients in a blender until well combined. Alternatively, mash with a fork in a bowl until smooth. Pour onto the salad or massage into salad leaves.

Calories: 218.7 | Total Fat: 23.2g | Carbs: 4.0g | Dietary Fiber: 2.3g | Protein: 0.7g

Mango Salad Dressing

This dressing goes great over avocado and sesame seeds!

Total time: 5 minutes | Serves 4

INGREDIENTS:

⅓ cup olive oil
Juice of 1 lemon
1 mango, peeled and seeded

ACTIONS:

- Mix all ingredients in a blender until well combined.

Calories: 179.5 | Total Fat: 18.0g | Carbs: 5.5g | Dietary Fiber: 0.6g | Protein: 0.3g

Sesame Ginger Dressing

Total time: 3 minutes | Serves 4

INGREDIENTS:

⅓ cup olive oil
Juice of 1 lemon
1 tablespoon sesame seeds, toasted
1 tablespoon ginger, grated

ACTIONS:

- Mix all ingredients in a bowl until well combined.

Calories: 174.9 | Total Fat: 19.1g | Carbs: 1.6g | Dietary Fiber: 0.3g | Protein: 0.4g

Thai Curry Dressing

This goes great over mixed greens, snow peas, and bean sprouts!

Total time: 3 minutes | Serves 4

INGREDIENTS:

Juice of 1 lemon
⅓ cup extra-virgin olive oil
2 tablespoons Thai Red Curry Paste or Thai Green Curry Paste

ACTIONS:

- Mix all ingredients in a bowl until well combined.

Calories: 172 | Total Fat: 18.5g | Carbs: 2.0g | Dietary Fiber: 1.1g | Protein: 0.1g

Balsamic Apple Cider Vinegar Dressing

Total time: 2 minutes | Serves 2

INGREDIENTS:

1 tablespoon apple cider vinegar
1 tablespoon organic balsamic vinegar
1 teaspoon honey

ACTIONS:

- Mix all ingredients in a bowl until well combined.

Calories: 14.6 | Total Fat: 0.0g | Carbs: 3.9g | Dietary Fiber: 0.0g | Protein: 0.0g

Citrus Salad Dressing

Total time: 3 minutes | Serves 4

INGREDIENTS:

Juice of 1 lemon
Juice of 1 orange
Juice of 1 grapefruit
2 tablespoons olive oil

ACTIONS:

- Mix all ingredients in a bowl until well combined.

Calories: 190.7 | Total Fat: 18.1g | Carbs: 7.8g | Dietary Fiber: 0.1g | Protein: 0.4g

Caesar Salad Dressing

Total time: 3 minutes | Serves 4

INGREDIENTS:

Juice of 1 lemon
⅓ cup extra-virgin olive oil
¼ teaspoon mustard powder
2 tablespoons nutritional yeast
½ teaspoon honey
1 teaspoon garlic, minced
¼ teaspoon salt
¼ teaspoon black pepper

ACTIONS:

- Mix all ingredients in a bowl until well combined.

Calories: 184.8 | Total Fat: 18.4g | Carbs: 4.0g | Dietary Fiber: 1.1g | Protein: 2.1g

Mustard Vinaigrette

Total time: 3 minutes | Serves 4

INGREDIENTS:

⅓ cup extra-virgin olive oil
1½ teaspoons apple cider vinegar
1 teaspoon garlic, minced
1 tablespoon mustard
¼ teaspoon black pepper
¼ teaspoon salt

ACTIONS:

- Mix all ingredients in a bowl until well combined.

Calories: 162.8 | Total Fat: 18.1g | Carbs: 0.6g | Dietary Fiber: 0.2g | Protein: 0.2g

Asian Dressing

If you are craving a vacation to somewhere like Thailand or Bali, this is a great dressing to infuse those vibes into your life! Add it to a simple green salad, raw cabbage, rice noodles, or gluten-free noodles.

Total time: 5 minutes | *Serves 4*

INGREDIENTS:

3 tablespoons rice vinegar

3 tablespoons amino acids (like Bragg Liquid Aminos or soy sauce) or 1 teaspoon salt and 2 teaspoons water

1 tablespoon sesame oil

¼ cup coconut sugar

2 scallions, diced

1 tablespoon sesame seeds, toasted

1 tablespoon fresh cilantro, chopped

ACTIONS:

- Mix all ingredients in a bowl until well combined.

Calories: 182.8 | Total Fat: 20.8g | Carbs: 7.9g | Dietary Fiber: 0.5g | Protein: 2.0g

CHAPTER 12

Raw Vegan Main Dishes

At dinnertime, even if you came home from work late and you only have an hour until bed, or if you're flat out exhausted and don't want to make a major production out of food preparation, you can still dedicate 10 minutes to whipping up something scrumptious. The Earth Diet provides food for every type of eater: raw vegan, cooked vegan, or meat eater. Want something on the lighter side? Try a salad or a soup. Want a more substantial meal with some protein? One of the main dishes is sure to appeal.

If you're aiming to lose weight or cleanse, opt for one of these Raw Vegan Main Dishes. Raw foods are extremely nutrient-dense and fibrous, so they'll fill you up and satisfy you with fewer calories—naturally.

Walnut "Meatballs"

You can make Raw Tacos by wrapping up a few of these "meatballs" in lettuce with the toppings of your choice. They also go well on a bed of brown rice pasta, bean pasta, or zucchini pasta. Serve with dipping sauce and organic corn chips for a great party snack.

Total time: 10 minutes | *Serves 4 to 6*

INGREDIENTS:

1½ cups walnuts
1 cup sun-dried tomatoes
2 tablespoons extra-virgin olive oil
1 teaspoon dried sage
1 teaspoon fennel seeds
1 teaspoon dried thyme
1 teaspoon dried rosemary
1 teaspoon dried oregano
1 pinch black pepper
1 pinch cayenne pepper
1 pinch salt

ACTIONS:

- Add all ingredients to your blender and mix for 5 minutes or until well combined. The mixture should be moist and stick together. Roll the mixture with your hands to make "meatballs."

TIPS:

- If you do not have a blender, you can use a mortar and pestle to crush the walnuts. Then dice the sun-dried tomatoes, and mix everything together in a bowl.
- For a nut-free version, use pumpkin seeds or sunflower seeds instead of walnuts.
- If you use essential oils instead of dried herbs, be sparing. Start with just the amount of oil you get when you dip a clean toothpick in the bottle, then increase, to taste.

Calories: 274 | Total Fat: 25g | Carbs: 10g |
Dietary Fiber: 4g | Protein: 6g

Zucchini Spaghetti with Tomato Sauce and Walnut "Meatballs"

This is a completely raw, plant-based vegan dish, no cooking required. It is extremely nutrient rich, leaving you fulfilled yet light so you can continue on with your day without feeling sluggish!

Total time: 10 minutes | Serves 4

INGREDIENTS:

2 large zucchini
1 batch Raw Tomato Sauce
1 batch Walnut "Meatballs"
Nutritional yeast, to taste (optional)

ACTIONS:

- Use a spiralizer or vegetable peeler to make spaghetti strips with the zucchini. Place in the bowls. Evenly divide the Tomato Sauce and "Meatballs" between the bowls, and sprinkle nutritional yeast, if desired, on top.

TIPS:

- To save some time, you can make this recipe without the Walnut "Meatballs," and just have the Zucchini Spaghetti and Tomato Sauce.
- Top with Cashew Cheese.

Calories: 377 | Total Fat: 28.6g | Carbs: 26g | Dietary Fiber: 9g | Protein: 10.4g

Raw Zucchini Alfredo

Total time: 10 minutes | Serves 2

INGREDIENTS:

1 large zucchini
Alfredo Sauce
Fresh parsley (optional)

ACTIONS:

- Use a spiralizer or vegetable peeler to make spaghetti strips from the zucchini. Serve in bowls, and top with Alfredo Sauce and fresh parsley, if desired.

Calories: 241 | Total Fat: 16.0g | Carbs: 22.2g | Dietary Fiber: 4.9g | Protein: 7.0g

Raw Pad Thai

Total time: 10 minutes | Serves 4

INGREDIENTS:

4 zucchini
1 tablespoon garlic, minced (or garlic powder)
4 green onions, diced
1 tablespoon apple cider vinegar
1 tablespoon maple syrup
1 teaspoon amino acids, like Bragg Liquid Aminos or soy sauce
1 teaspoon peanut butter
Dash of cayenne pepper or ¼ teaspoon red pepper flakes
1 cup bean sprouts
1 lime
½ cup peanuts, crushed

ACTIONS:

- Use a spiralizer or vegetable peeler to make noodle shapes with the zucchini. Place these in a large bowl.
- Make the sauce for your Raw Pad Thai by mixing together the garlic, green onions, apple cider vinegar, maple syrup, amino acids, peanut butter, and cayenne. Massage into the zucchini noodles.
- Serve in bowls and top with bean sprouts, lime juice, and peanuts.

Calories: 156 | Total Fat: 8.6g | Carbs: 19g | Dietary Fiber: 5.5g | Protein: 13.3g

Raw Lasagna

Total time: 10 minutes | Serves 1 to 2

INGREDIENTS:

1 zucchini
¼ batch Walnut "Meatballs"
¼ batch Cashew Cheese
2 tablespoons extra-virgin olive oil
1 tablespoon dried oregano

ACTIONS:

- Use a vegetable peeler to create thick layers of zucchini strips. Place the first layer on a plate.
- Add some Walnut "Meatballs" mixture and then a layer of Cashew Cheese. Add a middle layer of zucchini strips.
- Add another layer of the walnut meat and cashew cheese, followed by a final layer of zucchini. Drizzle with olive oil and sprinkle oregano on top!

TIP:

- Spend more time layering your lasagna with fresh basil, peppers, pesto, and Raw Tomato Sauce.

Calories: 223 | Total Fat: 21g | Carbs: 16g | Dietary Fiber: 4g | Protein: 6.6g

Zucchini Pasta with Pesto

Total time: 10 minutes | Serves 2

INGREDIENTS:

2 large zucchini
½ cup fresh basil
Juice of ½ lemon
2 cloves garlic
¼ teaspoon salt
¼ cup spinach
1 cup raw walnuts
¼ cup extra-virgin olive oil

ACTIONS:

- Make thin strips of zucchini using a peeler or a spiralizer. Set aside in 2 serving bowls.
- Blend the other ingredients in a blender until the mixture reaches the desired consistency. Add more oil if you want a smoother consistency.
- Pour the sauce over the pasta.

VARIATION:

- Zucchini Pasta with Nut-Free Pesto: Use pumpkin seeds instead of walnuts.

Calories: 312 | Total Fat: 30g | Carbs: 10g | Dietary Fiber: 3.5g | Protein: 6g

Raw Tomato Soup

Total time: 7 minutes | Serves 3

INGREDIENTS:

One 28-ounce can whole tomatoes, in juice
1 rib celery, roughly chopped
¼ small onion
1 clove garlic
1 teaspoon dried parsley
1 teaspoon dried thyme
1 bay leaf
1 tablespoon pure maple syrup
1 tablespoon fresh lemon juice
¼ teaspoon salt
¼ teaspoon black pepper

ACTIONS:

- Puree all ingredients and 1 cup water together in a blender until smooth. Taste. Season with more salt and pepper, if desired.

TIP:

- This also substitutes as a sauce when cooking ground beef, spaghetti, lasagna, or any other recipe that calls for "pasta sauce."

VARIATIONS:

- Creamy Tomato Soup: Add ¼ cup Vegan Sour Cream.
- Hot Tomato Soup: Add soup to a pot, bring to a boil, then let simmer for a few minutes.

Calories: 110 | Total Fat: 1.5g | Carbs: 20.8g | Dietary Fiber: 2g | Protein: 4.1g

CHAPTER 13

Cooked Vegan Main Dishes

Cooked vegan main dishes are an excellent source of the "good stuff" we need. Food should be a feast for the eyes, nose, and taste buds as well as giving us vital nutrients. Fortunately, vegetables meet all of these requirements.

Vegetables are so colorful that when we cook our vegan main dishes, we can view ourselves as painters drawing upon a vibrant palette. Red, orange, yellow, blue, green, and purple—with every color you consume, you're nourishing your cells with different phytochemicals and the life force of the sun that fed them.

Bean Burgers

Bean burgers are a light, plant-based alternative to beef burgers. These vegan burgers are a hit even with meat lovers because the herbs and spices make them so flavorful. Make a batch to store in the freezer and just pull one out whenever you need to fulfill a craving.

Total time: 10 minutes | *Serves 4*

INGREDIENTS:

2 tablespoons extra-virgin coconut oil, for cooking

One 15-ounce can organic beans, drained (butter, kidney, or black beans work best)

½ cup almond meal

1 small yellow onion, chopped

¼ cup nutritional yeast

½ teaspoon cumin

¼ teaspoon garlic powder

¼ teaspoon fennel

¼ teaspoon thyme

¼ teaspoon sage

¼ teaspoon salt

¼ teaspoon black pepper

Pinch of cayenne pepper

1 Flax Egg Alternative

ACTIONS:

- Heat the oil in a large pan over medium heat.
- Mash the beans with the rest of the ingredients. Taste and add more spices to your liking.
- Divide mixture into 4 equal parts, then shape into patties.
- Fry the patties until golden, about 4 minutes on each side.

TIPS:

- Top these burgers with fresh parsley, cilantro, and basil.
- Serve on gluten-free rolls, kale, collard greens, lettuce, or Gluten-Free Tortillas.
- Nonvegans can use one egg in this recipe instead of Flax Egg Alternative.
- Replace the nutritional yeast with more almond meal for a less cheesy flavor.

VARIATIONS:

- Bean Balls: Roll the mixture into 10 balls and serve on brown rice pasta or Zucchini Pasta.
- Nut-Free Bean Burgers: Replace the almond meal with pumpkin seed, sunflower seed, or hemp seed meal.
- Spicy Bean Burgers: Add extra cayenne pepper.
- Lentil Burgers: Use lentils instead of beans.
- Tigernut Bean Burgers: Replace the brown rice flour and flax meal with ½ cup tigernut flour.

Calories: 248 | Total Fat: 12g | Carbs: 27g |
Dietary Fiber: 11g | Protein: 13g

Cooked Vegan Main Dishes

Chickpea Burgers

Total time: 10 minutes | Serves 4

INGREDIENTS:

2 tablespoons extra-virgin coconut oil, for cooking
¼ cup brown rice flour
1 tablespoon flax meal
One 14-ounce can chickpeas, drained
2 teaspoons crushed garlic
1 teaspoon salt
1 teaspoon onion powder
¼ teaspoon cumin seeds
½ teaspoon cumin powder
¼ teaspoon turmeric
¼ teaspoon fennel
¼ teaspoon sage
¼ teaspoon rosemary
⅛ teaspoon oregano

ACTIONS:

- Heat the oil in a large pan over medium heat. Mash the beans with the rest of the ingredients. Taste and add more spices or salt to your liking. Divide into 4 equal parts and shape into patties.
- Fry the patties until golden, about 4 minutes on each side.

VARIATION:

- Tigernut Chickpea Burgers: Replace the brown rice flour and flax meal with ½ cup tigernut flour.

Calories: 181.5 | Total Fat: 8.8g | Carbs: 18.5g | Dietary Fiber: 4.4g | Protein: 5.6g

Black Bean Salsa Pasta

Total time: 10 minutes | Serves 4

INGREDIENTS:

One (7-ounce) packet black bean pasta
1 teaspoon garlic, minced
1 teaspoon salt
1½ cups 10-Minute Salsa
2 tablespoons nutritional yeast (optional)
½ cup fresh cilantro

ACTIONS:

- Prepare pasta according to package directions. Once cooked, drain the water and add all ingredients to pot. Stir until the pasta is well coated.

Calories: 105 | Total Fat: 1.2g | Carbs: 18.9g | Dietary Fiber: 4.8g | Protein: 6.3g

Thai Wraps

Total time: 10 minutes | Serves 4

INGREDIENTS:

Wrapper:
4 large collard greens, kale, or lettuce
Sauce:
1 tablespoon garlic, minced
1 tablespoon ginger, minced
2 teaspoons apple cider vinegar
1 carrot, grated
Juice of 2 oranges
¼ cup scallions, diced
Filling:
1 avocado, sliced
1 mango, sliced
½ cup fresh mint
½ cup fresh cilantro
½ cup bean sprouts
1 cup cabbage, diced (roughly ¼ of a
   whole cabbage)

ACTIONS:

- Combine all sauce ingredients well
  and set aside.
- Lay out a large lettuce leaf and layer
  it with the avocado and mango slices,
  mint, cilantro, sprouts, and cabbage.
  Repeat for all the leaves, then top with
  sauce, to taste.

Calories: 135 | Total Fat: 6g | Carbs: 22g |
Dietary Fiber: 5g | Protein: 3g

Vegan Pad Thai

Total time: 10 minutes | Serves 4

INGREDIENTS:

3 tablespoons coconut oil, for cooking
1 tablespoon garlic, minced (or garlic
   powder)
4 green onions, diced
1 packet soft rice noodles
1 tablespoon apple cider vinegar
1 tablespoon maple syrup
1 tablespoon soconut sugar
Dash of cayenne pepper or
   ¼ teaspoon red pepper flakes
2 cups bean sprouts
½ cup roasted peanuts, crushed
1 lime

ACTIONS:

- Heat the oil in a wok or large frying
  pan on medium heat. Add the garlic
  and half of the green onions. Stir-fry
  for 40 seconds.
- Add the rice noodles to the pan. Stir-
  fry for 3 minutes.
- Add the apple cider vinegar, maple
  syrup, coconut sugar, cayenne pepper,
  and bean sprouts. Stir-fry for 2
  minutes or until noodles are cooked
  and everything is well blended.
- Serve on plates, and then add roasted
  peanuts and squeeze fresh lime over
  the dish.

TIP:

- Be sure to check the rice noodle box
  directions, as some may require
  soaking or other preparations before
  use.

Calories: 536.7 | Total Fat: 19.4g | Carbs:
83.5g | Dietary Fiber: 6.4g | Protein: 10.6g

Vegetable Stir-Fry

Super simple, yet packed with layers of textures and flavors, this is a great weekly staple to prepare in large batches and keep in your fridge.

Total time: 10 minutes | *Serves 4*

INGREDIENTS:

¼ cup extra-virgin coconut oil, for cooking

1 yellow onion, chopped

3 teaspoons garlic, minced

1 teaspoon ginger, diced, or ½ teaspoon ginger powder

1 teaspoon turmeric powder

½ teaspoon cumin

½ teaspoon thyme

¼ teaspoon salt

1 large carrot, chopped

½ head of broccoli, chopped

½ head of cauliflower, chopped

1 cup spinach

1 cup green beans

1 tablespoon sesame seeds

ACTIONS:

- Heat the oil in a wok or frying pan on medium-high heat. Add onion and garlic, then sauté for 2 minutes.
- Add ginger, turmeric powder, cumin, thyme, salt, and all vegetables to the pan, and then stir-fry until tender, about 7 minutes.
- Serve, sprinkling sesame seeds over each dish, along with salt and pepper to taste.

TIPS:

- Add your favorite spices or other vegetables like peppers, snow peas, zucchini, beets, or peas.
- Add a squeeze of lemon right before serving for added health benefits.

VARIATIONS

- Vegetable Pasta Stir-Fry: Serve over 1½ cups cooked brown rice pasta.
- Vegetable Rice Stir-Fry: Serve over 1 cup cooked rice.
- Sesame Vegetable Stir-Fry: Use sesame seed oil instead of coconut oil.
- Artichoke Vegetable Stir-Fry: Add artichokes.
- Spicy Vegetable Stir-Fry: Add ½ teaspoon or more cayenne pepper.
- Sweet Vegetable Stir-Fry: Add 1 tablespoon or more honey or maple syrup when adding the vegetables.
- Meat and Veg Stir-Fry: If you are a meat eater, add chicken, beef, or scrambled eggs to this dish.

Calories: 190 | *Total Fat: 16g* | *Carbs: 11g* | *Dietary Fiber: 5g* | *Protein: 4g*

10-Minute Mac 'n' Cheese

This dairy-free, gluten-free mac 'n' cheese is incredibly creamy, and surprisingly, it really satisfies classic mac 'n' cheese lovers!

Total time: 10 minutes | Serves 3

INGREDIENTS:

2 cups quinoa or brown rice macaroni pasta, uncooked
3 tablespoons nutritional yeast
1 teaspoon salt

ACTIONS:

- In a pot, add the pasta to 3¼ cups boiling water. Stir the pasta and reduce the heat to medium. Keep stirring until the pasta is soft. As it cooks, the pasta will soak up the water and begin to take on a creamy appearance. Do not drain!
- Add the nutritional yeast and the salt to the pot of pasta and stir until well combined with the water to form the sauce.

TIPS:

- Usually when we cook pasta, there is so much water in the pot that the pasta needs to be drained. For this dish to succeed and achieve natural creaminess, however, we need the pasta to soak up the water. The residual liquid in the pot will become the base for the creamy sauce, so do not drain it.
- Make sure to read the directions to ensure that your chosen brand of pasta can be cooked in about 7 minutes.

Calories: 453 | Total Fat: 4.5g | Carbs: 90g | Dietary Fiber: 5g | Protein: 14g

Vegan Nachos

Total time: 10 minutes | Serves 4

INGREDIENTS:

1 packet organic chips (black bean, organic corn, or rice chips)
½ can (about 7.5 ounces) black beans
½ teaspoon salt
½ cup organic salsa
¼ cup nutritional yeast

ACTIONS:

- Preheat the oven to 400°F.
- On a baking tray, spread out the chips. Add the beans on top, and then sprinkle the salt over them. Add a layer of salsa, and sprinkle nutritional yeast on top.
- Bake for about 8 minutes.

TIPS:

- Serve with fresh toppings like diced onion, cilantro, avocado, and Vegan Sour Cream.
- For a nonvegan option, use the filling from Beef Tacos and organic cheese.

Calories: 255.5 | Total Fat: 10.8g | Carbs: 33.0g | Dietary Fiber: 7.0g | Protein: 6.4g

Cumin Turmeric Quinoa Pasta

Total time: 10 minutes | *Serves 3*

INGREDIENTS:

1 cup uncooked quinoa pasta
1 tablespoon cumin
½ teaspoon turmeric powder
1 teaspoon salt
1 teaspoon extra-virgin coconut oil
1 teaspoon black pepper
Dash of cayenne pepper
Fresh thyme (optional)

ACTIONS:

- In a pot, add the quinoa pasta to boiling water. Reduce the heat to medium, and continue cooking for 7 minutes or until the pasta is done.
- Drain the pasta and add the remaining ingredients. Stir well, and then serve with fresh thyme as a garnish, if desired.

Calories: 252 | Total Fat: 5.7g | Carbs: 42.8g | Dietary Fiber: 4.4g | Protein: 8.5g

Quinoa Pasta with Greens

Total time: 10 minutes | *Serves 2*

INGREDIENTS:

1 cup uncooked quinoa pasta
¼ cup extra-virgin coconut oil, for cooking
½ yellow onion, sliced
1 clove garlic
¼ head of broccoli, chopped into bite-sized pieces
8 asparagus stems, cut in thirds
½ cup fresh or frozen peas
Cracked black pepper and salt, to taste

ACTIONS:

- In a pot, add the quinoa pasta to boiling water. Reduce the heat to medium, and continue cooking for 7 minutes or until the pasta is done.
- While the pasta cooks, heat oil in a frying pan over medium and add the onion and garlic. Stir-fry for 3 minutes until golden brown. Add the broccoli and asparagus and continue to stir-fry for another 4 minutes. Add the peas and cook for another minute.
- Drain the pasta and add the cooked pasta to the vegetables and toss to combine. Add salt and pepper to taste.

Calories: 152 | Total Fat: 15g | Carbs: 20g | Dietary Fiber: 3.5g | Protein: 5.5g

Immune-Boosting Soup

This soup is incredibly immune boosting because it combines onion and tomato with garlic and spices. Did you know onions are high in vitamin C? This might be why you crave them when you're feeling run down.

Make a large batch of this up, and keep it in your freezer. Then just defrost some in a pot when you need some. Fresh herbs are best for immune-boosting properties, but if you do not have access to fresh, you can make this recipe with dried herbs only.

Total time: 10 minutes | Serves 2

INGREDIENTS:

1 tablespoon extra-virgin olive oil
1 small yellow onion, chopped
1 tablespoon garlic, minced
1 teaspoon cumin powder
1 teaspoon turmeric powder
1 teaspoon salt
½ teaspoon cracked black pepper
Pinch or two of cayenne pepper
8 fresh basil leaves, or 1 teaspoon dried
1 tablespoon fresh thyme, or 1 teaspoon dried
1 tablespoon fresh parsley, or 1 teaspoon dried
1 tablespoon fresh cilantro, or 1 teaspoon dried
3 fresh sage leaves, or 1 teaspoon dried
3 medium tomatoes

ACTIONS:

- Heat the oil in a pot on medium heat, then add the onion and cook for 2 minutes. (I like to gather up all my spices now, while the onion softens.)
- Mix all the herbs and spices into the pot.
- Cut the tomatoes in half and squeeze their juice into the pot. Then chop up the tomatoes into bite-size pieces, and add them to the pot.
- Add 2 cups water and let cook for 7 minutes.
- Taste, then season with more salt and pepper, if desired.

TIP:

- Top with additional fresh herbs like basil, parsley, and cilantro.

Calories: 149 | Total Fat: 7.9g | Carbs: 17.8g | Dietary Fiber: 4.8g | Protein: 2.5g

Vegetable Broth

You can make your vegetable broth in double and triple batches and keep it in the fridge or even the freezer so you always have it on hand for recipes.

Total time: 10 minutes | *Makes 4 cups*

INGREDIENTS:

1 tablespoon onion powder
1 tablespoon garlic powder
1 tablespoon celery powder
1 tablespoon coriander powder
1 tablespoon fresh parsley
1 tablespoon fresh thyme
2 bay leaves
1 teaspoon salt
¼ teaspoon black pepper

ACTIONS:

- Add the spices to a large pot of 4 cups of water brought to a boil. Allow it to boil for 8 minutes.
- When cooled, store it in an airtight jar or container, and keep it in the fridge or freezer.

Calories: 91 | Total Fat: 3.5g | Carbs: 15.8g | Dietary Fiber: 5.4g | Protein: 3.1g

Vegetable Soup

Total time: 10 minutes | *Serves 4*

INGREDIENTS:

1 teaspoon salt
¼ teaspoon black pepper
½ teaspoon dried thyme, or 1 tablespoon fresh thyme
½ teaspoon dried parsley, or 1 tablespoon fresh parsley
½ teaspoon dried oregano
½ teaspoon cumin powder
½ head of cauliflower
½ head of broccoli
1 carrot
2 celery stalks
Dash of cayenne pepper (optional)

ACTIONS:

- Add all ingredients except cayenne pepper to a large pot of 5 cups of water brought to a boil. Allow it to boil for 7 minutes, or until vegetables reach desired consistency.
- Serve soup with a dash of cayenne pepper, if you want some kick.

Calories: 56.5 | Total Fat: 0.6g | Carbs: 10.6g | Dietary Fiber: 5.5g | Protein: 4.0g

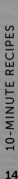

Indian Ramen

Total time: 10 minutes | *Serves 2*

INGREDIENTS:

2 packets of ramen noodles
2 teaspoons cumin powder
1 teaspoon turmeric
Dash salt
Fresh saffron, to taste
Cumin seeds, to taste
1 cucumber, diced

ACTIONS:

- Add the ramen noodles, cumin, turmeric, and salt to a pot with 5 cups of water brought to a boil. Cook until the noodles are done, approximately 5 minutes.
- Season with a dash of saffron and cumin seeds, and top with cubes of fresh cucumber.

TIPS:

- Drizzle with truffle oil at the end.
- Drain the water from this one. It is also good dry!

Calories: 395 | Total Fat: 14.6g | Carbs: 54.4g | Dietary Fiber: 2.7g | Protein: 10.8g

Butternut Squash Ramen

Total time: 10 minutes | *Serves 2*

INGREDIENTS:

1½ cups butternut squash soup
2 packets of ramen noodles
¼ teaspoon salt
1 teaspoon amino acids, like Bragg Liquid Aminos or soy sauce
Dash of sesame oil

Toppings:

Sprinkle of sesame seeds
1 cup bean sprouts or pea shoots
Dash of cayenne pepper or ¼ teaspoon red pepper flakes
Handful of arugula leaves

ACTIONS:

- Add all soup ingredients to a pot with 4 cups of water brought to a boil. Cook until the noodles are done, approximately 5 minutes.
- Add the toppings and enjoy.

Calories: 456 | Total Fat: 15.8g | Carbs: 69.2g | Dietary Fiber: 6.6g | Protein: 12.4g

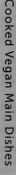

Red Curry Ramen

Total time: 10 minutes | Serves 2

INGREDIENTS:

1 tablespoon extra-virgin coconut oil
1 teaspoon garlic paste
½ pound shrimp, peeled and deveined
½ head of broccoli
3 tablespoons Thai Red Curry Paste
¼ cup coconut sugar or coconut nectar
2 packets ramen noodles
Toppings:
Handful of fresh basil
Handful of fresh cilantro
1 to 2 tablespoons crushed peanuts
¾ cup bean sprouts
2 green onions, sliced
Juice of 1 lime

ACTIONS:

- Add coconut oil, garlic paste, shrimp, broccoli, curry paste, and coconut sugar to a pot with 5 cups of water brought to a boil. Cook approximately 4 minutes, or until the shrimp starts to turn pink.
- Add the ramen noodles to the pot, and cook until done, approximately 5 minutes.
- Serve in bowls with the broth, add the toppings, and enjoy.

TIP:

- Grated carrots make a nice topping.

Calories: 772.7 | Total Fat: 35.5g | Carbs: 75.0g | Dietary Fiber: 6.6g | Protein: 38.3g

Green Thai Ramen

Total time: 10 minutes | Serves 2

INGREDIENTS:

2 packets of ramen noodles
1 tablespoon garlic, minced (or garlic powder)
1 tablespoon apple cider vinegar
2 tablespoons Thai Green Curry Paste
1 tablespoon maple syrup
1 teaspoon amino acids, like Bragg Liquid Aminos or soy sauce
Toppings:
Juice of 1 lime
¼ cup crushed roasted peanuts
Handful of fresh cilantro
1 cup bean sprouts
1 green onion diced
Dash of cayenne pepper or ¼ teaspoon red pepper flakes

ACTIONS:

- Add all soup ingredients to a pot with 5 cups of water brought to a boil. Cook until the noodles are done, approximately 5 minutes.
- Add the toppings and enjoy.

Calories (toppings not included): 427.6 | Total Fat: 14.5g | Carbs: 63.7g | Dietary Fiber: 2.4g | Protein: 11.9g

White Bean Soup with Kale

Total time: 10 minutes | Serves 4

INGREDIENTS:

1½ tablespoons coconut oil
1 yellow onion, chopped
1 teaspoon garlic powder
Two 15-ounce cans organic cannellini
   beans, rinsed and drained
4 cups kale, chopped
½ teaspoon black pepper, freshly
   ground

ACTIONS:

- Heat the oil in a large pot over medium-high heat. Add onion and garlic powder, and cook for 1½ minutes.
- Add the rest of the ingredients and 3 cups water, and cook on high for another 7 minutes. Season, to taste.

Calories: 158 | Total Fat: 0.5g | Carbs: 28.8g | Dietary Fiber: 12.5g | Protein: 10.1g

Tomato, Basil, and White Bean Soup

Total time: 10 minutes | Serves 4

INGREDIENTS:

1¾ cups chicken broth
2 teaspoons chili powder
1 teaspoon ground cumin
One 16-ounce can navy beans, drained
   and rinsed
1 medium chili, halved and seeded
1 small yellow onion
1 pint grape tomatoes
½ cup fresh basil
¼ cup fresh cilantro
2 tablespoons fresh lime juice
1 tablespoon extra-virgin olive oil
½ teaspoon salt

ACTIONS:

- Combine broth, chili powder, cumin, and beans in a pot over medium-high heat.
- While that is cooking, add to a food processor the chili, onion, tomatoes, basil, and cilantro. Puree until smooth, then pour it into the pot.
- Allow soup to boil for 8 minutes, then remove from the heat and stir in the lime juice, oil, and salt. Garnish with more fresh basil, if desired.

Calories: 194 | Total Fat: 4.1g | Carbs: 36.1g | Dietary Fiber: 12g | Protein: 8g

CHAPTER 14

Meat Eaters' Main Dishes

Always eat organic, free-range meat and poultry and wild-caught fish when you make your meat eaters' main dishes, as these are healthier animal-protein options. When I started writing this book, I wasn't sure that red meat and chicken could be prepared so quickly. It's fascinating what can be accomplished in 10 minutes or less, everything from 10-Minute Burgers to Almond-Crusted Chicken Tenders.

10-Minute Beef Burgers

Accompany with Basic French Fries and top with Ketchup.

Total time: 10 minutes | *Serves 4*

INGREDIENTS:

¼ cup extra-virgin coconut oil, for cooking
1 pound ground beef
1 tablespoon fresh sage, or 1 teaspoon dried sage
2 teaspoons salt
1 teaspoon cumin
1 teaspoon turmeric powder
½ teaspoon black pepper

ACTIONS:

- Heat a large frying pan with the coconut oil over medium heat. Form 4 beef patties by hand and place them in the pan.
- Mix the herbs, and sprinkle half of them over the patties. When the undersides have browned, flip them over and sprinkle the remaining herbs. Cook until desired doneness.

TIP:

- Choose your bun: Either fresh lettuce or kale leaves, or organic bread rolls.

VARIATION:

- Chicken Burgers: Use ground chicken instead of beef.

Calories: 503 | Total Fat: 42g | Carbs: 6g | Dietary Fiber: 3g | Protein: 30g

10-Minute Fish Burgers

Accompany with a Cucumber Lime Cocktail and Basic French Fries.

Total time: 10 minutes | *Serves 4*

INGREDIENTS:

¼ cup extra-virgin coconut oil, for cooking
1 pound white fish
1 tablespoon fresh sage, or 1 teaspoon dried sage
1 teaspoon thyme
1 teaspoon salt
½ teaspoon black pepper
1 lemon

ACTIONS:

- Heat a large frying pan with the coconut oil over medium heat. Mash the fish in a bowl with the spices. Form 4 fish patties by hand and place them in the pan.
- Mix the herbs, and sprinkle half of them over the patties. When the undersides have browned, flip them over and sprinkle the remaining herbs. Cook until desired doneness.
- Squeeze lemon juice over the burgers.

TIP:

- Choose your bun: Either fresh lettuce or kale leaves, or organic bread rolls.

Calories: 232 | Total Fat: 13.8g | Carbs: 3.4g | Dietary Fiber: 1.6g | Protein: 24.4g

Beef Tacos

I love tacos and grew up eating them once per week. Thanks, Mum! I love to top mine with avocado, grated carrot, and lettuce.

Total time: 10 minutes | *Serves 3 (2 tacos each)*

INGREDIENTS:

Filling:

1 tablespoon extra-virgin coconut oil, for cooking

1 pound ground beef

1 teaspoon salt

1 teaspoon cumin

1 teaspoon turmeric

1 teaspoon garlic powder, or 1 tablespoon garlic, minced

1 teaspoon onion powder

½ teaspoon paprika

¼ teaspoon black pepper

Dash of cayenne pepper

Choose Your Shell:

6 organic taco shells

6 tortilla wraps

6 lettuce leaves

Choose Your Toppings:

Nutritional yeast

Organic cheese, grated

Carrots, grated

Lettuce, shredded

Avocado, cubed

Peppers, diced

Fresh cilantro

Black beans, cooked

Vegan Sour Cream

10-Minute Salsa

Mango Salsa

Ketchup

Taco Sauce

ACTIONS:

- If you are choosing taco shells, bake them in the oven at 350°F for 5 minutes while you prepare the filling.
- Heat a large frying pan with oil, then add the beef and spices. Use a wooden spoon to break up the beef and combine the mixture well.
- Cook for 8 minutes or until done.
- Wrap the meat in tortilla wraps, taco shells, or lettuce leaves.

TIPS:

- To make things even faster, use 2 tablespoons Taco Seasoning instead of the listed spices.
- Stretch out the filling and serve more people by adding ¼ cup Ketchup and ½ cup beans.
- Use large, soft organic tortillas to make burritos.
- Use this filling in the Vegan Nachos for Beef Nachos.

VARIATIONS:

- Chicken Tacos: Use ground chicken or cubed chicken breast instead of beef.
- Fish Tacos: Use white fish fillets instead of beef.

Calories: 204 | Total Fat: 8g | Carbs: 10g | Dietary Fiber: 1g | Protein: 26g

Meatballs

These make a great quick protein snack on their own, or add them to pasta, pizza, salad, or soup!

Total time: 10 minutes | Serves 4

INGREDIENTS:

2 tablespoons extra-virgin coconut oil, for cooking
2 large eggs
1 pound ground beef
1 teaspoon salt
½ teaspoon black pepper
1 teaspoon cumin
½ teaspoon dried sage
½ teaspoon dried oregano
½ teaspoon dried parsley
¼ teaspoon turmeric

ACTIONS:

- Heat a frying pan with the coconut oil over medium heat. Beat the eggs in a bowl and add the ground beef and spices. Use your hands to combine the ingredients well, then roll the mixture into balls.
- Add the balls to the frying pan and sauté for 8 minutes or until done.

TIP:

- Serve with Raw Tomato Sauce.

Calories: 404 | Total Fat: 33.0g | Carbs: 0.8g | Dietary Fiber: 0.3g | Protein: 23.4g

Honey Rosemary Chicken

Total time: 10 minutes | Serves 3

INGREDIENTS:

¼ cup extra-virgin coconut oil, for cooking
1 pound chicken breasts, cubed
1 teaspoon garlic powder
1 bunch fresh rosemary, destemmed, or ¼ cup dried rosemary
5 tablespoons raw honey

ACTIONS:

- Heat a frying pan with the coconut oil over medium-high heat.
- Add the chicken, then sprinkle with garlic powder and rosemary. Drizzle 1 tablespoon honey over the chicken as it cooks.
- Cook the chicken until done, roughly 7 minutes, turning so all sides are browned.
- Serve on plates and drizzle with the remaining honey.

TIP:

- This is a great recipe to use if you want to fire up the grill. It's fun to substitute rosemary stems for traditional wooden or metal skewers.

VARIATION:

- Honey Rosemary Chicken Wraps: Wrap cooked chicken pieces in lettuce leaves.

Calories: 144 | Total Fat: 7g | Carbs: 17g | Dietary Fiber: 1g | Protein: 10g

Almond-Crusted Chicken Tenders

Ask the butcher to cut chicken into strips for you, or buy prepackaged strips to save even more time. Serve with Sweet Potato Fries and Four-Ingredient Green Salad.

Total time: 10 minutes | Serves 4

INGREDIENTS:

¾ cup extra-virgin coconut oil, for cooking
1 cup almond flour
2 tablespoons turmeric powder
2 teaspoons salt
1 pound boneless, skinless chicken breast, cut into strips

ACTIONS:

- Add the oil to a large pan and heat on medium-high.
- Mix the almond flour, turmeric, and salt in a bowl or plate.
- Wet the chicken with water, then dip them in the almond flour mixture until well coated.
- Drop the tenders into the hot pan, and cook for 4 minutes on each side until golden brown and cooked through.

VARIATION:

- Tigernut Chicken Tenders: Use tigernut flour instead of almond flour.

Calories: 724 | Total Fat: 62g | Carbs: 10g | Dietary Fiber: 5g | Protein: 36g

Meat Eaters' Main Dishes

BBQ Chicken

This sweet chicken recipe is great as a quick meal on its own or as an addition to tacos, a burrito, a sandwich, salad, or a pizza!

Total time: 10 minutes | Serves 1 to 2

INGREDIENTS:

1 tablespoon extra-virgin coconut oil, for cooking
½ pound chicken breast strips
2 tablespoons organic BBQ sauce

ACTIONS:

- Heat a frying pan with the coconut oil over medium-high heat.
- Add the chicken. When the chicken starts to turn white (at about 6 minutes), add the BBQ sauce and sauté until cooked through.

TIP:

- Add 1 teaspoon minced garlic and ½ teaspoon onion powder for additional flavor.

Calories: 247 | Total Fat: 9.5g | Carbs: 4.5g | Dietary Fiber: 0.0g | Protein: 34.6g

Italian Tomato Sausages

Sausages are a hearty, go-to dish that provides a good source of protein. Pair sausages with fresh salad or vegetables, or top some pasta, Cauliflower Rice, gravy, mashed potatoes, fries, and soup—even pizza!

Total time: 10 minutes | Serves 4

INGREDIENTS:

1 tablespoon extra-virgin olive oil, for cooking
4 sausages
1 tomato, chopped
1 bell pepper, red or green, thinly sliced
1 yellow onion, thinly sliced
½ teaspoon dried parsley
½ teaspoon dried basil
½ teaspoon dried oregano
Fresh basil (optional)
Fresh parsley (optional)

ACTIONS:

- Heat a frying pan with the oil over medium heat.
- Add the sausages, vegetables, and dried herbs. Sauté for 7 minutes, or until sausages are cooked through.
- Garnish with fresh basil and parsley, if desired.

Calories: 119 | Total Fat: 9.3g | Carbs: 3.9g | Dietary Fiber: 1.0g | Protein: 4.5g

Chicken Apple Sausages

Total time: 10 minutes | *Serves 4*

INGREDIENTS:

1 tablespoon extra-virgin coconut oil, for cooking
4 organic chicken sausages
1 small apple, diced
½ cup Apple Juice

ACTIONS:

- Heat a frying pan with the oil over medium heat.
- Add the sausages and diced apple, and sauté for 5 minutes.
- Add apple juice, and continue to cook until sausages are done.

Calories: 240 | Total Fat: 15.6g | Carbs: 12.3g | Dietary Fiber: 0.7g | Protein: 13.1g

Honey Rosemary Sausages

Total time: 10 minutes | *Serves 4*

INGREDIENTS:

1 tablespoon extra-virgin coconut oil, for cooking
4 organic chicken sausages
1½ tablespoons fresh rosemary
2 tablespoons honey

ACTIONS:

- Heat a frying pan with the coconut oil over medium heat.
- Add the sausages and rosemary, and sauté for about 6 minutes. Right before the sausages are cooked through, drizzle them with the honey.
- Remove from the heat and garnish with more fresh rosemary.

Calories: 245 | Total Fat: 15.5g | Carbs: 13.8g | Dietary Fiber: 0.1g | Protein: 13.1g

Sweet Cherry Tomato Sausages

Total time: 10 minutes | *Serves 4*

INGREDIENTS:

1 tablespoon extra-virgin coconut oil, for cooking
4 organic beef or pork sausages
1 small yellow onion, sliced thinly
1½ cups cherry tomatoes
Fresh basil, parsley, and oregano, for garnish (optional)

ACTIONS:

- Heat a frying pan with the coconut oil over medium heat. Add the sausages and onion slices.
- Squeeze half the cherry tomatoes into the pan. Slice the other tomatoes in half and add to the pan.
- Continue cooking until the sausages are done. Garnish with fresh herbs.

Calories: 54 | Total Fat: 4.7g | Carbs: 2.2g | Dietary Fiber: 0.5g | Protein: 0.8g

10-Minute Chicken Curry

Total time: 10 minutes | Serves 2

INGREDIENTS:

3 tablespoons coconut oil, for cooking
½ pound chicken strips
1 teaspoon garlic, minced
½ teaspoon onion powder
One (12-ounce) can organic coconut milk
¼ cup Thai Red or Green Curry Paste

ACTIONS:

- Heat a frying pan with the coconut oil over medium heat.
- Add the chicken, garlic, and onion.
- When the chicken starts to turn white (at about 6 minutes), add the coconut milk and curry paste.
- Cook for another 3 minutes or until the chicken is cooked through.

TIPS:

- Serve with Cauliflower Rice.
- Add vegetables like broccoli, cauliflower, and carrot. Add them to the pan with the coconut milk and curry paste.

Calories: 483 | Total Fat: 41.6g | Carbs: 14.6g | Dietary Fiber: 0.1g | Protein: 10.3g

Fish Fingers

Total time: 10 minutes | Serves 4

INGREDIENTS:

¾ cup extra-virgin coconut oil, for cooking
1 cup almond flour
2 tablespoons turmeric powder
2 teaspoons salt
1 pound fish fillets, sliced into finger-sized strips

ACTIONS:

- Heat a frying pan with the coconut oil over medium-high heat.
- Mix the almond flour, turmeric, and salt in a bowl or plate.
- Wet the fish with water, then dip the fillets in the almond flour mixture until well coated.
- Drop the fish into the hot pan, and cook for 3 minutes on each side until golden brown and cooked through

TIP:

- To make a wrap, use lettuce or tortillas and your choice of toppings, including: salsa, Vegan Sour Cream, avocado, onion, cucumber, tomato, celery, lettuce, spinach, alfalfa sprouts, fresh cilantro, fresh parsley, and fresh basil.

Calories: 606 | Total Fat: 54.6g | Carbs: 7.4g | Dietary Fiber: 3.2g | Protein: 27.6g

10-Minute Fish and Chips

You can enjoy this classic recipe because it's cooked in clean oil.

Total time: 10 minutes | Serves 4

INGREDIENTS:

1 tablespoon coconut oil, for cooking chips
2 small potatoes
2 tablespoons extra-virgin coconut oil, for cooking fish
1 pound fish such as tuna, swordfish, or salmon—just ensure that it is less than ½ inch thick
Lemon wedges (optional)

ACTIONS:

- Start the chips first: Add the coconut oil to a pan on high heat. As the oil is heating, cut the potatoes in thin strips. (If you cut them too big, they will take longer to cook.) Add the potatoes to the oil and let cook for 4½ minutes. When golden brown, flip them over and cook for another 4½ minutes.
- While the chips are cooking, heat a second pan with olive oil on medium heat. Add the fish, and let cook for 6 to 8 minutes, flipping midway through cooking, until opaque and flaky. Serve with lemon wedges, if desired.

TIP:

- Crumb your fish with tigernut flour or almond flour.

Calories: 227.5 | Total Fat: 10.3g | Carbs: 9.4g | Dietary Fiber: 1.8g | Protein: 25.1g

Simple Fish

Serve with Four-Ingredient Green Salad or Basic French Fries. Experiment with other seasonings, such as your favorite herbs, perhaps fresh cilantro, garlic, cayenne pepper, or oregano.

Total time: 10 minutes | Serves 1

INGREDIENTS:

1 tablespoon extra-virgin coconut oil, for cooking
1 (4-ounce) piece of fish, such as tuna, swordfish, or salmon—just ensure that it is less than ½ inch thick
1 teaspoon dried sage
1 teaspoon dried thyme
1 lemon
Salt and pepper, to taste

ACTIONS:

- Heat a frying pan with the coconut oil over medium heat.
- Add the fish to the pan. Sprinkle the herbs and half the lemon juice over the fish.
- Flip the fish after about 4 minutes, and cook until opaque and flaky.
- Remove the fish from the heat, squeeze the remaining lemon juice over it, and season with salt and pepper.

VARIATIONS:

- Simple Garlic Fish: Add 1 teaspoon garlic powder instead of sage.
- Simple Spicy Fish: Add a dash of cayenne pepper on each side of the fish while cooking.

Calories: 299 | Total Fat: 17.5g | Carbs: 12.9g | Dietary Fiber: 5.9g | Protein: 30.1g

Sautéed Scallops

Total time: 10 minutes | *Serves 2*

INGREDIENTS:

1 tablespoon chicken broth or
   Vegetable Broth
½ pound scallops
1½ teaspoons garlic, minced
2 tablespoons olive oil
1 tablespoon lemon juice
Salt and pepper, to taste
Fresh or dried dill, for garnish

ACTIONS:

- Heat the broth in a pan over medium heat. Add the scallops and garlic, and sauté for 1½ minutes. Then turn the scallops over and cook on the other side for 1½ minutes.
- Remove from the heat. Serve dressed with oil, lemon, salt, pepper, and dill.

TIP:

- For larger scallops, you may have to cook for an additional minute. Don't cook them for too long, as they can get tough.

Calories: 226.3 | Total Fat: 14.4g | Carbs: 4.4g | Dietary Fiber: 0.1g | Protein: 19.2g

Caramel Shrimp

Serve with the Ultimate Nourishing Detox Salad and a Margarita.

Total time: 8 minutes | *Serves 4*

INGREDIENTS:

¼ cup extra-virgin coconut oil,
   for cooking
1 pound raw shrimp, peeled and
   deveined
3 tablespoons raw honey

ACTIONS:

- Add the coconut oil and shrimp to a hot pan, sautéing over medium heat for 1 minute.
- Drizzle half of the honey over the shrimp, and continue to cook for 3 to 5 minutes, stirring occasionally, until the shrimp is cooked through.
- Drizzle the rest of the honey over the shrimp, then remove from the heat.

TIP:

- Replace the honey with maple syrup or coconut sugar, for another sweet alternative.

VARIATION:

- Spicy Caramel Shrimp: Add ½ teaspoon cayenne pepper to the shrimp along with the honey.

Calories: 284 | Total Fat: 16g | Carbs: 14g | Dietary Fiber: 0g | Protein: 23g

Seafood Sticks

These make a great entertaining platter and party food.

Total time: 10 minutes | *Serves 4*

INGREDIENTS:

1 pound white fish
1 pound shrimp, peeled and deveined
Salt and pepper, to taste
8 skewers
1 tablespoon coconut oil, for cooking
1 lemon

ACTIONS:

- Cut the fish into cubes and sprinkle with salt and pepper. Alternate shrimp and fish cubes on each skewer.
- Place the skewers on a hot grill or lightly oiled frying pan. Cook for about 3 minutes on each side, or until done. Squeeze lemon juice over the cooked skewers.

TIP:

- You can also use crabmeat for these Seafood Sticks.

Calories: 271.5 | *Total Fat: 6.3g* | *Carbs: 2.1g* | *Dietary Fiber: 0.1g* | *Protein: 48.4g*

Quinoa Pasta with Alfredo and Meatballs

Total time: 10 minutes | *Serves 4*

INGREDIENTS:

1½ cups uncooked quinoa pasta
1 batch Alfredo Sauce
1 batch Meatballs
Black pepper, to taste

ACTIONS:

- Add the pasta to a pot with 3½ cups of water brought to a boil. Reduce the heat to medium, and continue to cook for 7 minutes or until done. Drain the pasta.
- Add the Alfredo Sauce to the pot and stir until the pasta is well coated with the sauce. Serve into bowls and then add meatballs. Serve with pepper.

TIP:

- This recipe also tastes great with black bean pasta.

Calories: 835.8 | *Total Fat: 52.5g* | *Carbs: 55.9g* | *Dietary Fiber: 5.8g* | *Protein: 37.7g*

Cheesy Chicken Pasta

This recipe brings back memories of a nice summer day in Australia, hanging out with my dear family friend Carol Lucas. She is the one who inspired this recipe! One day, she added chicken to the Mac 'n' Cheese recipe for more protein, and now it's a favorite dish to share every time I visit her.

Total time: 10 minutes | Serves 3

INGREDIENTS:

2 cups uncooked quinoa or brown rice macaroni pasta

3 tablespoons nutritional yeast

1 teaspoon salt

1 pound ground chicken or chicken strips

1 tablespoon extra-virgin coconut oil, for cooking

ACTIONS:

- In a pot, add the pasta to 3¼ cups boiling water. Stir and reduce the heat to medium. Keep stirring until the pasta is soft. As it cooks, the pasta will soak up the water and begin to take on a creamy appearance. Do not drain!
- Add the nutritional yeast and the salt to the pot of pasta, and stir until well combined to form the sauce.
- While the pasta is cooking, add the chicken and oil to a hot pan and sauté for 6 minutes, or until the chicken is cooked through. Once the pasta is done, add the chicken and stir well.

TIPS:

- Usually when we cook pasta, there is so much water in the pot that the pasta needs to be drained. For this dish to succeed and achieve natural creaminess, however, we need the pasta to soak up the water. The residual liquid in the pot will become the base for the creamy sauce, so do not drain it.
- Make sure to read the directions to ensure that your chosen brand of pasta can be cooked in about 7 minutes.

Calories: 798.7 | Total Fat: 28.5g | Carbs: 87.6g | Dietary Fiber: 10.0g | Protein: 48.2g

Thai Shrimp Soup

Total time: 10 minutes | Serves 4

INGREDIENTS:

1 tablespoon coconut oil
2 tablespoons fresh ginger, grated
1 tablespoon Thai Red or Green
   Curry Paste
4 cups chicken broth
1 cup Vegetable Broth
3 tablespoons coconut sugar or maple
   syrup
½ teaspoon salt
1 teaspoon amino acids, like Bragg
   Liquid Aminos or soy sauce
One 14-ounce can coconut milk
1 pound shrimp, peeled and deveined
2 tablespoons fresh lime juice
¼ cup fresh cilantro, chopped
1 cup bean sprouts

ACTIONS:

- Add oil, ginger, and curry paste to a
  hot pot, and sauté for 1 minute. Add
  the rest of the ingredients except for
  the cilantro and bean sprouts. Bring to
  a boil for about 5 minutes.
- When the shrimp is no longer
  translucent, it is ready. Serve with
  fresh cilantro and bean sprouts.

TIP:

- Mince a stalk of lemongrass, if you
  have an extra minute to chop.

*Calories: 269 | Total Fat: 10.7g | Carbs: 16.9g
| Dietary Fiber: 0.6g | Protein: 25.5g*

Chicken Noodle Soup

Total time: 10 minutes | Serves 4

INGREDIENTS:

1 tablespoon coconut oil
2 celery stalks, chopped
1 tablespoon onion powder
1 teaspoon garlic powder
½ teaspoon dried basil
½ teaspoon dried oregano
½ teaspoon dried thyme
¼ teaspoon salt
¼ teaspoon black pepper
7 cups chicken broth
1¾ cups Vegetable Broth
½ pound chicken, in small cubes
2 packets organic ramen noodles

ACTIONS:

- Add oil, celery, onion powder, and
  garlic powder to a hot pot, and sauté
  for 1 minute. Add in the rest of the
  ingredients, except for the noodles.
- Bring to a boil for about 5 minutes.
- Add the ramen noodles and cook
  for another minute until the ramen
  noodles and chicken are cooked
  through.

*Calories: 228 | Total Fat: 8.6g | Carbs: 20.3g |
Dietary Fiber: 1.2g | Protein: 17.9g*

Beef Pho

Inspired by a delicious bowl of pho in London, I knew that I could make a quick, fulfilling version. This soup is warming, comforting, and exciting!

Total time: 10 minutes | Serves 2

INGREDIENTS:

2 packets of ramen noodles

1 teaspoon ginger powder

½ teaspoon salt

¼ teaspoon black pepper

¼ teaspoon star anise powder or seeds

2 tablespoons coconut sugar or maple syrup

1 tablespoon extra-virgin coconut oil

½ pound steak strips

1 tablespoon garlic, minced (or garlic powder)

2 large eggs

Toppings:

1 cup bean sprouts

1 green onion, diced

Dash of cayenne pepper, or ¼ teaspoon red pepper flakes

Juice of 1 lime

Handful of fresh cilantro

Handful of fresh basil

ACTIONS:

- In a pot, add the ramen noodles, ginger powder, salt, pepper, star anise, and coconut sugar to 5 cups of boiling water.
- While the noodles are cooking, heat the coconut oil in a skillet, and sauté the steak strips and garlic until done, approximately 6 minutes.
- Add the eggs to another pot of water. Bring to a boil, then reduce the heat and cook for 2 more minutes. Remove eggs from the pot and run under cold water, then set aside.
- Serve the ramen in bowls, with the liquid broth. Top with the steak pieces and other toppings. Lastly, peel the eggs and add them whole.

TIP:

- Add 1 tablespoon grated fresh ginger instead of ginger powder if you have more time.

Calories: 827.4 | Total Fat: 28.0g | Carbs: 89.6g | Dietary Fiber: 2.6g | Protein: 53.2g

Meat Eaters' Main Dishes

CHAPTER 15

Sides and Snacks

The body can't function optimally when it's low on fuel. Food is our fuel. We thrive when we graze on food throughout the day. Snacks are a great quick way to top up the "gas tank." A proper snack is a small, yet delicious and nourishing, amount of food eaten between meals. It could be a simple, raw whole food, like a handful of berries—a one-minute solution for hunger—or one of the delectable recipes you'll find in this chapter. You will always save time by opting for snacks that come directly from nature and do not require you to cook, chop, or blend.

Keep in mind that it's highly nourishing to go for nature's candy. Eat handfuls of strawberries, blueberries, pineapple, blackberries, nuts, tigernuts, shredded coconut, pomegranate, and carrots with dip. Or purchase snacks like organic cookies, That's It bars, and Earth Diet Chocolate Almond Butter Cups.

Make-Your-Own Trail Mix Formula

Use this easy formula to make your own trail mix! Choose your ingredients, shake them up in a bag, and eat at your pleasure on the trails, at the park, or in the office. Share with your friends!

CHOOSE YOUR NUTS:

Almonds
Brazil nuts
Cashew nuts
Hazelnuts
Macadamia nuts
Peanuts
Pecans
Pistachios
Walnuts

CHOOSE YOUR SEEDS:

Hemp seeds
Pumpkin seeds
Sunflower seeds

CHOOSE YOUR FRUITS:

Banana chips
Dried apricots
Dried cherries
Dried cranberries
Dried mulberries
Goji berries
Golden berries
Raisins

CHOOSE YOUR ADD-ONS:

Almond Granola
Cacao nibs
Cinnamon
High-Protein Granola
Peanut Butter Granola
Salt
Tigernuts
Toasted oats

Fruit Skewers

Eating fruit on a stick makes fruit-eating more fun, like eating cotton candy at a street fair. In Australia, we call this fairy floss. Because kids love eating this way, skewers are a way to get them to consume more antioxidants. If you're hosting a party, you can make beautiful table displays of vibrantly colored fruit skewers. Skewers can be dipped into Vegan Yogurt or Whipped Coconut Cream. You can drizzle Chocolate Sauce over them. Serve them in rows on rectangular trays, or arrange them in a circle on a large plate. Or stand a few skewers in a jar to make a fruit bouquet.

Depending on the fruit, you can put them on the skewers whole, chopped, cubed, or in balls. Try these skewer combinations:

Rainbow Skewer

INGREDIENTS:

Strawberries
Orange
Pineapple
Kiwifruit
Blueberries
Cherries

ACTIONS:

• Arrange fruits in order on a skewer.

Tropical Skewer

INGREDIENTS:

Pineapple
Papaya
Mango
Lychees
Cherries

ACTIONS:

• Alternate pieces of fruit on a skewer.

Joyful Skewer

INGREDIENTS:

Pineapple
Orange

ACTIONS:

• Alternate pieces of fruit on a skewer.

ABC Skewer

INGREDIENTS:

Apple
Banana
Cantaloupe

ACTIONS:

• Alternate pieces of fruit on a skewer.

Summer Skewer

INGREDIENTS:

Watermelon
Grapes

ACTIONS:

• Alternate pieces of fruit on a skewer.

Romance Skewer

INGREDIENTS:

Cherries
Chocolate-Covered Strawberries
Raspberries
Blueberries

ACTIONS:

• Alternate pieces of fruit on a skewer.

Aussie Skewer

Since I originate from Australia, these are a favorite of mine.

INGREDIENTS:

Pineapple
Kiwi

ACTIONS:

• Alternate pieces of fruit on a skewer.

American Flag Skewer

INGREDIENTS:

Banana
Strawberries
Blueberries

ACTIONS:

• To make a Fourth of July table display, you'll need 10 skewer sticks:
• On 5 skewers: Alternate between banana chunks and strawberries. (These will be the stripes.)
• On 5 skewers: Fill half the length with blueberries, then alternate between banana chunks and strawberries on the other half.
• Line up the skewers on a tray so that the blueberries are all next to each other in the top left corner, and all the strawberries and bananas line up to make the stripes of the American flag. If you're feeling creative, use Whipped Coconut Cream to make stars.

TIP:

• Make another country's flag by using fruit in the colors you need.

Basic Fruit Leather Formula

Add your fruit ingredients to a food processor, and blend until smooth.

Dehydrator method: Place parchment paper on the mesh screens in your dehydrator. Pour the fruit mixture on the paper to ¼ inch thick. Dehydrate at 115°F for 8 to 12 hours, or until no longer wet.

Oven method: Bake in your oven at 150°F for 4 to 6 hours.

Fruit Leathers

I put this recipe in the book for candy lovers! You can satisfy your candy cravings and feel fulfilled as a cook in the process by making homemade Fruit Leathers. Simply puree your favorite fruits and flavors, then dehydrate them in flat sheets until they are sticky and sweet like candy. Each one takes less than 10 minutes of hands-on time to prepare, but they do need to be dehydrated for a few hours.

If you squish the leather together or make a rollup with it, this can fulfill gummy bear cravings. The Cherry Leather is my favorite fruit leather!

Strawberry Banana Leather

INGREDIENTS:

3 cups strawberries
4 bananas, peeled

Calories: 69 | Total Fat: 0.2g | Carbs: 17.5g | Dietary Fiber: 2.8g | Protein: 0.8g

Strawberry Banana Blueberry Leather

INGREDIENTS:

2 cups strawberries
3 bananas, peeled
2 cups blueberries

Calories: 90 | Total Fat: 0.2g | Carbs: 22g | Dietary Fiber: 3.8g | Protein: 1g

Strawberry Kiwifruit Leather

INGREDIENTS:

2 cups strawberries
10 kiwifruit, peeled

*Calories: 75 | Total Fat: 0.6g | Carbs: 18g |
Dietary Fiber: 4.5g | Protein: 1.2g*

Cherry Leather

INGREDIENTS:

8 cups cherries, seeded

*Calories: 91 | Total Fat: 0.2g | Carbs: 23g |
Dietary Fiber: 3g | Protein: 1.5g*

Plum Leather

INGREDIENTS:

8 cups plums, seeded

*Calories: 75 | Total Fat: 0.5g | Carbs: 18.7g |
Dietary Fiber: 2.2g | Protein: 1g*

Strawberry Apple Leather

INGREDIENTS:

2 cups strawberries
4 apples, cored and peeled

*Calories: 51 | Total Fat: 0.1g | Carbs: 13.6g |
Dietary Fiber: 3.3g | Protein: 0.2g*

Strawberry Nectarine Leather

INGREDIENTS:

2 cups strawberries
4 nectarines, seeded

*Calories: 41 | Total Fat: 0.3g | Carbs: 9g |
Dietary Fiber: 2g | Protein: 1g*

Peach Apple Leather

INGREDIENTS:

4 apples, cored and peeled
4 peaches, seeded

*Calories: 57 | Total Fat: 0.2g | Carbs: 15g |
Dietary Fiber: 2.6g | Protein: 0.5g*

Apricot Leather

INGREDIENTS:

8 cups fresh apricots, seeded

*Calories: 74 | Total Fat: 0.6g | Carbs: 17g |
Dietary Fiber: 3g | Protein: 2g*

Blueberry Leather

INGREDIENTS:

8 cups blueberries

*Calories: 81 | Total Fat: 0g | Carbs: 20g |
Dietary Fiber: 3.9g | Protein: 1g*

Strawberry Peach Leather

INGREDIENTS:

2 cups strawberries
4 peaches, seeded

Calories: 33 | Total Fat: 0.2g | Carbs: 8g | Dietary Fiber: 1.8g | Protein: 0.5g

Green Apple Leather

INGREDIENTS:

8 apples, cored and peeled

Calories: 71 | Total Fat: 0.2g | Carbs: 19g | Dietary Fiber: 3.2g | Protein: 0.3g

Peach Goji Berry Leather

INGREDIENTS:

1 cup goji berries
8 peaches, seeded

Calories: 154 | Total Fat: 1.6g | Carbs: 29.7g | Dietary Fiber: 3.9g | Protein: 3g

Mango Banana Leather

INGREDIENTS:

3 mangoes, peeled and seeded
3 bananas, peeled

Calories: 65 | Total Fat: 0g | Carbs: 16.8g | Dietary Fiber: 1.8g | Protein: 0.75g

Raspberry Leather

INGREDIENTS:

6 cups raspberries

Calories: 45 | Total Fat: 0.5g | Carbs: 10.6g | Dietary Fiber: 6.3g | Protein: 0.8g

Apple and Pear Leather

INGREDIENTS:

4 apples, cored and peeled
4 pears, cored and peeled

Calories: 76 | Total Fat: 0.2g | Carbs: 20g | Dietary Fiber: 3.8g | Protein: 0.4g

Sweet Potato Leather

INGREDIENTS:

3 sweet potatoes, peeled
3 apples, cored and peeled
½ teaspoon cinnamon powder
¼ teaspoon nutmeg powder
¼ teaspoon ginger powder
Pinch of clove

Calories: 104.9 | Total Fat: 0.2g | Carbs: 25.8g | Dietary Fiber: 3.8g | Protein: 1.2g

Raw Cauliflower Popcorn

Total time: 10 minutes | *Serves 4*

INGREDIENTS:

2½ tablespoons extra-virgin olive oil
½ cup nutritional yeast
¾ teaspoon salt
1 head cauliflower, chopped into bite-sized pieces

ACTIONS:

- In a large bowl, mix the oil, nutritional yeast, and salt until combined.
- Add the cauliflower pieces to the bowl, and toss until the pieces are well coated.

TIP:

- Add 1 tablespoon sesame seeds for extra flavor.

VARIATION:

- Baked Cauliflower Popcorn: If you have the time, you can make this cooked variant. Simply bake for 20 minutes at 325°F.

Calories: 135 | Total Fat: 4.5g | Carbs: 11g | Dietary Fiber: 5g | Protein: 9g

Basic French Fries

Did you know that potatoes are high in vitamin C? This makes them immune boosting. As root vegetables, they have grounding properties. So if you are experiencing anxiety, depression, or stress, potatoes can help provide relief for your mind. Coconut oil is best for frying because it has a higher smoke point than olive oil and creates a buttery flavor.

But you don't have to be depressed to love French fries. They're a classic, mouthwatering comfort food: salty and savory with excellent mouthfeel, crunchy on the outside and soft in the middle! No need to beat yourself up when you eat them.

Total time: 10 minutes | *Serves 2*

INGREDIENTS:

2 tablespoons extra-virgin coconut oil, for cooking
2 small potatoes
Salt, to taste

ACTIONS:

- Add the coconut oil to a pan and heat on high.
- As the oil is heating, wash the potatoes, and then cut them into thin strips. (If you cut them too big, they will take longer to cook.)
- Add the potatoes to the oil and let cook until golden brown, about 4½ minutes. Then flip and cook for another 4½ minutes.
- Turn off the heat, and then season the fries with salt.

TIP:

- Use a spiralizer to make fun "Curly Wurly Fries."

VARIATIONS:

- Chipotle Fries: Add a dash of cayenne and 1 teaspoon chipotle powder to the fries before cooking.
- Garlic Fries: Add 2 teaspoons garlic powder to the fries before cooking.
- Cheese Fries: Add 2 tablespoons nutritional yeast to the fries before cooking.
- Lemon Herb French Fries: Sprinkle 2 tablespoons tigernut flour or almond flour and 1 to 2 teaspoons thyme over the fries before cooking. Then squeeze the juice of 1 lemon over the finished fries.

Calories: 754 | Total Fat: 55g | Carbs: 68g | Dietary Fiber: 8g | Protein: 7g

Sweet Potato Fries

Total time: 10 minutes | *Serves 2*

INGREDIENTS:

2 tablespoons extra-virgin coconut oil,
   for cooking
2 small sweet potatoes
Salt, to taste

ACTIONS:

- Add the coconut oil to a pan and heat
  on high.
- As the oil is heating, wash the
  potatoes and then cut them into thin
  strips. (If you cut them too big, they
  will take longer to cook.)
- Add the potatoes to the oil and let
  cook until golden brown, about 4½
  minutes. Then flip and cook for
  another 4½ minutes.
- Turn off the heat, and then season the
  fries with salt.

*Calories: 227 | Total Fat: 14.3g | Carbs: 21.6g
| Dietary Fiber: 2.7g | Protein: 1.6g*

Sweet Potato Coconut Basil Fries

Total time: 10 minutes | *Serves 2*

INGREDIENTS:

2 tablespoons extra-virgin coconut oil,
   for cooking
2 small sweet potatoes
2 tablespoons shredded coconut
2 tablespoons fresh or dried basil

ACTIONS:

- Add the coconut oil to a pan and heat
  on high.
- As the oil is heating, wash the
  potatoes and then cut them into thin
  strips. (If you cut them too big, they
  will take longer to cook.)
- Add the potatoes and coconut to the
  oil and let cook until golden brown,
  about 4½ minutes. Then flip and cook
  for another 4½ minutes.
- Turn off the heat, and then season the
  fries with salt and basil.

*Calories: 245.4 | Total Fat: 16.0g | Carbs:
22.5g | Dietary Fiber: 3.3g | Protein: 1.8g*

Cauliflower Rice

This dish goes great with spicy food, curries, soups, and salads.

Total time: 10 minutes | *Serves 4*

INGREDIENTS:

1 head of cauliflower
1 tablespoon coconut oil, for cooking
Salt and pepper, to taste

ACTIONS:

- Use a food processor or vegetable
  chopper to dice the cauliflower into
  tiny rice-sized pieces.

- Add the oil and cauliflower to a pan, and sauté
  on high heat for 9 minutes. Season with salt
  and pepper.

TIP:

- Add one diced yellow onion, for extra flavor.
- You can dice the cauliflower by hand, but it
  will take longer.

*Calories: 130.5 | Total Fat: 7.4g | Carbs: 15.0g |
Dietary Fiber: 7.2g | Protein: 5.7g*

Battered French Fries

Total time: 10 minutes | *Serves 2*

INGREDIENTS:

2 tablespoons extra-virgin coconut oil, for cooking
2 small sweet potatoes
3 tablespoons almond flour

ACTIONS:

- Add the coconut oil to a pan and heat on high.
- As the oil is heating, wash the potatoes and then cut them into thin strips. (If you cut them too big, they will take longer to cook.)
- Rinse the potatoes in water and then dredge them in a plate of almond flour. Coat them well.
- Add the potatoes to the oil and let cook until golden brown, about 4½ minutes. Then flip and cook for another 4½ minutes.

VARIATION:

- Tigernut French Fries: Replace almond flour with tigernut flour.

Calories: 263.3 | Total Fat: 17.3g | Carbs: 22.6g | Dietary Fiber: 3.5g | Protein: 2.9g

Baked Kale Chips

Purchasing prewashed and chopped kale will save you a lot of time. Simply season the kale and bake it in the oven.

Total time: 10 minutes | *Serves 1 to 4*

INGREDIENTS:

1 bunch (or bag) of kale
1 tablespoon extra-virgin olive oil
1 teaspoon salt

ACTIONS:

- Preheat the oven to 400°F. Line a baking sheet with parchment paper. (Lining with paper instead of oil will ensure a faster bake time.)
- Add the kale to a bowl along with the oil and salt, and massage until the leaves are well covered.
- Bake kale for 9 minutes or until the edges are brown and crisp. They will dry out when given time to rest after baking. Store in a dry place if you don't eat them all at once!

TIP:

- If you begin with a bunch of whole kale, wash it and drain the water really well, as wet leaves will make soggy chips. Use a paper towel to blot excess water. Tear the leaves from the stems in as big pieces as possible, keeping in mind the chips shrink as baked. Discard the stems or save for making broth.

VARIATIONS

- Cheesy Kale Chips: While seasoning, add ⅓ cup nutritional yeast.
- Spicy Kale Chips: While seasoning, add cayenne pepper, to taste.

Calories: 80 | Total Fat: 7.3g | Carbs: 4.0g | Dietary Fiber: 1.0g | Protein: 1.5g

Garlic Bread

Garlic Bread is so simple to make yourself.

Total time: 10 minutes | Serves 4 to 6

INGREDIENTS:

1 organic baguette
1 tablespoon garlic, minced
1½ tablespoons extra-virgin olive oil
¼ teaspoon salt

ACTIONS:

- Preheat the oven to 375°F. Cut the baguette into slices, keeping ¼ inch of the bottom part together.
- In a small bowl, mix the garlic, oil, and salt until well combined. Brush the oil mixture on each slice of the bread until well coated.
- Add the garlic bread to a tray and bake for 5 to 6 minutes until the bread is crunchy on the outside and melted in the middle.

Calories: 218.5 | Total Fat: 5.2g | Carbs: 28.6g | Dietary Fiber: 1.0g | Protein: 5.1g

Gluten-Free Onion Rings

You can eat these as a snack on their own or add them to a salad, soup, or sandwich.

Total time: 10 minutes | Serves 2 to 4

INGREDIENTS:

½ cup tigernut oil or coconut oil, for cooking
2 large white onions, sliced into rings
1 large egg, beaten
1 cup tigernut flour
¼ teaspoon salt
¼ teaspoon black pepper

ACTIONS:

- Heat a large frying pan with the oil on medium to high heat. Drop the onion rings into the beaten egg and coat well.
- In a bowl, add the tigernut flour, salt, and pepper, and mix until combined. Add onion rings one by one to the flour bowl and coat them well.
- Drop the onion rings into the oil and cook until their outsides are golden brown.

Calories: 513.1 | Total Fat: 36.3g | Carbs: 35.0g | Dietary Fiber: 5.4g | Protein: 13.4g

Chocolate Goji Berry Balls

Total time: 10 minutes | Makes 12 balls

INGREDIENTS:

1 cup almond flour
¼ cup cacao powder
3 tablespoons honey or maple syrup
¼ cup goji berries

ACTIONS:

- Mix all the ingredients and 1 tablespoon water together in a bowl until well combined.
- Roll the mixture into ½-inch balls.

Calories: 126.4 | Total Fat: 6.8g | Carbs: 16.4g | Dietary Fiber: 2.3g | Protein: 5.0g

Raw Chocolate Chip Almond Butter Granola

Total time: 8 minutes | *Makes 21 bars*

INGREDIENTS:

1½ cups almond butter
1 cup almond flour
1 cup organic chocolate chips or cacao nibs
¼ cup maple syrup
½ cup chia seeds

ACTIONS:

- Mix all the ingredients in a bowl until they are moist enough to stick together. If too dry to mold, add water.
- Pat the mixture into a 9 x 13-inch glass baking dish. Cut into squares.

VARIATION:

- Raw Chocolate Chip Tigernut Granola Bars: Replace almond flour with tigernut flour.

Calories: 215.4 | Total Fat: 18.3g | Carbs: 12.8g | Dietary Fiber: 7.1g | Protein: 6.0g

Protein Bars

Total time: 10 minutes | *Makes 5 bars*

INGREDIENTS:

7 tablespoons almond butter or peanut butter
½ cup almond meal
5 tablespoons raw honey or maple syrup
3 tablespoons hemp seeds
3 tablespoons pumpkin seeds

ACTIONS:

- Mix all the ingredients until they are moist enough to stick together. If too dry to mold, add water.
- Pat the mixture into a 9 x 13-inch glass baking dish. Sprinkle with additional hemp and pumpkin seeds, and press them in.
- Set in the freezer for 5 minutes, then cut into 5 bars.

VARIATION:

- Protein Balls: Form the mixture into balls, then roll in extra hemp seeds.

Calories: 329.4 | Total Fat: 23.1g | Carbs: 23.1g | Dietary Fiber: 4.0g | Protein: 10.7g

Raw High-Protein Granola Bars

Total time: 8 minutes | *Makes 21 bars*

INGREDIENTS:

1½ cups peanut butter
1 cup oats
1 cup organic chocolate chips or cacao nibs
¼ cup maple syrup
¼ cup chia seeds
¼ cup hemp seeds

ACTIONS:

- Mix all the ingredients until they are moist enough to stick together. If too dry to mold, add water.
- Pat the mixture into a 9 x 13-inch glass baking dish. Cut into squares.

Calories: 220.8 | Total Fat: 16.6g | Carbs: 16.7g | Dietary Fiber: 6.8g | Protein: 8.7g

Fruit and Nut Bar

Total time: 10 minutes | *Makes 5 bars*

INGREDIENTS:

7 tablespoons (14 ounces) almond
    butter or peanut butter
½ cup almond meal
5 tablespoons raw honey or maple
    syrup
3 tablespoons sunflower seeds
2 tablespoons crushed walnuts
5 dates, diced
3 tablespoons raisins
4 dried apricots, diced

ACTIONS:

* Mix all the ingredients and 1
  tablespoon water until they are moist
  enough to stick together. If too dry to
  mold, add more water.
* Pat the mixture into a 9 x 13-inch
  glass baking dish. Sprinkle with
  additional fruit and nuts on top and
  press them in.
* Set in the freezer for 5 minutes, then
  cut into 5 bars.

*Calories: 352 | Total Fat: 21.5g | Carbs: 38.0g
| Dietary Fiber: 5.7g | Protein: 7.6g*

Chocolate Almond Butter Bars

Total time: 10 minutes | *Makes 5 bars*

INGREDIENTS:

7 tablespoons (14 ounces) almond
    butter
½ cup almond meal
5 tablespoons raw honey or maple
    syrup
2 to 3 tablespoons cacao powder

ACTIONS:

* Mix all the ingredients and 1
  tablespoon water together in a bowl
  until well combined. If too dry to
  mold, add more water.
* Press the mixture into a baking tray.
  Set in the freezer for 5 minutes, and
  then cut into 5 bars.

VARIATION:

* Chocolate Peanut Butter Bars:
  Substitute peanut butter for the
  almond butter.

*Calories: 264.4 | Total Fat: 18.7g | Carbs:
24.4g | Dietary Fiber: 4.0g | Protein: 6.9g*

Almond Butter Superfood Balls

Total time: 10 minutes | *Makes 15 balls*

INGREDIENTS:

7 tablespoons almond butter
½ cup almond meal
¼ cup raw honey or maple syrup
1 teaspoon chia seeds
1 teaspoon hemp seeds
¼ teaspoon vanilla extract
2 teaspoons cacao nibs

ACTIONS:

- Mix all the ingredients together in a bowl until well combined. If too dry to mold, add water.
- Roll into balls, then roll the balls in more hemp seeds to coat.

VARIATION:

- Chocolate Peanut Butter Superfood Ball: Substitute peanut butter for the almond butter.

Calories: 80.1 | Total Fat: 5.6g | Carbs: 6.5g | Dietary Fiber: 1.4g | Protein: 2.2g

Alkalizing Chocolate pHresh Balls

Total time: 6 minutes | *Makes 15 balls*

INGREDIENTS:

7 tablespoons almond butter or peanut butter
½ cup almond meal
5 tablespoons raw honey or maple syrup
¼ cup cacao powder
2 tablespoons pHresh Greens
1 tablespoon sunflower seeds
2 teaspoons hemp seeds

ACTIONS:

- Mix all the ingredients, except the sunflower seeds and hemp seeds, together in a bowl with 1 tablespoon water until well combined. If too dry to mold, add more water.
- Roll into balls, then roll the balls in the sunflower seeds and hemp seeds.

Calories: 93.6 | Total Fat: 6.5g | Carbs: 7.4g | Dietary Fiber: 1.5g | Protein: 2.3g

Chickpea Fries

Chickpea Fries are an excellent snack eaten hot, or even cold. You can take them to lunch the next day or even add them to soups and salads! Some say this recipe is more like a "Chickpea Popcorn," but I titled it "fries" because people often tell me that it's their new fries.

Total time: 10 minutes | *Serves 1 to 2*

INGREDIENTS:

1 tablespoon extra-virgin olive oil, for cooking

One 14-ounce can organic chickpeas, drained of liquid

¼ teaspoon salt

Black pepper, to taste

ACTIONS:

- Heat a frying pan with oil on medium heat. When hot, add the drained chickpeas and season with salt and pepper.
- Cook for 5 to 7 minutes or until golden brown on the outside.

TIP:

- Save some to add to a wrap or the Chickpea Cucumber Cumin Salad.

VARIATIONS:

- Lemon Chickpea Fries: Squeeze juice of 1 lemon over the fries before serving.
- Lemon Thyme Chickpea Fries: Add 1½ teaspoons thyme while seasoning. Squeeze juice of 1 lemon over the fries before serving.
- BBQ Chickpea Fries: Add ½ teaspoon paprika, dash of cayenne pepper, and ½ teaspoon honey or maple syrup while seasoning. Squeeze juice of 1 lemon over the fries before serving.
- Cumin Chickpea Fries: Add 1 teaspoon cumin while seasoning.
- Totally Seasoned Chickpea Fries: Add ½ teaspoon cumin, ½ teaspoon oregano, and ½ teaspoon thyme while seasoning.
- Curry Chickpea Fries: Add 1 to 2 teaspoons curry powder while seasoning.

Calories: 204.1 | Total Fat: 10.5g | Carbs: 19.4g | Dietary Fiber: 4.9g | Protein: 8.6g

CHAPTER 16

Desserts

Before making any recipe and spending money and time on multiple ingredients, remind yourself that you can always simplify and focus on "nature's candy": blueberries, blackberries, raspberries, strawberries, apples, pineapple, dates, and coconuts.

Then again, what's better than eating our favorite desserts and getting vitamins and minerals at the same time? We can have our cake and eat it, too. When I realized that this was possible, it changed my life for the better. Eating 20 nutrient-dense Earth Diet Chocolate Balls a day for an entire year helped me eliminate refined sugar, dairy, soy, gluten, and preservatives from my diet without any sense of deprivation.

All these dessert recipes are meals in themselves so you never have to feel guilty for savoring them when you're hungry. These recipes are all nutrient-rich, so you can enjoy getting vitamins and minerals at the same time as fulfilling your dessert desires.

Chocolate Sauce

Serve as a dip for strawberries and other fruits. Chocolate Sauce also makes a great topping for any of the Instant Ice Creams.

Total time: 5 minutes | Makes 1½ cups, Serves 6

INGREDIENTS:

⅔ cup cacao powder
½ cup maple syrup
¼ cup extra-virgin coconut oil

ACTIONS:

- In a blender, blend all ingredients on high speed until they become a smooth sauce.

TIPS:

- For a more intense chocolate flavor, add more cacao powder.
- For a sweeter flavor, add more maple syrup.
- For a raw dish, substitute raw honey for maple syrup.
- If you don't have a blender, beat well in a bowl with a spoon.

VARIATIONS

- Raspberry Chocolate Sauce: Add ¾ cup raspberries.
- Cherry Chocolate Sauce: Add ¾ cup pitted cherries.

Calories: 170 | Total Fat: 11g | Carbs: 22g | Dietary Fiber: 3g | Protein: 2g

Vanilla Coconut Frosting

Total time: 5 minutes | Serves 12

INGREDIENTS:

1¾ cups dates
¼ maple syrup
1 cup macadamia nuts
1 teaspoon vanilla extract
½ cup coconut oil
½ cup shredded coconut

ACTIONS:

- Blend all ingredients and 1 cup water together in a blender until smooth.

Calories: 254 | Total Fat: 19g | Carbs: 24g | Dietary Fiber: 4g | Protein: 1.5g

Chocolate Hazelnutella

Total time: 5 minutes | Makes 1 cup, Serves 8

INGREDIENTS:

1 cup raw or roasted hazelnuts
¼ cup maple syrup
1 teaspoon vanilla extract
⅛ teaspoon salt (if using raw nuts, increase to ¼ teaspoon)
¼ cup raw cacao powder
3 tablespoons Almond Milk

ACTIONS:

- Blend all ingredients in a blender until smooth.

Calories: 151.1 | Total Fat: 11.6g | Carbs: 13.0g | Dietary Fiber: 2.1g | Protein: 3.8g

Whipped Coconut Cream

Enjoy this vegan, dairy-free alternative to whipped cream! Goes great on fruit salads, ice cream, yogurt parfaits, pies, French toast, mousse, and cake.

Total time: 10 minutes | Makes 2 cups

INGREDIENTS:

Two 14-ounce cans coconut cream, chilled overnight
¼ cup organic powdered sugar
¼ teaspoon vanilla extract

ACTIONS:

- Add all ingredients to a high-speed blender or hand mixer, and beat until thick and creamy.

TIPS:

- To properly chill the coconut cream, just leave it in the fridge overnight. The next day, don't shake it; open the can and scoop out the top layer, which should be really thick. You won't need to use the runny liquid, so reserve it for another recipe, such as a curry!
- Chill your mixing bowl to help you get a nice consistency when beating.
- If you let it rest in the fridge, it will harden and set.

Calories: 457.5 | Total Fat: 41.6g | Carbs: 23.1g | Dietary Fiber: 2.7g | Protein: 4.4g

Chocolate Avocado Mousse

Total time: 5 minutes | Serves 1

INGREDIENTS:

1 avocado
2 tablespoons cacao powder, or more to taste
2 tablespoons raw honey or maple syrup, or more to taste

ACTIONS:

- Blend all ingredients in a food processor until smooth and creamy. (Alternatively, whisk all the ingredients well in a bowl with a fork.)
- Taste. Add more cacao if you want it more chocolaty. Add more honey if you want it sweeter.

TIPS:

- Serve this mousse with fresh raspberries or strawberries.
- Add ¼ teaspoon pure vanilla extract for enhanced flavor.
- Serve this mousse on top of ice cream or cupcakes.

Calories: 379 | Total Fat: 22g | Carbs: 52g | Dietary Fiber: 13g | Protein: 5g

Chocolate Avocado Brownies

Total time: 5 minutes | *Makes 12 brownies*

INGREDIENTS:

Brownie:
1½ cups walnuts
1 cup dates, seeded
¼ cup cacao powder
Icing:
2 avocados, seeded
½ cup maple syrup or honey
¼ cup cacao powder
2 tablespoons coconut oil
1 teaspoon vanilla extract
Pinch of salt

ACTIONS:

- Make the brownies by blending all ingredients in a food processor until moist. Take the mixture and press it down in a baking tray. Set it in the fridge while you make the icing.
- Add the icing ingredients in a blender and whip until smooth and creamy. Ice the brownies and then cut into 12 pieces.

TIPS:

- Put fresh strawberries or raspberries on top!

VARIATION:

- Chocolate Avocado Tigernut Brownies: Replace half the walnuts with tigernut flour.

Calories: 226.2 | Total Fat: 14.4g | Carbs: 28.5g | Dietary Fiber: 3.4g | Protein: 4.4g

Chocolate Mint Balls

Total time: 10 minutes | *Makes 12 balls*

INGREDIENTS:

1 cup nut meal (finely ground almonds or other nuts)
¼ cup cacao powder
3 tablespoons maple syrup or raw honey
2 drops mint essence or essential oils
Fresh mint, as garnish

ACTIONS:

- Mix the nut meal, cacao powder, maple syrup, and mint essence in a bowl. Taste, then add another drop as needed. Roll the mixture into 1-inch balls with your hands. If dough sticks to your hands, add more nut meal. If dough is too dry, add water.
- Garnish the balls with fresh mint.

VARIATION:

- Chocolate Chip Mint Balls: Add 5 teaspoons cacao nibs or organic chocolate chips and 1 tablespoon water.

Calories: 69.9 | Total Fat: 4.8g | Carbs: 7.4g | Dietary Fiber: 1.3g | Protein: 2.5g

Raw Three-Ingredient Chocolate Balls

This recipe is made with just three ingredients, so it will be easy for you to remember how to make it for the rest of your life. Making healthy chocolate is easier than you may think. This is one of the most popular recipes I offer. This chocolate can stay fresh in the fridge for two weeks and in the freezer for three months.

Total time: 10 minutes | *Makes 12 balls*

INGREDIENTS:

1 cup nut meal (finely ground almonds or other nuts)

¼ cup cacao powder

3 tablespoons maple syrup or raw honey

ACTIONS:

- Mix all ingredients in a bowl, then roll the mixture into 1-inch balls with your hands. If dough sticks to your hands, add more nut meal. If dough is too dry, add water.

TIPS:

- Add ¼ teaspoon salt and ¼ teaspoon pure vanilla extract for enhanced flavor.
- Sprinkle balls with more cacao powder, crushed nuts, or another topping.
- You can use this mixture to make brownies (just make square forms) or a dessert pie (simply press into a pie plate with your fingertips).
- These are ready to eat now, but can also be stored in the fridge or freezer for a different texture.

VARIATIONS:

- Chocolate Vanilla Balls: Add ¼ teaspoon pure vanilla extract.
- Salty Chocolate Balls: Add ¼ teaspoon salt.

Calories: 106 | Total Fat: 7g | Carbs: 13g | Dietary Fiber: 4g | Protein: 4g

Desserts

Chocolate Coconut Balls

Total time: 10 minutes | Makes 12 balls

INGREDIENTS:

- 1 cup nut meal (finely ground almonds or other nuts)
- ¼ cup cacao powder
- 3 tablespoons maple syrup or raw honey
- 1 tablespoon coconut oil
- ¼ teaspoon salt
- 3 tablespoons shredded coconut

ACTIONS:

- Mix all ingredients in a bowl, then roll the mixture into 1-inch balls with your hands. If dough sticks to your hands, add more nut meal. If dough is too dry, add water.
- Roll the balls in shredded coconut to coat.

Calories: 86.4 | Total Fat: 6.4g | Carbs: 8.0g | Dietary Fiber: 1.6g | Protein: 2.6g

Chocolate Truffle Balls

Total time: 10 minutes | Makes 12 balls

INGREDIENTS:

- 1 cup nut meal (finely ground almonds or other nuts)
- ¼ cup cacao powder
- 3 tablespoons maple syrup or raw honey
- ¼ cup melted cacao powder
- 1 teaspoon rum (optional)

ACTIONS:

- Mix all ingredients in a bowl, then roll the mixture into 1-inch balls with your hands. If dough sticks to your hands, add more nut meal. If dough is too dry, add water.

TIPS:

- These are ready to eat now, but can also be stored in the fridge or freezer for a different texture.
- Roll the balls in chopped almonds or walnuts.

Calories: 141 | Total Fat: 3.9g | Carbs: 5.1g | Dietary Fiber: 1g | Protein: 1.7g

Raw Tigernut Chocolate Balls

Total time: 5 minutes | Makes 12 balls

INGREDIENTS:

- 1 cup Organic Gemini TigerNut Flour
- ¼ cup cacao powder
- 3 tablespoons maple syrup

Chocolate Almond Butter Balls

Total time: 5 minutes | Makes 15 balls

INGREDIENTS:

7 tablespoons almond butter
½ cup almond meal
¼ cup raw honey, or maple syrup
2 teaspoons cacao powder

ACTIONS:

- Mix all ingredients in a bowl, then roll the mixture into 1-inch balls with your hands. If dough sticks to your hands, add more nut meal. If dough is too dry, add water.

TIP:

- These are ready to eat now, but can also be stored in the fridge or freezer for a different texture.

VARIATION:

- Chocolate Peanut Butter Balls: Use peanut butter instead of almond butter.

Calories: 124 | Total Fat: 9g | Carbs: 8g | Dietary Fiber: 2g | Protein: 4g

Tigernut Raw Cookies

Total time: 3 minutes | Makes 10 cookies or balls

INGREDIENTS:

1 cup Organic Gemini TigerNut Flour
1 teaspoon pure vanilla extract
5 teaspoons maple syrup
¼ teaspoon salt
3 tablespoons cacao nibs or organic chocolate chips

ACTIONS:

- Place all ingredients and 1 tablespoon water in a bowl and mix with a spoon or your hands. Once the mixture is bound together and moist, it is done! Adjust water or flour, as needed, for desired texture.
- Roll the dough into balls, and they're ready to eat! You can also flatten the balls into cookie shapes, if desired.

VARIATION:

- Baked Tigernut Cookies: Bake the cookies at 325°F for 7 minutes.

Calories: 129 | Total Fat: 7g | Carbs: 21.3g | Dietary Fiber: 10g | Protein: 2g

ACTIONS:

- Mix all ingredients and 1 teaspoon water in a bowl, then roll the mixture into 1-inch balls with your hands. If dough sticks to your hands, add more flour. If dough is too dry, add more water.

TIP:

- These are ready to eat now, but can also be stored in the fridge or freezer for a different texture.

Calories: 90 | Total Fat: 7.5g | Carbs: 26.6g | Dietary Fiber: 11.4g | Protein: 3g

Raw Melt-in-Your-Mouth Chocolate Chip Cookies

These are my all-time favorite cookies! You can enjoy them as a raw cookie dough or bake them, or do both with each batch for the best of both worlds. These are "clean" as they are vegan. Without eggs, they are safe to eat raw, yet completely moist and delicious. They are also packed with protein and nutrition. Whenever I am having a craving for cookies, I know I can make these nourishing treats! Within 10 minutes, you too can be eating delicious cookies that melt in your mouth!

Total time: 10 minutes | *Makes 8 large cookies*

INGREDIENTS:

2 cups almond meal or flour
1 teaspoon pure vanilla extract
5 teaspoons maple syrup
¼ teaspoon salt
2 tablespoons organic chocolate chips or cacao nibs (feel free to add more—I do!)

ACTIONS:

- In a large bowl, combine all ingredients with 1 tablespoon water, and mix until well combined. It should be a moist dough, so add a dash of water if needed to reach desired consistency.
- Roll the dough into balls, and they're ready to eat! You can also flatten the balls into cookie shapes, if desired.

TIPS:

- Roll the balls in cacao powder or dust the powder on top of the flattened cookies!
- This can also be made without cacao nibs.
- For a softer cookie, use blanched almond flour. If you use almond flour that was made with almonds with skins on, you will need to add a little more water and maple syrup.

VARIATIONS:

- Raw Chocolate Chip Cookie Dough: Skip the final step of rolling the dough into balls or cookie shapes. You can just eat the dough out of the bowl with a spoon!
- Baked Melt-in-Your-Mouth Chocolate Chip Cookies: Bake the cookies at 325°F for 7 to 8 minutes.

Calories: 128 | Total Fat: 10.3g | Carbs: 6.5g | Dietary Fiber: 2.1g | Protein: 4.3g

10-MINUTE RECIPES

Cashew Oat Raw Cookies

Total time: 10 minutes | *Makes 12 cookies or balls*

INGREDIENTS:

1 cup cashew nuts
1 cup gluten-free rolled oats
1 teaspoon pure vanilla extract
5 teaspoons maple syrup
¼ teaspoon salt
2 tablespoons cacao nibs

ACTIONS:

- Blend the cashews and oats in a food processor, so the mixture resembles the consistency of flour meal. Combine in a large bowl with the vanilla, maple syrup, and salt.
- Once the mixture is well blended, stir in the cacao nibs.
- Roll the dough into balls, and they're ready to eat! You can also flatten the balls into cookie shapes, if desired.

TIP:

- This can also be made without cacao nibs.

Calories: 315 | Total Fat 18g | Carbs: 34g | Dietary Fiber 4g | Protein 10g

Healthy Raw Oatmeal Fruit Cookies

Total time: 10 minutes | *Makes 10 cookies or balls*

INGREDIENTS:

1 cup cashew nuts
1 cup gluten-free oats
1 teaspoon pure vanilla extract
2 tablespoons honey or maple syrup
¼ teaspoon salt
3 tablespoons raisins
5 dates, seeded
4 dried apricots, diced
1 tablespoon hemp seeds

ACTIONS:

- Blend cashews and oats in a food processor until they reach a fine meal consistency.
- In a large bowl, add all remaining ingredients and 1 tablespoon water to the cashew-oat mixture and combine well. The dough should be moist to be moldable. Add more water if needed.
- Roll the dough into balls, and they're ready to eat! You can also flatten the balls into cookie shapes, if desired.
- They're ready to eat!

Calories: 161.3 | Total Fat: 6.9g | Carbs: 22.6g | Dietary Fiber: 2.7g | Protein: 5.2g

Tigernut Raw Chocolate Brownies

Total time: 6 minutes | Makes 9 brownies

INGREDIENTS:

1 cup Organic Gemini TigerNut Flour
¼ cup cacao powder
3 tablespoons maple syrup
Pinch of real salt
¼ teaspoon vanilla extract
1 teaspoon coconut oil

ACTIONS:

- Place all ingredients and 1 teaspoon water in a bowl, and mix with a spoon or your hands. When the mixture is combined and moist, it is ready.
- Add the mixture to a baking dish that's at least ½ inch deep. Cut into squares to make 9 pieces. These are ready to eat, but can also be stored in the fridge or freezer for an enhanced texture.

Calories: 140 | Total Fat: 8g | Carbs: 20.6g | Dietary Fiber: 11.4g | Protein: 3g

Raw Lemon Coconut Bars

Total time: 10 minutes | Makes 12 bars

INGREDIENTS:

1 cup dates
½ cup macadamia nuts
½ cup cashews
2 tablespoons maple syrup
1 teaspoon vanilla extract
1 teaspoon coconut oil
1 teaspoon salt
Zest of 1 lemon
Juice of 1 lemon
¾ cup shredded coconut, plus 1 tablespoon for a topping

ACTIONS:

- Mix all ingredients together in a blender until smooth.
- Press into an 8 x 8-inch baking dish, then sprinkle with additional shredded coconut.
- Set in freezer for 5 minutes and then cut into 12 bars.

Calories: 162.6 | Total Fat: 6g | Carbs: 16.4g | Dietary Fiber: 2g | Protein: 1g

Raw Doughnut Holes

Total time: 10 minutes | Makes 15 doughnut holes

INGREDIENTS:

1 cup almonds
¾ cup cashews
¾ teaspoon vanilla extract
½ teaspoon salt
1 cup dried pineapple
1 cup dried apple
2 cups seedless dates
⅓ cup shredded coconut
1 teaspoon cinnamon (optional)
1 tablespoon coconut sugar (optional)

ACTIONS:

- Add the almonds and cashews to a food processor, and pulse to a fine powder.
- Add the vanilla, salt, pineapple, apple, dates, and shredded coconut to the food processor, and mix until well combined.
- Using a small ice-cream scoop or a tablespoon, scoop into the mixture to form doughnut "holes." Sprinkle cinnamon and coconut sugar on top of the doughnut holes, if desired.

Calories: 182.7 | Total Fat: 6.5g | Carbs: 33.9g | Dietary Fiber: 3.1g | Protein: 3.0g

Chocolate-Covered Strawberries

Total time: 10 minutes | Makes 4 servings

INGREDIENTS:

1 batch Chocolate Sauce
2 cups strawberries

ACTIONS:

- Dip the strawberries into Chocolate Sauce and place on a tray. Let set for a few minutes in the freezer or eat right away!

VARIATIONS:

- Dip different kinds of nuts and fruits in Chocolate Sauce. Try: Chocolate-Covered Macadamia Nuts, Chocolate-Covered Almonds, Chocolate-Covered Blueberries, Chocolate-Covered Hazelnuts, or Chocolate-Covered Bananas.

Calories: 151.6 | Total Fat: 25.4g | Carbs: 8.3g | Dietary Fiber: 2.5g | Protein: 1.2g

Raw Vanilla Cupcakes

The cupcakes will stay good in the fridge for 14 days, and in the freezer for 2 months.

Total time: 8 minutes | Makes 8 to 12 cupcakes

INGREDIENTS:

For the cupcakes:

½ cup walnuts, ground into a fine meal

½ cup almond meal

1½ teaspoons pure vanilla extract

1 teaspoon salt

3 tablespoons maple syrup

For the vanilla frosting:

¼ cup coconut oil

2 cups organic powdered sugar or coconut sugar

¼ cup Coconut Milk or Almond Milk

1 teaspoon vanilla extract

ACTIONS:

- Mix all the cake ingredients in a bowl. Once well combined, the batter should be slightly moist and moldable. Add water, if needed.
- Mold the batter into ½-inch balls and press each one into a paper baking cup.
- Allow to set in the fridge or freezer for a few minutes. While they're setting, whisk all the frosting ingredients in a bowl.
- Frost the cupcakes and eat.

TIPS:

- Make pink icing by adding a few drops of plain beet juice.
- Substitute Chocolate Sauce or Chocolate Avocado Mousse for the vanilla frosting.

(12 Cupcakes w/ Frosting) Calories: 180 | Total Fat: 9.1g | Carbs: 24.5g | Dietary Fiber: 0.4g | Protein: 1.0g

Raw Chocolate Cupcakes

The cupcakes will stay good in the fridge for 14 days, and in the freezer for 2 months.

Total time: 8 minutes | *Makes 8 to 12 cupcakes*

INGREDIENTS:

For the cupcakes:

1 cup **walnuts ground into a fine meal**

1½ teaspoons **pure vanilla extract**

1 teaspoon **salt**

3 tablespoons **maple syrup**

2 tablespoons **cacao powder**

For the chocolate frosting:

²/₃ cup **cacao powder**

½ cup **maple syrup**

¼ cup **extra-virgin coconut oil**

1 tablespoon **organic powdered sugar**

ACTIONS:

- Mix all the cake ingredients in a bowl. Once well combined, the batter should be slightly moist and moldable. Add water, if needed.
- Mold the batter into ½-inch balls and press each one into a paper baking cup.
- Allow to set in the fridge or freezer for a few minutes. While they're setting, whisk all the frosting ingredients in a bowl.
- Frost the cupcakes and eat.

TIPS:

- Top with Vanilla Coconut Frosting, Whipped Coconut Cream, or the frosting recipe from the Raw Vanilla Cupcakes.
- Make pink icing by adding a few drops of plain beet juice.
- Add more cacao powder for a darker chocolate cupcake.

(12 Cupcakes w/ Frosting) Calories: 93 | Total Fat: 6.8g | Carbs: 7.5g | Dietary Fiber: 0.9g | Protein: 1.8g

Desserts

197

Raw Chocolate Avocado Cupcakes

The cupcakes will stay good in the fridge for 14 days and in the freezer for 2 months.

Total time: 8 minutes | *Makes 15 cupcakes*

INGREDIENTS:

1 cup walnuts ground into a fine walnut meal
1 avocado, seeded and peeled
3 tablespoons cacao powder
1½ teaspoons pure vanilla extract
1 teaspoon salt
¼ cup maple syrup

ACTIONS:

- Mix all ingredients in a bowl. Once well combined, the batter should be slightly moist and moldable. Add water, if needed.
- Mold the batter into ½-inch balls and press each one into a paper baking cup.

TIPS:

- You can let them set in the fridge or freezer, but they are ready to eat immediately.
- Ice the cupcakes with Chocolate Sauce or Chocolate Avocado Mousse.

Calories: 72 | Total Fat: 5.2g | Carbs: 6.2g | Dietary Fiber: 0.9g | Protein: 1.3g

Mini Cashew Cheesecakes

You'll need 20 little paper cupcake liners or a metal cupcake tray for this recipe.

Total time: 10 minutes | *Makes 20 mini cheesecakes*

INGREDIENTS:

3 cups cashew nuts
½ cup lemon juice
¾ cup maple syrup
¾ cup coconut oil
1 tablespoon pure vanilla extract
Pinch of salt

ACTIONS:

- Put all ingredients in a high-speed blender and whip until completely smooth.
- Spoon 1 heaping tablespoon of the cheesecake mixture into each cupcake cup.
- Set in the freezer for 6 minutes. Enjoy!

TIPS:

- Make the cashews softer and easier to blend by soaking them for 3 hours before preparing this recipe.
- Garnish each cupcake with a pecan, walnut, or macadamia nut.
- Let these cheesecakes set longer in the freezer for a different texture.

Calories: 90 | Total Fat: 10g | Carbs: 8g | Dietary Fiber: 3g | Protein: 3.5g

Raw Pecan Pear Cake

Total time: 10 minutes | *Makes 12 servings*

INGREDIENTS:

2 cups pecans
6 soft pears
3 cups seedless dates
1 teaspoon vanilla
Dash cinnamon
½ teaspoon salt

ACTIONS:

- Blend all ingredients together in a food processor until moist. Mold the mixture into the shape of a cake using a cake tin.

TIP:

- Ice this with Vanilla Coconut Frosting.

Calories: 277 | Total Fat: 14g | Carbs: 39g | Dietary Fiber: 6g | Protein: 3g

Raw Chocolate Brazil Nut Cake

Brazil nuts are high in magnesium, which is important for nerve and muscle function. This is a great restorative, especially postworkout.

Total time: 10 minutes | *Makes 4 large slices*

INGREDIENTS:

1¾ cups Brazil nuts
½ teaspoon salt
3 cups shredded coconut
¾ cup cacao powder
3 cups seedless dates

ACTIONS:

- In a food processor add the Brazil nuts, salt, and coconut. Blend until a fine flour consistency.
- Add the cacao powder and dates until well combined and moist. Form into a shape of a cake either in a square or round tin.

TIP:

- Use parchment paper to line a cake tin, and then you can just peel away the paper and enjoy the cake with no mess.

Calories: 983 | Total Fat: 51.8g | Carbs: 130.6g | Dietary Fiber: 25.6g | Protein: 16g

Raw Carrot Cake

This recipe is a fun way to use the carrot pulp leftover from juicing!

Total time: 10 minutes | Makes 12 servings

INGREDIENTS:

Cake:

5 cups carrot pulp

¾ cup sunflower seeds

1 cup hemp seeds

¾ cup pumpkin seeds

2 cups dates

¼ cup maple syrup

2¾ cups shredded coconut

1 teaspoon grated nutmeg, or ½
     teaspoon nutmeg powder

3 teaspoons cinnamon

Zest of ¼ lemon

Frosting:

1½ cups cashews

Juice of 1 lemon

2 tablespoons maple syrup or honey

ACTIONS:

- Blend all cake ingredients together in a food processor until moist. Mold the mixture into the shape of a cake using a cake tin.
- Blend all frosting ingredients and ½ cup water together in a food processor until smooth. Frost the cake, then slice and serve.

Calories: 241 | Total Fat: 12g | Carbs: 33g | Dietary Fiber: 6g | Protein: 4g

Gluten-Free Pie Crust

Walnuts make an excellent piecrust! Crunchy and crisp.

Total time: 10 minutes | Makes 9-inch pie crust, Serves 12

INGREDIENTS:

2 cups walnuts

2 tablespoons maple syrup or honey

1 teaspoon extra-virgin coconut oil

¼ teaspoon salt

½ teaspoon pure vanilla extract

ACTIONS:

- Put the walnuts into a food processor and blend until it forms the consistency of a fine meal (a few chunks of walnut are okay to give it a nice crusty texture).
- Make the pie crust by adding the walnut meal and other ingredients to a bowl, and mix together until all is moist and moldable.
- Line a 9-inch pie pan with the pie-crust mixture and press on the bottom as well as the sides until it is even, about ¼ inch thick.

Calories: 88 | Total Fat: 84.5g | Carbs: 30.2g | Dietary Fiber: 8g | Protein: 18.2g

Raw Apple Pie

Total time: 10 minutes | *Makes 12 servings*

INGREDIENTS:

4 apples, peeled and cored
½ teaspoon cinnamon powder
1 tablespoon honey or maple syrup
Dash of salt
1 Gluten-Free Pie Crust

ACTIONS:

- Combine the apples, cinnamon, honey, and salt together in a food processor. Blend until smooth, or leave some apple chunks if you like that texture. Press into the Pie Crust.

TIPS:

- Serve with Instant Vanilla Ice Cream, Whipped Coconut Cream, or Almond Granola for some crunch.

Calories (for whole pie): 1231 | *Total Fat: 85.4g* | *Carbs: 123.9g* | *Dietary Fiber: 21.3g* | *Protein: 19.6g*

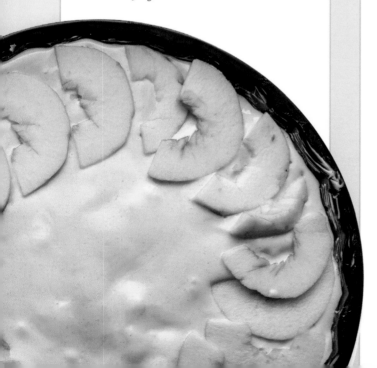

Gluten-Free Tigernut Pie Crust

Tigernuts are actually *nut-free!* This ancient superfood is a vegetable root.

Total time: 10 minutes | *Makes 9-inch pie crust, Serves 12*

INGREDIENTS:

½ cup walnuts
1½ cups tigernut flour
2 tablespoons maple syrup or honey
1 teaspoon extra-virgin coconut oil
¼ teaspoon salt
½ teaspoon pure vanilla extract

ACTIONS:

- Put the walnuts into a food processor and blend until it forms the consistency of a fine meal (a few chunks of walnut are okay to give it a nice crusty texture).
- Make the pie crust by adding the walnut meal and other ingredients to a bowl, and mix together until all is moist and moldable.
- Line a 9-inch pie pan with the pie-crust mixture and press on the bottom as well as the sides until it is even, about ¼ inch thick.

Calories: 112 | *Total Fat: 9g* | *Carbs: 7g* | *Dietary Fiber: 1g* | *Protein: 2g*

Raw Chocolate Pecan Pie

Total time: 10 minutes | Makes 16 servings

INGREDIENTS:

Crust:
1½ cups pecans
1½ tablespoons maple syrup
1½ tablespoons coconut oil
½ teaspoon vanilla extract
½ teaspoon salt
Filling:
½ cup cacao powder
1½ cups pecans
⅓ cup maple syrup
½ tablespoon coconut oil
½ teaspoon salt
Topping:
¼ cup whole pecans

ACTIONS:

- Mix the crust ingredients in a food processor until moist and well combined. Chunks are okay. Press the crust into a tart pan or pie pan (about 9 inches in diameter).
- Make the filling by blending all ingredients until completely smooth. Pour the filling into the pie crust and top with pecans.

TIPS:

- This is ready to eat immediately, but will become firmer if allowed to set in the refrigerator or freezer for a couple of hours.
- You can also use the Gluten-Free Pie Crust recipe.

Calories: 250 | Total Fat: 22g | Carbs: 12g | Dietary Fiber: 3g | Protein: 6g

Raw Apple Crumble

Total time: 10 minutes | Makes 4 servings

INGREDIENTS:

1 batch Almond Granola
4 apples, peeled and cored
½ teaspoon cinnamon powder
1 tablespoon honey or maple syrup
Dash of salt

ACTIONS:

- Create a layer of Almond Granola in four bowls.
- Blend the filling ingredients together in a food processor, leaving some chunks of apples. It should be moist and creamy. Pour into the bowls over the granola.

TIP:

- Garnish the bowls with Instant Vanilla Ice Cream or Whipped Coconut Cream and fresh berries.

Calories: 239.7 | Total Fat: 8.2g | Carbs: 41.4g | Dietary Fiber: 6.3g | Protein: 4.3g

Vanilla Pudding

Total time: 10 minutes | Makes 4 servings

INGREDIENTS:

1 cup Almond Milk
1 cup Vegan Yogurt
2 tablespoons maple syrup
1 teaspoon vanilla extract
Dash of salt
½ cup chia seeds
Toppings:
¼ cup almonds, sliced
Handful of walnuts
1 cup strawberries, chopped

ACTIONS:

- Whisk all ingredients together in a bowl, except the chia seeds. Add the chia seeds and then set in fridge for 9 minutes so it can gelatinize.
- Serve in bowls and add toppings.

TIPS:

- If the texture is not to your liking after 9 minutes, let it set an additional 20 minutes.
- Add additional vanilla extract or use Vanilla Almond Milk, for more flavor.

Calories: 327.7 | Total Fat: 24.8g | Carbs: 21.1g | Dietary Fiber: 8.4g | Protein: 11.1g

Blueberry Chia Seed Pudding

This also makes a great breakfast!

Total time: 10 minutes | Makes 2 to 4 servings

INGREDIENTS:

1 cup fresh blueberries
2 cups Almond Milk
½ teaspoon vanilla extract
2 tablespoons honey or maple syrup
¼ teaspoon salt
½ cup chia seeds

ACTIONS:

- Combine all ingredients together in a bowl, except the chia seeds. Add the chia seeds and then set in fridge for 9 minutes so it can gelatinize.

TIPS:

- If the texture is not to your liking after 9 minutes, let it set an additional 20 minutes.
- Garnish with fresh blueberries.

Calories: 175.8 | Total Fat: 7.0g | Carbs: 29.8g | Dietary Fiber: 8.0g | Protein: 3.5g

Chocolate Pudding

This pudding will stay good in the fridge for three days.

Total time: 10 minutes | Makes 4 servings

INGREDIENTS:

2 cups almonds
¼ cup seedless dates
1 tablespoon cacao powder
1 tablespoon chia seeds

ACTIONS:

- Combine all ingredients and 1 cup water together in a blender, until completely smooth. Eat right away or store in fridge to allow to set further.

Calories: 327.7 | Total Fat: 24.8g | Carbs: 21.1g | Dietary Fiber: 8.4g | Protein: 11.1g

Ice Cream Bites with Chocolate Sauce

Total time: 10 minutes | Makes 15

INGREDIENTS:

1½ cups cashews
Juice of 1 small lemon
½ cup maple syrup
¼ cup coconut oil
1 tablespoon vanilla extract
Dash of salt
2 teaspoons maca powder or lucuma
    powder (optional)
1 batch Chocolate Sauce

ACTIONS:

- Blend the cashews, lemon juice, maple syrup, coconut oil, vanilla, salt, and maca powder, if desired, in a blender on high speed until smooth. There should be absolutely no lumps.
- Scoop the ice cream mixture into a mini cupcake tin or onto a baking sheet (as shown), then place in the freezer for 5 minutes.
- Add a spoonful of Chocolate Sauce to each ice cream bite. They are ready to eat! Keep them in the freezer longer, and they will set even harder.

TIP:

- Soak the cashews for 4 hours to get a creamy, easier-to-whip ice cream.

(Ice Cream only) Calories: 112 | Total Fat: 8.9g | Carbs: 11.1g | Dietary Fiber: 0.4g | Protein: 2.1g

(Ice Cream and Sauce) Calories: 197.9 | Total Fat: 14.5g | Carbs: 23.8g | Dietary Fiber: 1.2g | Protein: 4.1g

Strawberry Sorbet

Experiment with different fruits and added flavorings to make a variety of delicious sorbet flavors!

Total time: 5 minutes | Makes 2 servings

INGREDIENTS:

2 cups strawberries
4 cups ice

ACTIONS:

- Place ingredients in a high-speed blender and blend for 1 minute or until you achieve an icy sorbet consistency. Serve immediately.

TIPS:

- Add 1 to 2 tablespoons honey, maple syrup, or coconut sugar if you like it sweeter.
- Add some nut milk for a creamier sorbet.

VARIATIONS:

- Blueberry Sorbet: Use 2 cups of blueberries instead of strawberries.
- Raspberry Sorbet: Use 2 cups of raspberries instead of strawberries.
- Cherry Sorbet: Use 2 cups of pitted cherries instead of strawberries.
- Passion Fruit Sorbet: Use 2 cups of passion fruit pulp (about 10 fruits) instead of strawberries.
- Pineapple Sorbet: Use 2 cups of chopped fresh pineapple instead of strawberries.

Calories: 62 | Total Fat: 0g | Carbs: 15g | Dietary Fiber: 3g | Protein: 1g

Acai Banana Ice Cream

Total time: 5 minutes | Makes 1 serving

INGREDIENTS:

1 cup acai puree (for convenience, use two 100-gram packs of Sambazon Acai Superfruit)
1 frozen banana
2 tablespoons your choice of liquid: water, coconut water, Almond Milk, or Apple Juice
Your choice of toppings: roasted nuts like almonds, cacao powder, cacao nibs, or Chocolate Sauce

ACTIONS:

- Blend the Acai, banana, and liquid until completely smooth.
- Serve in a bowl and then add your toppings!

VARIATION:

- Acai Blueberry Ice Cream: Add ½ cup frozen blueberries to blender.

Calories: 256.8 | Total Fat: 12.0g | Carbs: 35.4g | Dietary Fiber: 5.0g | Protein: 3.0g

Mixed Berry Sorbet

Total time: 5 minutes | Makes 2 servings

INGREDIENTS:

¼ cup strawberries
¼ cup blueberries
¼ cup raspberries
¼ cup blackberries
4 cups ice

ACTIONS:

- Place ingredients in a high-speed blender and blend for 1 minute or until you achieve an icy sorbet consistency. Serve immediately.

TIPS:

- Add 1 to 2 tablespoons honey, maple syrup, or coconut sugar if you like it sweeter.
- Add some nut milk for a creamier sorbet.

Calories: 33 | Total Fat: 0.2g | Carbs: 8g | Dietary Fiber: 2.9g | Protein: 0.5g

Orange Sorbet

Total time: 5 minutes | Makes 2 servings

INGREDIENTS:

2 oranges, peeled
4 cups ice

ACTIONS:

- Place ingredients in a high-speed blender and blend for 1 minute or until you achieve an icy sorbet consistency. Serve immediately.

TIPS:

- Add 1 to 2 tablespoons honey, maple syrup, or coconut sugar if you like it sweeter.
- Add some nut milk for a creamier sorbet.

VARIATION:

- Chocolate Orange Sorbet: Add 1 to 2 tablespoons dark chocolate, grated.
- Grapefruit Sorbet: Use 1 grapefruit, peeled, in place of the oranges.

Calories: 62 | Total Fat: 0.1g | Carbs: 15.4g | Dietary Fiber: 3.1g | Protein: 1.2g

Apple Sorbet

Total time: 5 minutes | Makes 2 servings

INGREDIENTS:

3 apples, peeled and cored
4 cups ice

ACTIONS:

- Place ingredients in a high-speed blender and blend for 1 minute or until you achieve an icy sorbet consistency. Serve immediately.

TIPS:

- Add 1 to 2 tablespoons honey, maple syrup, or coconut sugar if you like it sweeter.
- Add some nut milk for a creamier sorbet.

Calories: 57.2 | Total Fat: 0.2g | Carbs: 15.2g | Dietary Fiber: 2.6g | Protein: 0.3g

Instant Ice Cream Formula

You can't get any simpler than this ice cream made with just one ingredient: frozen bananas! To adjust the flavor, just add your favorite ingredients in the blender. Try any of the following flavor combinations.

Total time: 5 minutes | *Serves 1 or 2*

INGREDIENTS:

2 frozen bananas

ACTIONS:

- Add the bananas to a blender and mix until all is smooth and fluffy, exactly like ice cream. At first, it will appear chunky, and then it will become juicy and smooth.

TIPS:

- To freeze bananas, peel them and then wrap them in plastic and put them in the freezer. Grab however many you need whenever you want to make a smoothie or ice cream.
- Sprinkle with coconut sugar or cinnamon.

Calories: 210 | Total Fat: 0.0g | Carbs: 54.0g | Dietary Fiber: 6.0g | Protein: 2.0g

Instant Vanilla Ice Cream

INGREDIENTS:

2 frozen bananas
1 teaspoon vanilla extract

Calories: 222.1 | Total Fat: 0.0g | Carbs: 54.5g | Dietary Fiber: 6.0g | Protein: 2.0g

Instant Chocolate Ice Cream

INGREDIENTS:

2 frozen bananas
2 teaspoons cacao powder (plus 1 or 2 more, if you like dark chocolate)

Calories: 252.9 | Total Fat: 0.9g | Carbs: 60.4g | Dietary Fiber: 8.5g | Protein: 3.8g

Instant Chocolate Peanut Butter Ice Cream

INGREDIENTS:

2 frozen bananas
2 teaspoons cacao powder
4 teaspoons peanut butter
1 teaspoon water

Calories: 319.4 | Total Fat: 2.2g | Carbs: 69.1g | Dietary Fiber: 9.8g | Protein: 6.4g

Instant Chocolate Almond Butter Ice Cream

INGREDIENTS:

2 frozen bananas
2 teaspoons cacao powder
4 teaspoons almond butter
1 teaspoon water

Calories: 383.2 | Total Fat: 12.7g | Carbs: 65.0g | Dietary Fiber: 10.6g | Protein: 7.0g

Instant Strawberry Ice Cream

INGREDIENTS:

2 frozen bananas
1/3 cup strawberries
1 teaspoon Almond Milk

Calories: 225.8 | Total Fat: 0.3g | Carbs: 57.6g | Dietary Fiber: 7.2g | Protein: 2.3g

Instant Blueberry Ice Cream

INGREDIENTS:

2 frozen bananas
1/3 cup blueberries
1 teaspoon Almond Milk

Calories: 237.7 | Total Fat: 0.1g | Carbs: 60.9g | Dietary Fiber: 7.3g | Protein: 2.4g

Parfaits

Fruit Parfaits make an incredibly delicious yet sweet and healthy dessert, breakfast, and snack! You can get creative with your layers, too! You can even buy special parfait glasses to make the experience more official. Experiment with the number of layers and types of ingredients.

A classic beginners' parfait has three layers:

(1) Something wet like yogurt, ice cream, smoothie, or whipped cream
(2) Something crunchy like nuts or granola
(3) Fruit like strawberries, blueberries, or mangoes

Beginners' Parfait

Banana Smoothie
Almond Granola
Strawberries, chopped

Chocolate Avocado Mousse Parfait

Strawberries, chopped
Almond Granola
Chocolate Avocado Mousse
Raspberries
Almond Granola
Strawberries and fresh mint, for
    garnish

Sunrise Parfait

Pineapple cubes
Vegan Yogurt
Almond Granola
Strawberries

Ice Cream Parfait

Mangoes, cubed
Macadamia nuts, chopped
Instant Ice Cream
Banana slices
Walnuts, chopped
Whipped Coconut Cream and
    strawberries, for garnish

Popular Yogurt Parfait

Strawberries, chopped
Vegan Yogurt
Almond Granola
Strawberries, chopped
Banana slices
Blueberries
Vegan Yogurt
Almond Granola

Summer Parfait

Peaches, chopped
Instant Ice Cream
Peanut Butter Granola
Nectarines, chopped
Vegan Yogurt
Apple, diced
Banana slices
Vegan Yogurt
Pineapple slice, for garnish

Fruit and Yogurt Parfait

Blueberries
Almond Granola
Vegan Yogurt
Strawberries, chopped
Almond Granola
Strawberries and fresh mint, for
    garnish

Strawberries and Cream Parfait

Strawberries, chopped
Almonds, sliced
Strawberry Smoothie
Strawberries, chopped
Walnuts, chopped
Whipped Coconut Cream and
    strawberries, for garnish

Raspberry Chocolate Cream Parfait

Chocolate Smoothie
Raspberries
Whipped Coconut Cream
Chocolate Smoothie
Raspberries
Whipped Coconut Cream
Blackberries and raspberries,
    for garnish

Pink Princess Parfait

Almond Granola
Strawberries, chopped
Strawberry Smoothie
Almond Granola
Raspberries
Strawberry Smoothie
Strawberries and raspberries,
    for garnish

American Flag Parfait

Blueberries
Whipped Coconut Cream
Strawberries, chopped
Whipped Coconut Cream
Blueberries
Whipped Coconut Cream
Strawberries, chopped

Chocolate Nut Berry Parfait

Strawberries, chopped
Almond Granola
Chocolate Nut Berry Smoothie
Blueberries
Almond Granola
Instant Ice Cream
Walnuts, cacao nibs, strawberries, for
    garnish

CHAPTER 17

Condiments, Sauces, and Bases

Here are recipes for sauces, dips, condiments, and bases to supplement your other dishes. You'll find recipes for things like tortillas, seasonings, ketchup, tahini, guacamole, cashew cheese . . . recipes that complement others rather than stand on their own.

Gluten-Free Almond Flour Breading

This makes an excellent base for crusting chicken and fish, and you can add other spices to it. If you have fine almond flour, you will get a totally smooth, even dish. If you have almond flour that still has chunks, you can create a nice, crispy, crunchy effect when cooking with it. You can also use alternate flours that are gluten-free and also nut-free. These recipes are to crumb 1 pound of meat.

Total time: 5 minutes | Makes 1 cup (enough for 1 pound of meat)

INGREDIENTS:

1 cup almond flour
1 teaspoon salt

ACTIONS:

• Mix the ingredients in a bowl until well combined.

VARIATIONS:

• Turmeric Almond Flour: Add 2 tablespoons turmeric powder.
• Thyme Almond Flour: Add 2 tablespoons dried thyme, ¼ teaspoon black pepper, and zest of ¼ lemon.

Calories: 640 | Total Fat: 56.0g | Carbs: 24.0g | Dietary Fiber: 12.0g | Protein: 24.0g

Tigernut Flour Breading

Remember, tigernuts are actually a root vegetable, so this breading is nut-free!

Total time: 5 minutes | Makes 1 cup

INGREDIENTS:

1 cup tigernut flour
1 teaspoon salt

ACTIONS:

• Mix all ingredients in a bowl until well combined.

VARIATIONS:

• Turmeric Tigernut Flour Breading: Add 2 tablespoons turmeric powder.
• Sweeter Breading: Add 1 tablespoon coconut sugar.
• Cheesy Breading: Add 2 tablespoons nutritional yeast.

Calories: 960 | Total Fat: 56.0g | Carbs: 104.0g | Dietary Fiber: 80.0g | Protein: 16.0g

Flax Egg Alternative

For every egg in an original recipe, use one serving of this flax mix. This is a great vegan alternative to egg.

Total time: 10 minutes | Makes 1 serving

INGREDIENT:

3 teaspoons ground flaxseed

ACTIONS:

- In a bowl, whisk the flaxseed and 4 teaspoons water together.
- Let the mixture sit for 7 minutes. During this resting period, it will become gummy, just like eggs.

Calories: 37 | Total Fat: 3g | Carbs: 2g | Dietary Fiber: 2g | Protein: 1g

Pumpkinseed Protein Powder

Make a large batch of this and keep it in your fridge so you always have home-made protein powder on hand! Mix this with water, or add it to your nut milks, juices, smoothies, salads, cereals, and soups for extra protein.

Total time: 5 minutes | Makes 1 serving

INGREDIENT:

½ cup pumpkin seeds

ACTIONS:

- Add to a blender, and mix until you get a fine powder.

Calories: 374 | Total Fat: 32g | Carbs: 13g | Dietary Fiber: 3g | Protein: 17g

Super Protein Powder

Total time: 6 minutes | Serves 4

INGREDIENTS:

½ cup pumpkin seeds
½ cup hemp seeds
½ cup almonds
½ cup uncooked quinoa

ACTIONS:

- Add all ingredients to a blender, and mix until you get a fine powder.

Calories: 344 | Total Fat: 18.5g | Carbs: 28.4g | Dietary Fiber: 5.1g | Protein: 18g

Gluten-Free Tortillas

A tortilla can be used as a wrap or as the base of a pizza. Slice tortillas into strips and they become suitable for dipping into guacamole, cashew cheese, salsa, tahini, and hummus.

Total time: 10 minutes | *Makes 6 tortillas*

INGREDIENTS:

1½ cups rice flour
1½ cups buckwheat flour
2 teaspoons apple cider vinegar
1 teaspoon flax meal

ACTIONS:

- Put the flours in a large bowl. While stirring, slowly add 1 cup warm water and the vinegar. When that is combined, stir in flax meal to form the dough. (If you need more water at this point, add it a teaspoon at a time.)
- Once well mixed, knead the dough for 2 minutes until the dough feels tougher, and then form it into a ball.
- Roll out the ball of dough with a rolling pin to make six 6-inch circles (⅓ cup dough each). This will be about ¼ inch thick.
- Heat a cast-iron pan on medium heat on the stove, and once hot, place the flat bread in it. Cover the pan while it cooks (this is important for the softness of the tortilla). Cook until the dough is no longer soft to the touch, about 1 minute on each side until there is no more soft dough anywhere on your tortilla. Set the tortillas aside as they come off the heat.
- Once the tortilla is ready, transfer to a plate and cover with a clean dish towel or cotton napkin to keep it soft. It is best eaten the day of preparation.

TIPS:

- Add 1 teaspoon salt for enhanced flavor.
- If you can tolerate gluten, you may substitute 3 cups whole-wheat flour for the rice flour and buckwheat flour.

VARIATIONS:

- Cheesy Tortillas: Add 2 tablespoons nutritional yeast to dough.
- Spicy Tortillas: Add 1 teaspoon cayenne pepper to dough.
- Tortilla Strips: Cut the finished tortillas into easy-to-eat sizes.

Calories: 250 | Total Fat: 3g | Carbs: 52g | Dietary Fiber: 5g | Protein: 7g

Walnut Crusting

This is great on salmon and lamb chops!

Total time: 5 minutes | Makes just over 1 cup

INGREDIENTS:

1 cup walnuts
1 teaspoon sage
1 teaspoon thyme
½ teaspoon salt

ACTIONS:

- Blend the walnuts until the mixture achieves the consistency of a fine flour. Add the spices to the walnut meal and mix until well combined.

Calories: 789.1 | Total Fat: 80.2g | Carbs: 17.8g | Dietary Fiber: 8.8g | Protein: 18.4g

Garlic Salt

This is delicious sprinkled on fries, vegetables, and meat.

Total time: 1 minute | Makes 6 tablespoons

INGREDIENTS: 3 tablespoons salt
3 tablespoons garlic powder

ACTIONS:

- Add ingredients to a spice jar and shake until well combined.

Calories: 84 | Total Fat: 0.2g | Carbs: 18.3g | Dietary Fiber: 2.5g | Protein: 4.2g

Oregano Sage Seasoning

Use this for roasted meats.

Total time: 1 minute | Makes 5 tablespoons

INGREDIENTS:

2 tablespoons fresh sage
2 tablespoons fresh oregano
1 teaspoon dried parsley
1 teaspoon cumin powder
½ teaspoon turmeric powder
½ teaspoon salt
¼ teaspoon black pepper
Dash of cayenne pepper

ACTIONS:

- Add ingredients to a spice jar and shake until well combined.

Calories: 50.8 | Total Fat: 2.0g | Carbs: 9.8g | Dietary Fiber: 6.0g | Protein: 1.9g

Taco Seasoning

A must-have staple in the kitchen for taco lovers! Keep this in the cupboard for whenever you want to have meat tacos (beef, chicken, and fish). It also makes a great seasoning for salads. This recipe creates enough seasoning to do three batches of the Beef Tacos.

Total time: 5 minutes | Makes just under ½ cup

INGREDIENTS:

1 tablespoon salt
1 tablespoon cumin
1 tablespoon turmeric
1 tablespoon garlic powder
1 tablespoon onion powder
1½ teaspoons paprika
¾ teaspoon black pepper
3 dashes of cayenne pepper

ACTIONS:

- Mix all the spices together in a bowl. Put it in a shaker bottle.

Calories: 36 | Total Fat: 0.9g | Carbs: 7g | Dietary Fiber: 1.6g | Protein: 1.6g

Vegetable Seasoning

Use for stir-fried vegetable dishes.

Total time: 1 minute | Makes ¼ cup

INGREDIENTS:

1 tablespoon thyme
1 teaspoon sage
1 teaspoon parsley
1 teaspoon basil
1 teaspoon coriander
½ teaspoon turmeric
½ teaspoon cumin
½ teaspoon salt
½ teaspoon garlic powder
¼ teaspoon ginger powder

ACTIONS:

- Add ingredients to a spice jar and shake until well combined.

Calories: 28.3 | Total Fat: 1.1g | Carbs: 5.4g | Dietary Fiber: 3.4g | Protein: 1.3g

Taco Sauce

Total time: 5 minutes | Makes 1½ cups (9 servings)

INGREDIENTS:

1¼ cup ketchup
1 teaspoon cumin powder
1 teaspoon onion powder
1 teaspoon garlic powder
1 teaspoon chili powder
¼ teaspoon salt

ACTIONS:

- Mix all ingredients and ¼ cup water in a small dish until well combined.

Calories: 47.2 | Total Fat: 0.1g | Carbs: 11.7g | Dietary Fiber: 0.1g | Protein: 0.1g

Vegan Mayonnaise

A blender is important in this recipe to make a thick, smooth, creamy mayonnaise.

Total time: 10 minutes | Makes 1½ cups (4 servings)

INGREDIENTS:

¾ cup Almond Milk or Cashew Milk
1½ tablespoons lemon juice
1 teaspoon mustard
¾ cup olive oil
Pinch of salt and pepper

ACTIONS:

- In a blender, add the Almond Milk, lemon juice, mustard, oil, salt, and pepper. Mix until well combined.
- After about 1 minute, add the oil until it thickens, after about 3 to 4 minutes. When emulsified, it is ready to eat. Store it in a jar or airtight container in the fridge.

Calories: 367.7 | Total Fat: 41.1g | Carbs: 0.9g | Dietary Fiber: 0.3g | Protein: 0.3g

3-Minute Instant Butter

Total time: 3 minute | Makes ⅓ cup

INGREDIENTS:

½ cup extra-virgin olive oil
½ teaspoon salt
⅛ teaspoon apple cider vinegar

ACTIONS:

- Blend all ingredients in a blender or food processor until whipped. It is ready to use now.

TIP:

- Store this butter in a container in the freezer, and it will set solid like a stick of dairy butter.

Calories: 954.7 | Total Fat: 108.0g | Carbs: 0.0g | Dietary Fiber: 0.0g | Protein: 0.0g

Vegan Butter

This butter can be stored in an airtight container in the refrigerator for up to one month, or up to one year in the freezer.

Total time: 10 minutes | *Makes ½ cup (16 servings)*

INGREDIENTS:

¼ cup plus 2 teaspoons Almond Milk

1 teaspoon apple cider vinegar

½ teaspoon salt

½ cup extra-virgin coconut oil, melted

1 tablespoon extra-virgin olive oil

ACTIONS:

- Place the Almond Milk, apple cider vinegar, and salt in a small cup and whisk together with a fork. Let this sit and it will curdle. While that sits, add the coconut oil and olive oil to a blender and mix on high speed until well combined and smooth.

- Add the Almond Milk mixture to the blender. Mix for 2 minutes until smooth and creamy.
- The mixture is now ready to use as butter! To solidify it more, place it in a mold in the freezer. An ice cube tray works well as a mold. It will be ready to use as a harder butter in 1 hour.

TIPS:

- To make your butter nut-free, use a seed milk instead of Almond Milk.
- Other butter alternatives for toast or pancakes are extra-virgin coconut oil, extra-virgin olive oil, or avocado oil. You can also use avocado as a substitute for butter on toast.

VARIATION:

- Cinnamon Butter: Add ¼ teaspoon cinnamon and 2 teaspoons maple syrup to the oil. (Make Cinnamon Toast by spreading the Cinnamon Butter on Gluten-Free Tortillas or toasted bread.)

Calories: 70 | *Total Fat: 8g* | *Carbs: 0g* | *Dietary Fiber: 0g* | *Protein: 0g*

Vegan Sour Cream

Refrigerated in an airtight container or jar, this sour cream lasts for up to two weeks. Use this in any recipe that calls for sour cream.

Total time: 5 minutes | *Makes 1 cup (8 servings)*

INGREDIENTS:

1 cup raw cashew nuts
¼ teaspoon salt
1 teaspoon apple cider vinegar
Juice of 1 small lemon (no more than ¼ cup)
½ teaspoon dill

ACTIONS:

- Blend the ingredients and ¼ cup water in a blender until the consistency is creamy. Add more water if necessary, to achieve desired smoothness.

TIPS:

- For a nut-free alternative, substitute sunflower seeds or hemp seeds for cashew nuts.
- For a creamier sour cream, soak the cashews for 4 hours in water. If you do soak the cashews, use half the amount of water in the recipe.

Calories: 119 | Total Fat: 9g | Carbs: 7g | Dietary Fiber: 1g | Protein: 4g

Ketchup

Ketchup keeps well in the refrigerator for up to eight weeks, and in the freezer for three to six months.

Total time: 10 minutes | *Makes 3 cups (48 servings)*

INGREDIENTS:

14 ounces organic tomato paste
1 teaspoon apple cider vinegar
2 tablespoons maple syrup
⅓ teaspoon garlic powder
⅓ tablespoon onion powder
⅓ teaspoon cayenne pepper
½ teaspoon cinnamon
Pinch of ground cloves
⅔ teaspoon salt

ACTIONS:

- Put all the ingredients and ⅓ cup water into a blender and mix well.
- Pour into a glass container and store in the fridge. Flavors will mesh well overnight.

TIP:

- Add a dash of allspice for added flavor.

VARIATION:

- Add 1 teaspoon dried mustard powder to make Mustard Ketchup.

Calories: 7 | Total Fat: 0g | Carbs: 2g | Dietary Fiber: 0g | Protein: 0g

Cashew Cheese

Serve on Raw Tacos made with Walnut "Meatballs" or in Raw Lasagna. Spread on lettuce leaves for raw lettuce wraps.

Total time: 10 minutes | Makes 1 cup (4 servings)

INGREDIENTS:

2 cups cashews
2 tablespoons nutritional yeast
Juice of 1 small lemon
(no more than ¼ cup)
½ teaspoon salt

ACTIONS:

- Put all ingredients and ½ cup water in your food processor, and blend until smooth. Add more water if you prefer a softer consistency.

TIPS:

- Soak the cashews for 4 hours for a smoother, creamier cheese.

- Instead of cashews, use almonds, macadamia nuts, walnuts, or Brazil nuts. For a nut-free version, use hemp seeds, pumpkin seeds, or sunflower seeds.
- Adjust the cheesy flavor by adding more or less nutritional yeast, to taste. You can also make this recipe without nutritional yeast.
- Add herbs for more flavor. My favorite is to add 1 teaspoon thyme.

VARIATIONS:

- Raw "Parmesan" Cheese: Add additional 3 tablespoons nutritional yeast to the mixture and spread the mixture ¼ inch thick on a dehydrator tray. Place it in a food dehydrator for 12 hours. It will crumble easily when you're ready to use it.
- Garlic Cashew Cheese: Add 1 clove garlic, or more to taste.
- Pesto Cashew Cheese: Add 1 cup fresh basil leaves.
- Spicy Cashew Cheese: Add a dash of cayenne pepper or chili flakes, to taste.

Calories: 486 | Total Fat: 37g | Carbs: 30g | Dietary Fiber: 4g | Protein: 17g

Hummus

Serve with carrot sticks and cucumber sticks.

Total time: 10 minutes | Serves 4 to 6

INGREDIENTS:

One 14-ounce can chickpeas
¼ cup chickpea water from the can
1 tablespoon extra-virgin olive oil
3 cloves garlic
1 tablespoon lemon juice
3 tablespoons Tahini
1 teaspoon salt

ACTIONS:

- Put all ingredients in your food processor, and blend until smooth.

TIPS

- As an alternative to chickpeas, use almonds, pumpkin seeds, sunflower seeds, or hemp seeds.
- Massage hummus into kale or lettuce leaves for a creamier texture.

Calories: 372 | Total Fat: 12g | Carbs: 51g | Dietary Fiber: 15g | Protein: 17g

Guacamole

Serve with carrot sticks or cucumber sticks.

Total time: 5 minutes | Serves 1

INGREDIENTS:

1 avocado
¼ teaspoon salt
¼ teaspoon black pepper
Juice of ½ lemon

ACTIONS:

- Mash the avocado in a bowl with a fork, then mix in the other ingredients.

TIP:

- Add flavor with ½ small red onion, diced, or ½ small bell pepper any color, diced.

Calories: 234 | Total Fat: 21g | Carbs: 14g | Dietary Fiber: 9g | Protein: 3g

Tahini

Total time: 10 minutes | Serves 4 to 6

INGREDIENTS:

½ cup sesame seeds
4 teaspoons sesame oil
¾ teaspoon salt

ACTIONS:

- Put ½ cup water and all ingredients in your food processor, and blend until smooth.

Calories: 143 | Total Fat: 13g | Carbs: 4g | Dietary Fiber: 2g | Protein: 3g

10-Minute Salsa

This salsa is a raw recipe, no cooking needed. It is extremely fresh! Serve with organic corn chips, Gluten-Free Tortillas, or add it to Vegan Nachos! Makes a great condiment on tacos, too! Goes well at a party with guacamole.

Total time: 10 minutes | *Serves 2 to 6*

INGREDIENTS:

1 red onion, diced

2 cups tomatoes, diced
(about 6 large tomatoes)

½ teaspoon cumin

½ teaspoon salt

¼ cup fresh cilantro

1 small lime, peeled

1 jalapeño, finely chopped

1 teaspoon garlic, minced

½ teaspoon maple syrup

1 tablespoon olive oil

¼ teaspoon black pepper

ACTIONS:

- Dice all vegetables and add to a bowl. Stir in the spices and mix until well combined.

TIPS:

- Add all ingredients to a blender and mix until smooth to save even more time and have no chunks in your salsa.
- You can make this oil-free for less fat and calories.

VARIATIONS:

- Red and Green Bell Pepper Salsa: Add 1 red and 1 green bell pepper, diced.
- Hot Chipotle Salsa: Add a dash of cayenne pepper, 1 finely chopped chipotle pepper, and 1 teaspoon chipotle powder.
- Mango Salsa: Add the flesh of 1 mango, diced.
- Pineapple Salsa: Add 1½ cups pineapple, cubed.
- Strawberry Salsa: Add 1½ cups strawberries, diced.

Calories: 142.7 | Total Fat: 7.5g | Carbs: 18.9g | Dietary Fiber: 4.9g | Protein: 3.8g

Condiments, Sauces, and Bases

Raw Tomato Sauce

Serve this sauce with the Zucchini Pasta and Walnut "Meatballs" and as an extra layer on the Raw Lasagna.

Total time: 10 minutes | Serves 4

INGREDIENTS:

2 large tomatoes
1 cup sun-dried tomatoes
1 clove garlic
¼ red or yellow onion
1 tablespoon extra-virgin olive oil
¼ teaspoon black pepper
¼ teaspoon chili flakes or cayenne pepper
1 tablespoon fresh basil, or ½ tablespoon dried basil
½ teaspoon dried thyme
½ teaspoon dried parsley
½ teaspoon dried oregano

ACTIONS:

- Add all ingredients to the blender and mix for 1 minute or until well combined.

TIP:

- Soak the sun-dried tomatoes for 1 hour to make the blender process easier and the sauce smoother.

Calories: 70 | Total Fat: 3g | Carbs: 10g | Dietary Fiber: 3g | Protein: 2g

Alfredo Sauce

This delightful, creamy, plant-based Alfredo Sauce is dairy-free, yet extremely creamy because of the cashews. Enjoy as much as you like as it is gluten-free and high in antioxidants! Because it is raw, you can make it in 5 minutes or less, no cooking involved. This means that the nutrients are intact. Goes great on pasta, steak, chicken, and pizza.

Total time: 5 minutes | Makes 1¼ cups (5 servings)

INGREDIENTS:

1¼ cup cashews
½ tablespoon lemon juice
1 clove garlic, peeled
¼ teaspoon dill
¼ teaspoon parsley
¼ teaspoon thyme
½ teaspoon salt

ACTIONS:

- Add all ingredients and ¾ cup water to a blender and mix until completely smooth.

TIPS:

- Make a big batch up and freeze what you don't eat for a later meal.
- Alfredo Sauce is delicious on brown rice pasta.

Calories: 198.3 | Total Fat: 15.9g | Carbs: 11.6g | Dietary Fiber: 1.1g | Protein: 5.3g

Thai Red Curry Paste

This is an incredibly rich-flavored red spice blend that you can use in curries, steamed vegetables, soups, and salads. You can also serve it over plain rice, quinoa, or brown rice pasta. Store covered in the fridge for 10 days or freeze for up to 2 months.

Total time: 7 minutes | Makes ½ cup

INGREDIENTS:

¼ cup fresh cilantro
3 tablespoons fresh lemon or lime juice
2 scallions
3 cloves garlic
2 tablespoons ginger, peeled
1 tablespoon lemon or lime peel
1 tablespoon coconut sugar or maple syrup
1 tablespoon ground coriander
1 teaspoon turmeric
½ teaspoon real salt
1 large fresh red chili

ACTIONS:

• Add all the ingredients to a blender and puree until smooth.

TIP:

• Add 2 teaspoons minced lemongrass (the inner stalk).

VARIATION:

• Thai Green Curry Paste: Replace red chili with 1 fresh green chili and add 1 Kaffir lime leaf.

Calories: 24 | Total Fat: 1g | Carbs: 5g | Dietary Fiber: 8g | Protein: 0g

Sweet Blueberry Syrup

Total time: 5 minutes | Serves 4

INGREDIENTS:

2 tablespoons maple syrup
2 cup blueberries

ACTIONS:

• Blend the ingredients together until completely smooth.

TIP:

• Add some water, if needed, to make it smooth.

Calories: 66.7 | Total Fat: 0.0g | Carbs: 17.0g | Dietary Fiber: 2.0g | Protein: 0.5g

Sweet Strawberry Syrup

Total time: 5 minutes | Serves 4

INGREDIENTS:

2 tablespoons maple syrup
2 cup strawberries

ACTIONS:

• Blend the ingredients together until completely smooth.

TIP:

• Add some water, if needed, to make it smooth.

Calories: 48.9 | Total Fat: 0.3g | Carbs: 12.1g | Dietary Fiber: 1.8g | Protein: 0.4g

CHAPTER 18

Meal Planning Ideas

"The **freedom to create** is a fruit of **personal growth** and evolution."

—Stephen Nachmanovitch

Y ou don't always need to follow a recipe. Once you understand the basic components to a dish, you can quickly throw together a meal with the ingredients you have on hand or whatever looks good at the farmers' market today.

10-Minute Noodle Soup Formula

Noodles are a fun part of life. Not only are they healthy and can be made in less than 10 minutes, they are versatile. Noodles can be made into a soup or drained and served with toppings. When you add fresh toppings, it packs this dish with a lot of nutrients! In particular, adding raw toppings makes for a great hybrid of raw and cooked.

CHOOSE YOUR NOODLES:

Organic ramen wheat noodles
Organic ramen brown rice noodles
    (gluten-free)
Organic ramen buckwheat noodles
    (gluten-free)
Rice noodles

CHOOSE YOUR TOPPINGS:

Boiled egg
Fried egg
Fresh cilantro, parsley, sage
Curry powder
Turmeric
Cumin
Salt and pepper
Cayenne pepper
Red chili flakes
Fresh bean sprouts
Shrimp
Chicken
Beef
Pork
Onion
Garlic

10-Minute Pasta Formula

The good news is we can enjoy a healthy pasta dish within 10 minutes! For the fastest-cooking pasta, use one of the following options below. You can make a raw pasta dish or a cooked dish.

CHOOSE YOUR PASTA:

Zucchini Pasta
Black bean pasta
Quinoa pasta
Chickpea pasta

CHOOSE YOUR SAUCE:

Raw Tomato Sauce
Alfredo Sauce
10-Minute Salsa

CHOOSE YOUR PROTEIN (OPTIONAL):

Walnut "Meatballs"
Meatballs

CHOOSE YOUR TOPPING:

Fresh parsley
Fresh basil

10-Minute Pizza Formula

The only way to make pizza in 10 minutes is to use a ready-made crust. There are some great organic ones on the market that are even gluten-free. Buy them frozen and keep them in your freezer so you always have one on standby. The smaller and thinner the crust, the shorter amount of time it takes to bake it. You can also buy nonrefrigerated, gluten-free pizza shells from Vitacost.com/TheEarthDiet.

For your pizza sauce, you can buy ready-made organic sauce or make your own. If you tolerate dairy, you can use regular cheese, or you can substitute a vegan cheese or nutritional yeast. You can have fun and get creative with the toppings of your choice.

Basic Pizza Recipe

Total time: 10 minutes | Serves 2 to 4

INGREDIENTS:

One (8-ounce) pizza crust
¼ cup sauce
¾ cup cheese

CHOOSE YOUR SAUCE:

Raw Tomato Sauce
Alfredo Sauce
BBQ sauce

CHOOSE YOUR CHEESE:

Organic cheese, such as mozzarella
Vegan cheese
Nutritional yeast

CHOOSE YOUR TOPPINGS:

Tomato slices
Basil
Mushrooms
Walnut "Meatballs"
Parsley
Sage
Sausage
Avocado
Bacon
Meatballs
BBQ Chicken

ACTIONS:

- Preheat the oven to 375°F. Cover the crust with the sauce of your choice and cover with cheese and toppings.
- Bake in the oven for 8 minutes or until the cheese is melted and bubbly. Top with fresh parsley or basil.

Alfredo Pizza

INGREDIENTS:

Pizza crust
Alfredo Sauce
Cheese
Mushrooms, sliced
Cooked chicken breast strips, steak strips, bacon, or Meatballs (optional)

Italian Pizza

INGREDIENTS:

Pizza crust
Raw Tomato Sauce
Cheese
Red or green peppers, sliced
Fresh or dried sage, parsley, oregano, and basil
Cooked sausage (optional)

BBQ Chicken Pizza

INGREDIENTS:

Pizza crust
BBQ Chicken
BBQ sauce of your choice
Cheese
Caramelized onions (optional)

Lunch Box Ideas

Treat yourself right. Always take a refreshing lunch break, a moment to press the pause button on other activities and reconnect. If you can plan ahead for your break, it's possible to whip up a very healthy meal that is portable. Whether you're at work or school, traveling on a plane or train or in a car, if you have time to sit down and eat a Protein Bar, toss and dress a Mason Jar Salad, or unwrap a Sandwich Stack, then you can enjoy a mouthwatering meal. Toss one of these portable goodies into your kid's lunch box and you'll get the award for Best Parent of the Year.

Hearty Lunch Box

Cherry tomatoes
1 raw carrot
Mini Cashew Cheesecake
1 Beef Taco loaded with greens

Sweet Tooth Lunch Box

Green tea or ginger tea would go great
  with this lunch box.
1 Raw Chocolate Chip Cookie
1 cup strawberries
1 cup blueberries
1 cup pineapple

Vibrant Kid's Lunch Box

1 orange
1 carrot
Handful of raw broccoli, chopped into
  bite-sized pieces
Handful of raw cauliflower, chopped
  into bite-sized pieces
Sandwich Stack
1 Raw Three-Ingredient Chocolate Ball

High-Protein Lunch Box

Chicken Wrap: Almond-Crusted
  Chicken Tenders in a Gluten-Free
  Tortilla with sprouts, avocado, and
  hemp seeds. Vegan Mayonnaise is
  optional.
1 tablespoon pumpkin seeds
1 Protein Bar
¼ raw head of broccoli, chopped into
  bite-sized pieces

Raw Food Lunch Box

1 whole avocado
2 tablespoons hemp seeds
1 tablespoon pumpkin seeds
Walnut "Meatballs" with a kale leaf to
  make a raw taco
1 orange

Detox Lunch Box

Detox Jar Salad
1 cucumber
1 orange
1 celery stick

Weight Loss Lunch Box

Chickpea Fries
1 apple
1 carrot with Hummus
1 cucumber

Wraps and Sandwich Stack Ideas

Choose your protein, salad, and toppings; then either wrap it up—or stack it up!

CHOOSE YOUR WRAP OR BREAD:

Lettuce

Collard green

Kale leaf

Tortilla

Whole-wheat bread, organic

White bread, organic

Multigrain bread, organic

Gluten-free bread

CHOOSE YOUR PROTEIN:

Boiled egg

Fish

Chickpeas

Beans

Turkey

Bean Burger

Beef Taco

Beef Burger

Chickpea Fries

Omelet

Almond-Crusted Chicken Tenders

CHOOSE YOUR SALAD:

Sprouts

Broccoli

Tomato

Celery

Spinach

Alfalfa sprouts

Carrot, grated

Avocado

Onion

Peppers

Lettuce

Cucumber

CHOOSE YOUR TOPPINGS:

10-Minute Salsa

Mango Salsa

Pineapple Salsa

Sesame seeds

Vegan Sour Cream

Vegan Yogurt

Ketchup

Guacamole

Nutritional yeast

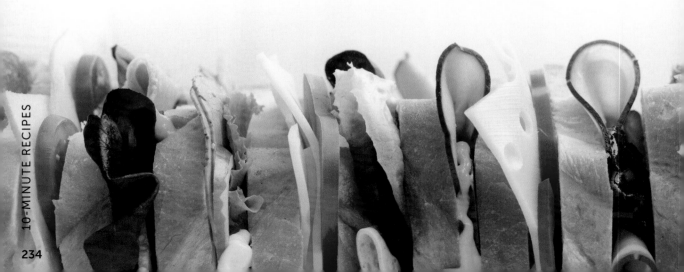

My Favorite Sandwich Stack Combinations

Take all the ingredients with you to school or work then stack them up at lunchtime:

Turkey Sandwich Stack

Bread
Guacamole
Lettuce
Turkey breast, salt, and pepper
Tomatoes, sliced
Green pepper, sliced
Vegan Mayonnaise
Bread

Chicken Tender Sandwich Stack

Bread
Lettuce
Avocado
Cucumber, sliced
Tomato, sliced
2 Almond-Crusted Chicken Tenders
Vegan Mayonnaise
Carrot, grated
Bread

Vibrant Veggie Sandwich Stack

Bread
Avocado
Sesame seeds
Mango Salsa
Lettuce
Carrot, grated
Yellow pepper, sliced
Cucumber, sliced
Purple onion
Bread

My Favorite Wrap Combination

- Wrap: Lettuce or soft Gluten-Free Tortilla

- Protein: Almond-Crusted Chicken Tender, Chicken Taco, or Beef Taco mix

- Salad: Sprouts, grated carrot, avocado, diced lettuce, cucumber

- Toppings: 10-Minute Salsa, Ketchup, and nutritional yeast

Fruit and Vegetable Platters

Fruit and vegetable platters can be served at parties, and also at meetings where you want to keep everyone's mind sharp and body energized. Express yourself! Create interesting shapes by cutting some of the produce into cubes and some into circles.

Basic Fruit Platter

Try these Party Platter combinations:

INGREDIENTS:

Kiwifruit
Strawberries
Grapes
Oranges
Cantaloupe

ACTIONS:

- Cut all the fruit into cubes and serve with lemon wedges and Vegan Yogurt in the middle as a dip.

Tropical Fruit Platter

INGREDIENTS:

Mangoes
Pineapple
Papaya
Lychees
Cherries

Coconut chips
  or the fresh flesh
  of a coconut
Strawberries
Halved passion fruit

ACTIONS:

- Cut all the fruit into cubes and serve with lemon wedges and Vegan Yogurt in the middle as a dip.

Fruit and Vegetable Platter

INGREDIENTS:

Carrot sticks
Cucumbers
Celery
Grapes

Green beans
Strawberries
Watermelon
Blueberries

ACTIONS:

- Cut all the fruit into bite-sized pieces and serve with Hummus and tortilla strips in the middle.

Stuffed Foods

Stuffed foods are fun to make, and make vibrant table decorations.
These are a hit at parties and social events. You could
even have them as your lunch or dinner.

CHOOSE YOUR SHELL:

Avocado
Peppers
Raspberries
Cherries
Olives
Mushrooms
Pineapple
Papaya
Coconut

CHOOSE YOUR STUFFING:

Cashew Cheese
Hummus
Chocolate
Vegan Mayonnaise
Smoothies
Fruit

The following are some of my favorite stuffed combinations!

Alfredo Stuffed Mushrooms

INGREDIENTS:

16 mushrooms
Alfredo Sauce
Fresh rosemary

ACTIONS:

- Cut the stems off each mushroom. Stuff Alfredo Sauce into each mushroom cap. Serve with fresh rosemary. (If you have the time, you can also bake these for 20 minutes at 375°F.)

Stuffed Raspberries

INGREDIENTS:

2 cups fresh raspberries
Chocolate Sauce

ACTIONS:

- Lay out the raspberries on a baking sheet or platter, hole side up. Pour a bit of Chocolate Sauce in each hole. (Alternatively, stuff each raspberry with a blueberry.) These can be refrigerated or even frozen for a delicious "ice cream" treat.

Stuffed Hummus Avocado

INGREDIENTS:

1 avocado
2 tablespoons Hummus
Paprika or cayenne pepper, to taste

ACTIONS:

- Cut the avocado in half and remove the pit. Add a scoop of Hummus in each hole. Sprinkle with fresh spices like paprika and cayenne pepper. Serve with celery or carrot sticks.

Stuffed Hummus Peppers

INGREDIENTS:

1 bell pepper
¾ cup Hummus
Paprika or cayenne pepper, to taste

ACTIONS:

- Cut the pepper in half and scoop out the seeds. Spread the Hummus on each half. Sprinkle with fresh spices like paprika and cayenne pepper. Serve with celery or carrot sticks.

Stuffed Olives

INGREDIENTS:

2 cups fresh olives, pitted
1 red pepper, diced

ACTIONS:

- Lay out the olives on a platter or baking sheet and fill with diced peppers.

PART III

MEAL PLANS FOR SPECIFIC GOALS

CHAPTER 19

The "Break an Addiction to Junk Food" Guide

"No one ever **achieved a goal** by being **interested** in **its** achievement. One **must be committed.**"

—Anthony Robbins

BODY

MIND

SPIRIT

The Earth provides us with everything we need to survive and thrive. Looking at nature, we can see that it supports our human existence by generating a variety of foods: vegetables, fruits, nuts, seeds, berries, herbs, spices, and different proteins. There is a biological reason why we crave fat, sugar, and salt, and the sensation of fullness. Where we can go wrong is in how we respond to our cravings: Too often we'll mindlessly grab a fast-food option, sacrificing nutrition for convenience. This starts a vicious cycle of emptiness and insatiability. We take in massive amounts of food and still long for more.

Ideally, once we've eaten, the brain sends a signal to the stomach saying that we've had enough. In the vicious cycle of a junk-food addiction, we never absorb the nutrients we need that should trigger this signal, so we keep eating. No one ever binges on a bowl of carrots!

Then there's the emotional component to the cycle. If we're not adequately nourished, we get blue. We feel disempowered, ashamed of our lack of control, stuck, and frustrated. The longer this goes on, the less confidence we have in our ability to end the pattern.

No matter how long you've been suffering with out-of-control, disorderly eating, hear me out on this promise: You absolutely can escape the addictive cycle and totally transform your life, health, and eating habits in ways that you may not even be able to imagine right now. It takes time. It's a process. But it can and will happen if you declare, "I will not suffer in this way for the rest of my life. Someday I will be free of it. I am committed and open to learning what I need to know to take care of myself."

Remember, I myself was addicted to junk foods. For five years, I ate them every day. Any type of junk food, I ate it! Pizza, burgers and fries, tacos, cakes, cookies, chocolate, gummy bears, caramel koalas, chips, red licorice. Let's not forget the deep-fried ice cream. I didn't just eat it every day; I binged on it every day. I overate, and I always ate to the point where I felt extremely sick. When my digestive system stopped working properly, I took laxatives. My situation was extreme.

Your situation may be different from mine. You may be a stress eater, an overeater, or someone who "self-medicates" with food when you don't want to feel bad. Food can numb us out. It's important to understand when we're using junk food in that way. Wholesome food can help us heal our lives, relieve stress, and feel better, but it is not the only answer. We also get nourishment from things other than food. We are fed by and get energy from oxygen, sunlight, our connection to our Source (call it God, Spirit, soul, as you prefer), and our connections to people: community, friends, family, and of course, ourselves. If one of these things is missing, we will feel imbalanced. That's when many of us seek comfort, love, and energy in junk food. We're simply looking in the wrong place for comfort.

When you make the decision to end your addiction, it will happen. I broke my addiction to junk food by committing to eat only foods that earth provides naturally for 365 days. My rule was: Eat whatever you are craving, just make sure that it's as natural a variation of that food as possible. If you usually eat an entire pack of cookies in one sitting, allow yourself to eat an entire batch of Raw Melt-in-Your-Mouth Chocolate Chip Cookies. This way you are getting protein, vitamins, minerals, and other nutrients from the cookie and you will feel more fulfilled. As long as you know you're on the path to a healthier life, you'll have peace of mind.

Follow Your Cravings

When an intense impulse to quickly grab some junk food takes you over, stop whatever you're doing for five minutes, close your eyes, relax, and breathe. Give time to yourself to feel however you feel, and take care of yourself by not beating yourself up for feeling as you do. Be with what is.

If you feel like eating potato chips, upgrade and grab an organic bag so you feel less guilt later. Slow down and enjoy them. You might as well take full pleasure in the moment. As you eat, use the affirmation, "I accept myself."

If you can pay attention to your cravings and fulfill them using upgrades or recipes from this book, you'll find it easy to stop craving junk foods. When you see how much color and variety you have to choose from, you'll be excited. How could anyone feel deprived?

10-Day Guide to Breaking an Addiction to Junk Food

Use this formula every day for 10 days. If you're still hungry, snack on pineapple, tigernuts, walnuts, blueberries, or sunflower seeds. Remember, the more you load your body with nutrient-rich foods, the less you'll crave junk food.

Start each day with Lemon Water and a fresh juice. Choose from:
- Green Lemonade
- Super Greens
- Fat Blaster
- Beet Juice

For breakfast, choose from:
- Chocolate Nut Berry Smoothie
- Strawberry Smoothie
- Pineapple Papaya Smoothie
- Chocolate Peanut Butter Smoothie

For a morning snack, choose from:
- Chocolate Chip Raw Cookies
- Raw Three-Ingredient Chocolate Balls
- Mini Cashew Cheesecake

For lunch, choose from:
- Four-Ingredient Green Salad
- Fish Tacos
- Vegetable Stir-Fry

For an afternoon snack, choose from:
- Chocolate Shake
- Basic French Fries
- Black Bean Salsa Pasta

For dinner, choose from:
- Superfood Kale Salad
- Almond-Crusted Chicken Tenders
- 10-Minute Beef Burgers

For dessert, choose from:
- Instant Ice Cream
- Smoothie Bowl
- Raw Apple Pie

An hour after dinner:
- Clay Drink or bentonite clay capsule

Before bed:
- Ginger Tea (to aid digestion and suppress cravings)

CHAPTER 20

The Alkalize Your Body Guide

"**The body** is **holographic**; therefore, when you change one biomarker you **influence** them **all**."

— Deepak Chopra, M.D., and David Simon, M.D.

It is my opinion—based on common sense—that we can assist our bodies in remaining healthy by consuming foods that are alkalizing, such as fruits and vegetables. When your body is alkaline, you can experience weight loss, energy, healing, a strong immune system, no pain and no bloating, and a feeling of vibrancy.

The research of Nobel Prize–winner Dr. Otto Heinrich Warburg indicated that cancer cells have a very narrow band of pH that they can tolerate. Because healthy human tissue is stressed by anything acidic that lies outside this range, some researchers have aimed to treat cancer instead with alkaline therapy—going outside the range in the opposite direction.

The range of pH goes from 0 (very acidic) to 14 (very alkaline). A pH of 7.0 is considered neutral; water has a pH of 7. Proper pH for the blood of human beings is as close to 7.4 as possible. The pH of our digestive juices is more acidic, however, because this helps us to break down food. Saliva ranges from 6.5 to 7.5. Hydrochloric acid and pepsin in the stomach can range from 1.5 to 6.5, depending on the phase of digestion that's occurring. The small intestine, where the vast majority of nutrient absorption occurs, is much more alkaline—pH naturally ranges from 7.0 to 8.5. To me, this explains why it is important to maintain a slightly alkaline body if you want to stay healthy.

If you tested your pH level right now, you could immediately determine if you are alkaline or acidic. If your body was alkaline, you could expect to feel great and have a light body, positive mood, and strong immune system. If your body was acidic, you could expect to feel heavy, gain weight, and experience pain and inflammation in the body.

Certain foods have an acidizing effect on the body after consumption, and certain foods have an alkalizing effect. You can assist your body to maintain its acid-alkaline balance to some degree by eating and drinking certain foods. (Refer to the following list as well as the Top Acid- and Alkaline-Forming Substances chart in Chapter 2.) Relaxation and feelings of love and joy create an alkaline environment, where stress creates an acidic environment within the body.

Top Alkalizing Foods

VEGETABLES
- Alfalfa
- Barley grass
- Beet greens
- Beets
- Broccoli
- Cabbage
- Carrot
- Cauliflower
- Celery
- Chard greens
- Chlorella
- Collard greens
- Cucumber
- Daikon
- Dandelion flowers and dandelion root
- Dulce
- Edible flowers
- Eggplant
- Fermented veggies
- Garlic
- Green beans
- Green peas
- Kale
- Lettuce
- Mushrooms
- Mustard greens
- Nori
- Onions
- Parsnips
- Peas
- Peppers
- Pumpkin
- Reishi
- Radishes
- Sea veggies
- Shiitake
- Spinach
- Spirulina
- Sprouts
- Sweet potatoes
- Tomatoes
- Wakame
- Watercress
- Wheatgrass
- Wild greens

FRUITS
- Apple
- Apricot
- Avocado
- Banana
- Berries
- Blueberries
- Cantaloupe
- Cherries
- Coconut, fresh
- Currants
- Dates
- Figs
- Grapes
- Grapefruit
- Honeydew melon
- Lemon
- Lime
- Melons
- Nectarine
- Orange
- Papaya
- Peach
- Pear
- Pineapple
- Raisins
- Raspberries
- Rhubarb
- Strawberries
- Tangerine
- Tomato
- Watermelon

PROTEINS
- Almonds
- Chestnuts
- Millet

SPICES & SEASONINGS
- Almonds
- Chili pepper
- Cinnamon
- Curry
- Ginger
- Herbs (all)
- Mustard
- Sea salt

WATERS
- Lemon Water: the juice of one lemon squeezed into a glass of water.
- pHresh Water: 1 teaspoon of the supplement pHresh Greens (or another alkaline supergreens powder) mixed into 1 cup water.
- Apple Cider Vinegar Water: 1 teaspoon apple cider vinegar mixed into 1 cup water.
- Clay Drink: Drink 1 teaspoon bentonite clay mixed in 2 cups water.
- Salt Water: ½ teaspoon salt in 1 or 2 cups water.

One-Day Alkalizing Guide

AFTER RISING:

- Lemon Water or Apple Cider Vinegar Water

BREAKFAST:

- Fresh juice and Chia Seed Cereal

MORNING SNACK:

- Smoothie or Smoothie Bowl

LUNCH:

- Salad

AFTERNOON SNACK:

- Ginger Lemon Shot and raw vegetable

DINNER:

- Cooked meal

BEFORE BED:

- Bedtime tea

Seven-Day Alkalizing Guide

- **DAY 1:** Lemon Water, Green Lemonade, Chia Seed Cereal, Avocado Smoothie, Ultimate Nourishing Detox Salad, Ginger Lemon Shot and carrot stick, Vegetable Soup, Immune-Boosting Tea

- **DAY 2:** Lemon Water, Green Lemonade, Chia Seed Cereal, Banana Berry Smoothie, Avocado Sesame Seed Salad, Ginger Lemon Shot and cucumber, Immune-Boosting Soup, Ginger Tea

- **DAY 3:** Apple Cider Vinegar Water, Berry Green, Chia Seed Cereal, Classic Green Smoothie, Chickpea Cucumber Cumin Salad, Ginger Lemon Shot and celery, Vegetable Stir-Fry, Skin Cleansing Tea

- **DAY 4:** Apple Cider Vinegar Water, Super Greens, Chia Seed Cereal, Antioxidant Vitamin Blast Smoothie, Seaweed Salad, Ginger Lemon Shot and carrot stick, Lemon Thyme Chickpea Fries, Skin Cleansing Tea

- **DAY 5:** pHresh Water, Detox Juice, Chia Seed Cereal, Banana Berry Smoothie Bowl, Thai Wraps, Ginger Lemon Shot and cucumber, Cauliflower Rice, Bedtime Tea

- **DAY 6:** pHresh Water, Detox Juice, Chia Seed Cereal, Acai Blueberry Bowl, Four-Ingredient Green Salad, Ginger Lemon Shot and celery stick, Sweet Potato Fries, Bedtime Tea

- **DAY 7:** Lemon Water, Energy Juice, Chia Seed Cereal, Avocado Smoothie, Four-Ingredient Green Salad, Ginger Lemon Shot and carrot stick, Vegetable Soup, Bedtime Tea

Make Your Own Alkalizing Meal Plan

— CHOOSE YOUR JUICE:

- Green Lemonade
- Berry Green
- Super Greens
- Detox Juice
- Energy Juice

— CHOOSE YOUR SMOOTHIE:

- Avocado Smoothie
- Banana Berry Smoothie
- Classic Green Smoothie
- Antioxidant Vitamin Blast Smoothie
- Banana Berry Smoothie Bowl
- Acai Blueberry Bowl

— CHOOSE YOUR SALAD:

- Avocado Sesame Seed Salad
- Ultimate Nourishing Detox Salad
- Chickpea Cucumber Cumin Salad
- Seaweed Salad
- Thai Wraps
- Four-Ingredient Green Salad

— CHOOSE YOUR DINNER:

- Vegetable Soup
- Immune-Boosting Soup
- Vegetable Stir-Fry
- Lemon Thyme Chickpea Fries
- Cauliflower Rice
- Sweet Potato Fries

— CHOOSE YOUR HERBAL TEA:

- Immune-Boosting Tea
- Skin Cleansing Tea
- Bedtime Tea

— CHOOSE YOUR SNACKS:

- Guacamole with carrot sticks
- Hummus with carrot sticks
- Baked Kale Chips
- Blueberry Leather
- Sweet Potato Leather
- Alkalizing Chocolate pHresh Balls

CHAPTER 21

The Detox Guide

"The **liver** is where the bulk of the **detox** chemistry happens, and it **requires** a whole shopping list of natural ingredients, such as **vitamins** and **minerals** found in whole foods as well as a good stock of **antioxidants**."

—Alejandro Junger, M.D.

Let's be realistic: we are human, so we tend to binge here and there, plus we live in a day and age where junk food is always being put in front of our faces. So when you've been tempted and do end up eating something you don't feel entirely good about, here are some things you can do to balance it out. These make your body more alkaline and also help with digestion, both contributing to a detox experience.

Drink This When You Need to Restore Balance After . . .

Green Lemonade ....Overeating

Lemon Water..............Eating candy made from refined sugar and preservatives

Ginger Tea ....Eating processed sweets, like cake or cookies

Fat Blaster.................Eating fried foods, like potato chips

Clay Drink ....Consuming alcohol

Beet Juice ....Overconsumption of meat

Salt Water...................Smoking, or exposure to secondhand smoke

Green tea....................Overconsumption of bread

Morning Detox Practice:

Oil Pulling

Oil pulling is an ancient Ayurvedic dental technique that draws toxins out of your body and reduces the bacterial load in your mouth. It is safe to do every day if you like, or just when you feel a little toxic and want to cleanse. Oral hygiene is important for the health of your teeth, your heart, and your digestive tract.

Do this practice first thing in the morning, for 10 to 20 minutes. Even before brushing your teeth! Be sure to spit out the oil when you're finished rather than swallowing it.

INGREDIENTS:

1 tablespoon sesame seed oil or coconut oil
½ cup salt water (or lemon water or plain warm water), for rinsing

ACTIONS:

- Put oil in your mouth and swish it around your teeth and gums.
- When you feel like you've had enough, spit out the oil in the trash (so as not to clog the sink). Start with 5 minutes at first, then work your way up to 20 as you get more familiar with this practice.
- Rinse your mouth out with salt water, then brush your teeth as you customarily do.

The Three-Day Detox Guide

Most of us indulge in food that our bodies don't tolerate well more often than we should. We are also exposed to environmental pollution. For this reason, I recommend doing the following detox once a month. If you cannot commit to a monthly detox, then at a bare minimum do it once every season: winter, spring, summer, and fall. In between, do the best you can and stick to the Earth Diet.

The basic premise of this three-day detoxifying program is to embody the concept: "Nutrition in, toxins out." This detox isn't about deprivation or starving the body. I view it as "overdosing" the body on nutrition, so that it can basically push the toxins out of the cells itself. Mostly the recipes are for salads and juices—all of which can be prepared in 10 minutes or less.

It's important to drink at least 16 cups of Detox Water every day and go to bed early so you get plenty of rest.

DAY 1

- *After rising:* Oil Pulling for 10 minutes, then drink a Lemon Water.
- *Breakfast:* Detox Juice
- *2 hours later:* Fat Blaster
- *Lunch:* Four-Ingredient Green Salad
- *2 hours later:* Beet Juice
- *Dinner:* Superfood Kale Salad
- *1 hour after dinner:* Clay Drink or bentonite clay capsule
- *Before bed:* Detox Water

Take a sauna for 15 to 30 minutes, and allow yourself to perspire profusely. If you don't have access to a sauna, take a hot bath or go in a steam room.

DAY 2

- *After rising:* Oil Pulling for 10 minutes, then drink a Lemon Water.
- *Breakfast:* Super Greens Juice
- *2 hours later:* Detox Juice
- *Lunch:* Superfood Kale Salad
- *2 hours later:* Fat Blaster
- *Dinner:* Four-Ingredient Green Salad
- *1 hour after dinner:* Clay Drink or bentonite clay capsule
- *Before bed:* Ginger Tea

Do one hour of a cardio workout, making sure that you're sweating and your heart rate is up.

DAY 3

- *After rising:* Oil Pulling for 10 minutes, then drink a Lemon Water.
- *Breakfast:* Detox Juice
- *2 hours later:* Fat Blaster
- *Lunch:* Four-Ingredient Green Salad
- *2 hours later:* Vegetable Smoothie
- *Dinner:* Ultimate Nourishing Detox Salad
- *1 hour after dinner:* Clay Drink or bentonite clay capsule
- *Before Bed:* Weight Loss Tea

Take a hot bath for 15 to 30 minutes with 1 or 2 cups Epsom salts dissolved in the water. The idea is to sweat profusely, so let the water be as hot as you can tolerate without scalding yourself. Use your best judgment on temperature.

CHAPTER 22

The Weight Loss Guide

"My philosophy to food and **healthy eating** has always been about enjoying **everything** in a **balanced** and sane way."

—Jamie Oliver

When the body is energized by receiving good nutrition, weight loss occurs almost effortlessly. For years, I was obsessed with losing weight, but I gained weight because I would binge on junk food after depriving myself. Once I started the Earth Diet, excess weight dropped off me, and I stopped my painful cycle of binge and restriction. I switched my focus to health, feeling good, and freedom from cravings. Obsessing about being skinny doesn't work. Nourishing our bodies with all the nutrients they need *does* work!

Losing weight can often be a matter of simply replacing processed foods with natural, organic, nutrient-rich foods. In my experience, the body will arrive at its natural weight as it gets healthier—gradually or sometimes quickly. The pace of transformation is different for every person. Sometimes the outer shape is changing, though the numbers on the scale are not immediately. If you stay on the earth-friendly path, your body will begin to remodel itself from the inside out. If this becomes a lifestyle.

It's important to maintain hope that you'll experience living in your dream body in this lifetime. The first you'll notice is a bit of relief and increased piece of mind from moving in the right direction. I've worked with clients whose doctors had told them they would never lose weight because of thyroid issues and other metabolic conditions. One lost 30 pounds in eight months on the Earth Diet after 20 years with no progress by following a plan that's like the Seven-Day Plan I'm going to give you here, tailored to her specific flavor preferences.

The way I coach people to lose weight on the Earth Diet is to emphasize detoxification, with recipes that are raw, whole, high in fiber, green, anti-inflammatory, and low in calories. In this guide, I'll give you a daily formula and you will choose from suitable recipe options.

The Seven-Day Weight Loss Formula

Start each day with Lemon Water and Ginger Tea.

FOR BREAKFAST, CHOOSE FROM:
- Super Greens Juice
- Beet Juice
- Fat Blaster

MORNING SNACK:
- A raw fruit or vegetable of your choice.

LUNCH:
- A salad of your choice.

AFTERNOON SNACK:
- A raw fruit or vegetable of your choice.

FOR DINNER, CHOOSE FROM:
- Superfood Kale Salad
- Ultimate Nourishing Detox Salad
- Four-Ingredient Green Salad
- Vegetable Stir-Fry
- Cauliflower Popcorn
- Any of the soups

BEFORE BED:
- Weight Loss Tea

Follow this guide every day for one week.

CHAPTER 23

The Anti-inflammatory, Immune-Boosting, and Healing Guide

> "The literal **meaning** of 'healing' is becoming 'whole.'"
>
> —Andrew Weil, M.D.

We can sometimes forget that it's in our best interest to feel good. When we get sick, we need to make time to take care of ourselves. The body's natural reaction is to do things to get better. It is so smart that it will do whatever needs to be done to heal. What we need to do is deliberately feed it the fuel it needs to run its metabolic processes. If you follow the Earth Diet on an ongoing basis, you'll find you are more energized and less stiff, have fewer aches and pains, sleep better, get fewer colds, and feel more positive. Anytime you feel bloated, puffy, down, or inflamed follow this formula for a day or to improve the situation.

The Anti-inflammatory, Immune-Boosting, and Healing Formula

To reduce inflammation and boost immunity in general, incorporate more anti-inflammatory foods in your diet and avoid things that cause inflammation and weaken the immune system.

AFTER RISING:

- Oil Pulling, then gargle with salt water. Drink a Lemon Water.

BREAKFAST:

- Super Greens Juice and Sick Kick Smoothie

MORNING SNACK:

- Four-Ingredient Green Salad

LUNCH:

- Immune-Boosting Soup

AFTERNOON SNACK:

- 1 stick raw celery and 1 whole cucumber

DINNER:

- Superfood Kale Salad

BEFORE BED:

- Ginger Tea

Top 21 Anti-inflammatory Foods

1. Ginger
2. Kale
3. Spinach
4. Arugula
5. Broccoli
6. Blueberries
7. Cauliflower
8. Onion
9. Garlic
10. Quinoa
11. Turmeric
12. Sweet Potato
13. Extra-virgin olive oil
14. Tigernuts
15. Fatty fish, like salmon and tuna
16. Almonds
17. Walnuts
18. Kelp
19. Mushrooms
20. Green tea
21. Papaya

Top 10 Things That Cause Inflammation

1. Stress
2. Gluten
3. Refined white sugar
4. Wheat
5. Chemicals
6. Dairy
7. Vegetable oils
8. Deep-fried foods
9. Soda
10. Preservative-laden foods, like many dried fruits

CHAPTER 24

The High-Protein Guide for Building Muscle Mass

"Working out gets your body fit, but true results come from what you eat."

—Donovan Green

Protein is one of the three macronutrients (along with carbohydrates and fat) that is essential to us. The by-product of digested protein is amino acids, which are the building blocks of our tissues.

There are many reasons that some people need to eat a higher protein diet. Athletes need protein to build muscle mass and recover after their workouts. I have also coached people who were underweight and wanted to gain weight with high-protein foods. Sometimes when people are in treatment for an illness, protein is called for.

A simple way to add more protein to your diet is to add Super Protein Powder to your soups, salads, smoothies, and cereals. High-protein snacks to reach for include: pumpkin seeds, hemp seeds, peanut butter, almond butter, Brazil nuts, and chickpeas. Make a point of eating high-protein meals, such as the following recipes in this book.

Plant-Based High-Protein Recipes

- Superfood Kale Salad
- High-Protein Granola
- Chia Hemp Seed Cereal
- Protein Salad
- High-Protein Smoothie
- Protein Bars
- Chickpea Burgers
- Hummus
- Bean Burgers
- Zucchini Pasta with Pesto
- Zucchini Spaghetti with Tomato Sauce and Walnut "Meatballs"
- Raw Lasagna
- Breakfast Cereal

Meat-Based High-Protein Recipes

- Almond-Crusted Chicken Tenders
- Chicken Burgers
- Honey Rosemary Chicken
- Honey Rosemary Chicken Wraps
- 10-Minute Beef Burgers
- Beef Burritos
- Beef Tacos
- Simple Fish
- Fish Tacos
- Caramel Shrimp
- Seafood Sticks
- Omelet
- Humpty Dumpty

The Daily High-Protein Meal Guide

AFTER RISING:

- Lemon Water

BREAKFAST:

- High-Protein Smoothie and Omelet or Humpty Dumpty

MORNING SNACK:

- Protein Bar

LUNCH:

- Superfood Kale Salad and Almond-Crusted Chicken Tenders

AFTERNOON SNACK:

- High-Protein Smoothie (make it a nut-topped smoothie bowl for added protein)

DINNER:

- Beef Burritos or Zucchini Spaghetti with Tomato Sauce and Walnut "Meatballs"

DESSERT:

- Chocolate Avocado Brownies, Raw Melt-in-Your-Mouth Chocolate Chip Cookies, or Protein Balls

CHAPTER 25

The Clear, Smooth, Radiant Skin Guide

"The moment you realize that **you create it all**, you will realize that **you can change it all.**"

—Howard Falco

Did you know that the skin . . .

- Is the largest organ of the body?

- Accounts for about 15 percent of our body weight (around 20 pounds for a 130-pound person)?

- Renews itself once a month?

- Gives us clues to changes in our internal health? (Rashes, acne, dryness, and dullness

  can be signs of deeper issues that need our attention and healing.)

- Is our first line of protection from the environment (bacteria, viruses, and pollution)?

- Can react poorly to gluten, dairy, soy, GMOs, and preservatives and other chemicals?

- Deserves our love and support?

After people have been following the Earth Diet for a while, they begin to glow as if they are illuminated from the inside out. This radiance is the result of receiving optimal nutrition. For skin you'll love the rest of your life, there are six main things to do:

---

1. Juice daily. This gives your cells a high dose of vitamins.

2. Remember, if you cannot eat it, do not put it on your skin. Your skin absorbs absolutely everything you put on it, so you must feed it well.

3. Every time you feel frustrated about your skin, look in the mirror and say, "I accept myself." Let this affirmation replace habitual negative feelings and self-criticism. (Never underestimate the power of affirmations. They have assisted in my transformation. Just try it!)

4. Drink plenty of water throughout the day. Make at least one glass of your water a Lemon Water.

5. Replace processed foods with fresh, raw, whole foods whenever possible. Aim for 70 percent raw intake.

6. Give your skin a quick wipe before bed each night with a toner made from equal parts water and apple cider vinegar. Apply with an organic cotton pad.

The One-Day Radiant Skin Formula

One of the ways we can promote this effect instantly is to nourish the body directly through the skin. The following is a formula for a one-day regimen of skin care. I recommend my clients follow this protocol once a month to help maintain clear, healthy skin and prevent wrinkles. It can also be useful for treating acne, scars, psoriasis, eczema, warts, and other skin conditions. What you eat and drink, and what you do, will be detoxifying and nourishing.

When you follow the One-Day Radiant Skin Formula, be sure to treat yourself as if you're at a high-quality beauty spa. Because of the nature of this regimen, I find that it's best done on a weekend when you have a whole day to pamper yourself and few obligations. If you wish to go deeper in healing your skin, try the Detox Guide.

— After rising, drink a glass of Lemon Water followed by a cup of Ginger Tea. Make up a triple-sized batch of Beauty Water to drink throughout the day.

— For breakfast, have a smoothie within an hour or so of rising. Choose from: Vegetable Smoothie, Antioxidant Vitamin Blast Smoothie, or Sick Kick Smoothie.

— Apply a Bentonite Clay Mask: Mix 1 teaspoon bentonite clay powder with 1 teaspoon water in a nonmetal bowl. Spread evenly on your face and neck, let rest for 50 minutes, then rinse your face with warm water.

(Optional hair mask: Double the recipe, and spread half the clay through your hair. To rinse your hair, you'll need to take a shower or a bath. If you run a bath, you can dunk your whole head underwater and then spend a few minutes soaking before giving yourself a final rinse in a shower. Your hair will be luxurious and shiny, and your entire body will feel silky smooth.)

A NOTE ON CLAY FACE MASKS: Bentonite clay, which is formed from volcanic ash, is high in minerals. When applied as a mask, it draws toxins—including heavy metals—out of the skin, shrinks pores, exfoliates, reduces the appearance of scars, and evens out skin tone.

It's important to remain completely still and silent for 50 minutes as the mask sets and does its job on your skin. While you're in repose, relax and repeat one of the following affirmations in your head (or substitute one of your own): "I accept myself," "I deserve smooth, clear, radiant skin," "I am beautiful."

You can expect to feel minor discomfort while you are wearing the mask. Many people report itching, tingling, and a kind of tightness. If you can hold completely still and tolerate it—not smiling, not gabbing on the phone—in my opinion, you're going to appreciate the results the most. Trust your intuition about the sensations you feel. If you rinse off sooner, you'll still get the benefit of detoxification and mineral enrichment. It's safe to repeat this face mask once a week.

— For your morning snack, sip a Green Lemonade while letting your face "air out."

— Apply an Avocado Face Mask to feed your skin with omega-3 fatty acids, antioxidants, and deep, penetrating hydration. Mash 1 ripe avocado with 1 teaspoon cacao powder (optional) until smooth. Apply mixture to your face and neck. Relax with cucumber slices over your eyes for 10 minutes, then rinse away with warm water. Pat your skin dry with a soft, fluffy towel.

— Lightly moisturize your whole body. Choose from: olive oil, coconut oil, tigernut oil, melted cacao butter, or aloe vera (fresh is best).

When I do this at home, I disrobe and apply the oil in front of a mirror, giving me the opportunity to connect with every inch of my skin in a loving manner.

— For lunch, have the Four-Ingredient Green Salad. It's light and alkalizing.

— For an afternoon snack, have 1 large whole cucumber.

— For dinner, have the Superfood Kale Salad.

— Before bed, drink a mug of Goddess Beauty Tea. Rub the inner flesh of an aloe vera plant over your face (avoiding your eyes) and let the juice seep in overnight.

In the morning, you should feel thoroughly refreshed and energized, and you'll look great. Your skin should be plump and practically shooting off sparks because your skin was so well fed.

CHAPTER 26

The Kid-Friendly Guide

"You're off to **great** places!
Today is your **day!**
Your **mountain** is waiting.
So . . . get on your **way!"**

—Dr. Seuss

Healthy food can be easy and fun, full of colors and flavors. If kids have a chance to touch their food and get a friendly feeling for it early in life, they'll develop a lifelong love of wholesome ingredients—and they'll enjoy food preparation, too. Making Raw Three-Ingredient Chocolate Balls or Raw Melt-in-Your-Mouth Chocolate Chip Cookies, for example, is awesome! Molding them into balls by rolling them in the palms of your hands, and then popping those perfect-sized balls into your mouth is a joyous and giggle-inducing experience no kid should miss.

Perhaps best of all, when kids are eating Earth Diet recipes, you know they're being properly nourished and getting every nutrient necessary for them to grow up strong and healthy. All while eating their favorite all-natural flavors!

Safety first! While all of the recipes in this guide are kid-friendly, if you're a parent or a babysitter, help younger children operate the stove or oven, run juicers and blenders, and chop vegetables with a knife. Use common sense about what is age appropriate in your household. If you're a kid, check with an adult before you use the stove or oven, sharp knives, and other equipment.

10 Tips for Kids Who Want to Grow Up Healthy

If you want to get good grades and have fun with your friends, you need a brain and body that are well nourished. You'll always have energy if you eat this way. When you're older and done with school and going after your dreams, you'll look back at your choices now and be proud if you made healthy choices. Start now while you're young. Kids who do lead better lives.

Here are 10 ways to grow up healthy.

1. Drink a fresh vegetable juice every day. This will give you a great start to your life!

2. Sing a song when you gather ingredients and clean the juice machine to make it more fun!

3. Ask your teachers and principal to have me come to the school to talk to your class about healthy living and nutrition! Send an e-mail to info@theearthdiet.org.

4. Always have your favorite Earth Diet desserts in the fridge and freezer.

5. Help your parents in the kitchen when making food. Learn as much as you can because one day you'll be living without them and you'll have to take care of yourself.

6. Be sure to have a big, bright, colorful Fruit Platter at your next birthday party!

7. Drink a delicious smoothie every day.

8. Take nutrient-rich lunches to school every day. Be cool and be a leader: show your classmates how to be healthy!

9. When you have a junk food craving, choose a healthier snack "upgrade"!

10. Have breakfast for dinner by making Smoothie Bowls. Make it bright and beautiful with tons of toppings. Post a picture of your work of art on Instagram and tag it #10MinuteRecipes.

The Most Popular Kid-Friendly Recipes

Kids are smart. They know what they like. Why not give it to them if it's healthy? From working with parents, I've learned that kids' favorite recipes to make and eat are:

- Raw Three-Ingredient Chocolate Balls
- Chocolate Avocado Tigernut Brownies
- Raw Melt-in-Your-Mouth Chocolate Chip Cookies
- ABC Juice
- Apple Juice
- Green Lemonade
- Kids' Paradise Juice
- Chocolate Shake
- Strawberry Milk
- Chocolate Peanut Butter Smoothie
- Lemon Water (and Lemon Ice Cubes!)
- Fruit Water
- Beginners' Breakfast Bowl
- Kids' Happy Face Breakfast Bowl
- Humpty Dumpty
- Fruit Leathers
- Sandwich Stack
- Zucchini Spaghetti with Tomato Sauce and Walnut "Meatballs"
- Chocolate Avocado Mousse
- Fruit Skewers
- Fruit Platter
- Baked Cauliflower Popcorn
- Fruit and Nut Bar
- Chickpea Fries
- Beef Burritos
- Almond-Crusted Chicken Tenders
- Taco Salad
- Raw Lemon Coconut Date Bars
- Instant Ice Cream

Kids (and adults) can eat as many whole raw fruits and vegetables as they want for snacks. Good snacks include: 1 cucumber, ½ avocado, 1 celery stick, a handful of raw broccoli, a handful of raw cauliflower, 1 orange, 1 apple, 1 pear, and 1 banana; or try: 1 spoonful of hemp seeds, sunflower seeds, pumpkin seeds, tigernuts, or walnuts.

Big Batch, Shareable Snacks for BFFs

- Mix up a large batch of Lemon Water and Fruit Water and keep it in your fridge to drink for a whole week. When your BFF comes over, offer him or her a refreshing drink so you both have more energy to play! These drinks go great with a Tigernut Raw Chocolate Brownie.

- Make a large batch of Raw Melt-in-Your-Mouth Chocolate Chip Cookies and keep them in the fridge for a week! Ask your parents to keep the freezer stocked. If you ever have a fight with a brother or sister, one of these will help you make peace. Be sure to give one to the new kid on your block.

- Once a month, make a huge batch of Fruit Leathers and hand them out to the kids in your class. It's just fruit, so even many of the kids with allergies can enjoy these treats a lot.

- Fill a couple of ice cube trays with Lemon Water. Stick a blueberry in the middle for decoration. These will keep you hydrated and give you nice clear skin. Pop one out and add it to a juice, smoothie, or infused water.

The 5-Day Menu for Kids

An idea of what to eat in one day for a well-balanced diet of protein, antioxidants, vitamins, minerals, and essential fatty acids.

DAY 1

- After rising: Lemon Water
- Breakfast: Kids' Happy Face Breakfast Bowl and Green Lemonade
- Morning snack: Grapes
- Lunch: Sandwich Stack
- Afternoon snack: Raw Lemon Coconut Date Bar
- Dinner: Almond-Crusted Chicken Tenders with Mango Avocado Salad
- Dessert: Mini Cashew Cheesecake

DAY 2

- After rising: Lemon Water
- Breakfast: Humpty Dumpty and ABC Juice
- Morning snack: Strawberry Milk
- Lunch: Chicken Burrito
- Afternoon snack: Blueberries
- Dinner: Baked Cauliflower Popcorn

DAY 3

- After rising: Lemon Water
- Breakfast: Beginners' Breakfast Bowl
- Morning snack: Baked Kale Chips
- Lunch: Taco Salad
- Afternoon snack: Fruit Leathers
- Dinner: Tigernut Chicken Tenders
- Dessert: Fruit Skewer

DAY 4

- After rising: Fruit Water
- Breakfast: Perfect Porridge and Kids' Paradise Juice
- Morning snack: Fruit and Nut Bar
- Lunch: Walnut "Meatballs"
- Afternoon snack: Tigernuts
- Dinner: Chickpea Fries with steamed or raw vegetables
- Dessert: Instant Ice Cream

DAY 5

- After rising: Fruit Water
- Breakfast: Apple Juice and Humpty Dumpty
- Morning snack: Raw carrots dipped into Hummus
- Lunch: Chocolate Avocado Mousse and raw broccoli
- Afternoon snack: Protein Bar
- Dinner: Beef Tacos
- Dessert: Raw Melt-in-Your-Mouth Chocolate Chip Cookies

RECIPE LIST

Metric Conversion Chart

The recipes in this book use the standard United States method for measuring liquid and dry or solid ingredients (teaspoons, tablespoons, and cups). The following charts are provided to help cooks outside the U.S. successfully use these recipes. All equivalents are approximate.

Standard Cup	Fine Powder (e.g., flour)	Grain (e.g., rice)	Granular (e.g., sugar)	Liquid Solids (e.g., butter)	Liquid (e.g., milk)
1	140 g	150 g	190 g	200 g	240 ml
¾	105 g	113 g	143 g	150 g	180 ml
⅔	93 g	100 g	125 g	133 g	160 ml
½	70 g	75 g	95 g	100 g	120 ml
⅓	47 g	50 g	63 g	67 g	80 ml
¼	35 g	38 g	48 g	50 g	60 ml
⅛	18 g	19 g	24 g	25 g	30 ml

Useful Equivalents for Liquid Ingredients by Volume				
¼ tsp				1 ml
½ tsp				2 ml
1 tsp				5 ml
3 tsp	1 tbsp		½ fl oz	15 ml
	2 tbsp	⅛ cup	1 fl oz	30 ml
	4 tbsp	¼ cup	2 fl oz	60 ml
	5⅓ tbsp	⅓ cup	3 fl oz	80 ml
	8 tbsp	½ cup	4 fl oz	120 ml
	10⅔ tbsp	⅔ cup	5 fl oz	160 ml
	12 tbsp	¾ cup	6 fl oz	180 ml
	16 tbsp	1 cup	8 fl oz	240 ml
	1 pt	2 cups	16 fl oz	480 ml
	1 qt	4 cups	32 fl oz	960 ml
			33 fl oz	1000 ml	1 l

Useful Equivalents for Dry Ingredients by Weight

(To convert ounces to grams, multiply the number of ounces by 30.)

1 oz	1/16 lb	30 g
4 oz	1/4 lb	120 g
8 oz	1/2 lb	240 g
12 oz	3/4 lb	360 g
16 oz	1 lb	480 g

Useful Equivalents for Cooking/Oven Temperatures

Process	Fahrenheit	Celsius	Gas Mark
Freeze Water	32° F	0° C	
Room Temperature	68° F	20° C	
Boil Water	212° F	100° C	
Bake	325° F	160° C	3
	350° F	180° C	4
	375° F	190° C	5
	400° F	200° C	6
	425° F	220° C	7
	450° F	230° C	8
Broil			Grill

Useful Equivalents for Length

(To convert inches to centimeters, multiply the number of inches by 2.5.)

1 in			2.5 cm	
6 in	1/2 ft		15 cm	
12 in	1 ft		30 cm	
36 in	3 ft	1 yd	90 cm	
40 in			100 cm	1 m

> At the Earth Diet, we're committed to supporting you in leading a natural, earth-friendly lifestyle. To this end, we have created lifestyle and eating programs catering to your specific needs.

Earth Diet Health Coaching

Work with me or another personal health coach to meet your personal dietary and lifestyle goals. We create personalized programs for each individual. Our coaching is for people whose goal is to take their health to the next level and experience transformative results, whether that means moving toward healing acne, diabetes, or cancer, or simply losing excess weight and gaining more energy. Those who receive coaching are held accountable for achieving their goals and get to experience powerful results.

While the Earth Diet is free for everyone to do, Earth Diet coaching is for people who want to commit to this lifestyle fully and want guidance at every step. The coaches on my team can teach you all the tools you need to live a powerful, natural lifestyle that you love. We look at the toxicities in your lifestyle and make a strategy with you to incorporate more nature, one step at a time. For more details, visit TheEarthDiet.com/health-coaches.

Connect with Me via Social Networks

I would love to connect with you after you've read this book. To keep in touch, either e-mail me and my team directly at info@theearthdiet.org, or join me through my various social media accounts.

FACEBOOK: Facebook.com/theearthdiet and Facebook.com/LianaWernerGray
TWITTER: Twitter.com/theearthdieter
PINTEREST: Pinterest.com/theearthdiet
INSTAGRAM: Instagram.com/theearthdiet

Connect with Me Live On Air

Tune in to my radio show on www.HayHouseRadio.com. You can connect for free from anywhere in the world through the internet or the free phone app. Each week I take callers live on air and give away hundreds of dollars worth of organic goodies.

Read My Original Blog

This is where the Earth Diet started. Fed up with a five-year addiction to junk food and binge eating, I created a challenge for myself to end the vicious cycle by eating only unrefined organic foods for the next 365 days. The posts focus on leading a wholesome lifestyle and offering hundreds of delicious and healing recipes. TheEarthDiet.blogspot.com

Earth Diet Food Demonstrations and Lectures

I frequently travel the world to give cooking demonstrations and food lectures. An appearance might include a demonstration on how to make raw chocolate balls, or some helpful tips on self-healing. To see when I might be coming to a town near you, visit TheEarthDiet.com/events.

To book me for your event, e-mail: info@theearthdiet.org.

Discounts and Recommended Brands

For a list of the first things to purchase as you begin the Earth Diet lifestyle, items that will assist you in living your healthiest life in only minutes a day, go to Vitacost.com/TheEarthDiet.

On that webpage, you'll find a shopping guide there and discount codes for online purchases of quality brands like Vitamix high-speed blenders, juice machines, pHresh Greens, Redmond Clay (bentonite), Real Salt, and Organic Gemini TigerNut products, and Earth Diet Raw Chocolate Cups and Bars, and more.

For a free book gift, visit
TheEarthDiet.com/10minutegift.

BIBLIOGRAPHY

Altered States. Managing Your Body's pH Levels. http://altered-states.net/barry/update178.

Cameron, Julia. *The Artist's Way*. New York: J.P. Tarcher, 1992.

Chopra, M.D., Deepak and David Simon, M.D. *Grow Younger, Liver Longer*.
New York: Harmony Books, 2001.

Falco, Howard. *I Am*. New York: J.P. Tarcher, 2010.

Green, Donovan. Private correspondence.

Hay, Louise. *Heal Your Life Blog*. http://www.healyourlife.com/my-vegetable-garden.

Hyman, M.D., Mark. *The Blood Sugar Solution 10-Day Detox Diet*. New York:
Little, Brown and Company, 2014.

Junger, M.D., Alejandro. *Clean,* expanded edition.
San Francisco, CA: HarperOne, 2012.

Kaytor, Marilyn. "Condiments: The Tastemakers," *Look*, January 1963.

Mateljan, George. *The World's Healthiest Foods*.
Seattle, WA: George Mateljan Foundation, 2007.

Nachmanovitch, Stephen. *Free Play*.
New York: J.P. Tarcher/Putnam, 1990.

Nobelprize.org. *The Nobel Prize in Physiology or Medicine 1931,
Otto Warburg*. http://www.nobelprize.org/nobel_prizes/medicine/laureates/1931/warburg-bio.html.

Northrup, M.D., Christiane, *Food Matters* (blog).
http://foodmatters.tv/articles-1/the-hormone-balancing-food-plan-for-women.

Oliver, Jamie. *Jamie Oliver* (website).
JamieOliver.com/philosophy.

Robbins, Anthony. *Awaken the Giant Within*.
New York: Free Press, 1991.

Dr. Seuss. *Oh, the Places You'll Go*.
New York: Random House, 1990.

Shaw, Nancy Elizabeth. *Green Med Info* (blog).
http://www.greenmedinfo.com/blog/why-alkaline-approach-can-successfully-treat-cancer.

Weil, M.D., Andrew. *Spontaneous Healing*. New York: Alfred A. Knopf, 1995.

ACKNOWLEDGMENTS

> "**We** need the **support of others** to make lasting shifts in how we eat, move, **and live. We're better together**—it's as simple as **that.**"
>
> —Mark Hyman, M.D.

Thank you to all my supporters, the people who are grateful, and readers of *The Earth Diet*.

Thank you to all the passionate cooks for sharing my recipes and requesting that I address the topic of quick healthy food. Thank you for encouraging me to do what I love doing.

These Acknowledgments would not be complete without honoring our beautiful Mother Earth for the goodness provided. To be able to nourish our beautiful bodies with the abundant offerings in 10 minutes or less is a truly epic thing.

Thank you to the Hay House team in the United States. Thank you, Reid Tracy, Patty Gift, Stacey Smith, Nicolette Salamanca Young, Bryn Starr Best, Chelsea Larson, Aurora Rosas, and Richelle Zizian for doing such a great job in producing this book. Thank you to the Hay House team in the United Kingdom: Ruth Tewkesbury, Michelle Pilley, Joe Burgess, Diane Hill, George Lizos, and Jessica Gibson. Thank you to the Hay House Radio team: Diane Ray, Steve Morris, Rocky George III, Mike Joseph, and Rachel Michelle,.

Thank you to my developmental editor, Stephanie Gunning. It was fun working side-by-side with you in NYC, snacking on raw 10-minute goodies, eating French fries and raw chocolate, and dancing around to celebrate each of the chapters we completed.

Ken Petersen, you are a true legend. You came through for my deadline at the last minute. Thank you for providing the nutritional information for every recipe in the book. The readers will appreciate this contribution forever. Not only are you a great Earth Diet Health Coach, you are a reliable, amazing human being.

Thank you, Wayne Dyer, for your generosity and love.

Thank you, Dr. Mark Hyman, for writing the foreword to this book. You are one of the most inspiring doctors on the planet.

Thank you, Roxana Ireland, for your friendship, support, amazing vegan cooking, and photography for the front cover and interior! You are truly epic and one of the most talented people I know—as I always tell you, lol! I appreciate how harmonious and beautiful our relationship is. You are a wonderful artist and soulful human being. I am so grateful for you in my life.

Thank you, Andrew Davis. You are a beautiful angel in my life.

Thank you to one of my favorite teams on the planet, Vitacost: Rebecca Choplin, Jay Topper, David Beren, Brian Helman, Tammy Rothman, Jorie Mark, Vee Sohan, and Lisa Weinberger.

Thank you, Darryl Bosshardt and the team at Redmond. I was the luckiest girl in the world to be able to visit your farm in Utah; that was a dream come true!

Thank you to Howard Hoffman, CEO of Phresh Greens, for your ongoing support. It's been such an incredible journey of growth.

Thank you to George and Miriam Papanastasatos, founders of Organic Gemini TigerNuts. I absolutely love working with you guys and the rest of the incredible team. You guys have made such an impact on my life—more than you know.

Thank you to Explore Cuisine, to the amazing team: Erika Wasserman, Jim Magner, and Joe Spronz. Pasta is so back, thanks to you guys. Joe, you will forever have the legacy of being one of the most amazing food scientists on the planet.

Thank you, Noah Loin, aka the Raw Chocolate Man, for your love, support, faith, and raw chocolate. Thank you for introducing me to Chickpea Fries and natural margaritas, and for the tip on how to get salt on the margarita glass—haha! The Chicken Tender recipe is for you. Thank you so much, Jody and John Loin. I love you guys forever.

Thank you to the brilliant Nutiva team, especially Madalyn Crum. John Roulac, you are such an inspiring leader, and now you've just done it again by making chocolate hazelnut butter. Now my life is complete—haha.

Thank you to my family for your support and solid love. You give me a foundation every single day that gives me strength. To my sisters: Nadine Gray, you are amazing and inspiring, my rock. Caitlin, I love you so much and can't wait to hug you again. To my Aunty Tammy, for being incredible and unstoppable, and for helping me deal with the haters. Thank you for giving me stripes—haha. To my uncle Unc and my cousin and godson, Bernie, thank you for brightening my life and being so cool. To my beautiful Nanna, you are so great! I love you so much and am always thinking of you gathering postcards from around the world. To Laurie, thank you for loving my Nanna so much and for being in our lives. To Rock, for promoting me in the Australian mining community—still, to this day, no one makes a better Humpty Dumpty than you! You really showed me how to boil eggs well. To my father, Bernard Werner, for passing down your great chef genes to me. To my strong mother, Vicki Gray, for sharing your green-thumb wisdom with me; I have learned so much from you. I love you forever.

Carol Lucas, you are family. Thank you for your consistent rock solid love and support—and making the best chicken pasta dish ever! Thank you also for the Lemon Ice Cube idea. I love our feasts together. You have been vital in my growth. Thank you for loving me so well. My words cannot explain how grateful I am for you.

Thank you to the Earth Diet team. You guys are my biggest supporters: Jason Colchiski, Mila and Lynn Hover, Debra Thacker, Sheila O'Brien, Ken Petersen, Renee Resnansky, Susan Misuraca, and Dave Tesla. Susie Tesla, thank you for everything, including letting me know that one of your favorite snacks is Mango Salsa, so I could make an Earth Diet version. The salsa recipes are dedicated to you, beautiful. Thank you, as always, to Demetra and Eleni Simos. Jason Colchiski, thank you as always for reminding me to include the research on the Nobel Prize–winner Dr. Otto Heinrich, who proved that cancer cannot live in an alkaline state.

Thank you to the Earth Diet Health Coaches for whom I am incredibly grateful: Mila Hover, Amanda Martindale, Andrew Braum, Angelina Ireland, Ann Gaboriault, Carrie Miller, Courtney Kohout, Cynthia Leeder, Danielle Winning, Elizabeth Corso, Emily Rose Shaw, Jennifer Ritter Russo, Jessica Bahr, Jessie Jean, Jessie Miller, Jo Grabyn, Kailey Donewald, Kathleen Barkley, Maura Nash Kennedy, Nick Fairbairn, Raini Forrest, Renee Resnansky, Renique Webster, Stephanie Clark, Summer Williams, Terry Hodges, Marcie Wingfield Shanks, Morena Escardo, and Zahra Carpenter.

Thank you to the Earth Diet Ambassadors: Kimberly Rossa, Derek Hall, Marie Wellens, and Debra Toomey.

Thank you to my friends: Marc Bryan Brown (it's always so fun to take photos with you in NYC—haha); Robert Scott Bell (I learned many of my radio skills from you—haha); Donovan Green (I am so grateful for your energy in my life); Lynnette Pate and our powerful prayers; Heidi Williams, soul sister; Angelina Brown (I love our time together); Salvatore Fiteni; and Ali Craddock in Australia.

Thank you, Jill DeJong, for your friendship. It blows my mind every day how beautiful you are.

Thank you, Monica Rowsom. You are the greatest client ever. Health coaching you has never been so enjoyable. I am so grateful to have built an incredible friendship. Alexander Rowsom, the Chicken Noodle Soup recipe is for you. The Taco Sauce recipe is for you, Peter Rowsom. Looking forward to your organic burgers again—haha.

Thank you, Lauri Thoday, for being a strong foundation for me and being a woman of God, which empowered me so much during the manuscript deadline process.

Thank you, Camille Turner, for being tenacious and unstoppable in your healing journey.

Thank you to the NY Hair Co team, Andrew Gould, Marie, and Olga.

Thank you, Craig and Jasmine Margulies and Heather Siegel from Organic Corner in Long Island, NY. I am always thinking about you guys, more than you know!

Thank you, Shawn Bowman, for reminding me to add Baked Kale Chips to the book when I met you on a plane that one time.

Thank you, Thomas Daniel, for your pug love, of course.

Thank you, Danielle Daugherty, for your amazing sister love. And Aden for blessing us all with his spark.

Thank you to Courtney Wiesman; I love how our friendship is blossoming. Girl, I am so grateful for your vibrant energy in my life and for having a brunette other half, lol. Real women don't cry, they wine—haha. Mazel tov.

Linda Hines-Skinner, you are an amazing Earth Angel. Thank you for keeping my skin so vibrant and clear with Herbal Face Foods.

To my amazing dedicated readers and passionate health sharers:

Stephanie Sheldon, the Pad Thai recipe is for you. I also hope you enjoy the array of vegan breakfasts, especially the Smoothie Bowls and Chia Seed Cereal to fill you up and start your day off right! I also cannot decide if I like the cookies better raw or baked, so usually I eat half the cookie dough raw and bake the other half—lol.

Thank you, Tina Woods, for realizing the importance of a good breakfast! I hope you enjoy the nourishing breakfasts and quality quick dinner options. I have dedicated the Red Curry Ramen Noodles to you, and I think you will also love the Curry Chickpea Fries and the Thai Curry Dressing for salads and stir fries. Curry and turmeric is one of my favorite flavor combinations, too—cheers to that, Tina!

Robin Dalton, enjoy the desserts and adult beverages!

Farzaneh Kazemi, enjoy the High-Protein Guide and all the deliciousness you get to eat to build your new body!

Kylie Innes, I hope you enjoy the gluten-free sauces and sides and that they are everything you imagined!

Karen Marley, I am happy I could fulfill most of your "dream list" of recipes to make in 10 minutes or less! Enjoy the Black Bean Burger, Burritos, Tacos, Granola Bars, Raw Pecan Pie, Cauliflower Popcorn, Vegan Nachos, and the Coffee Milk. I am excited for you to try it all!

Hetty de Vries, enjoy the Vegetable Stir Fry and the Cauliflower Rice, which can be a great base for any amazing vegetable dish!

Jopy Wikana, the colorful dishes are for you: the Smoothie Bowls, Fruit & Veggie Platters, and Parfaits. Enjoy the beautiful vibrant dishes that remind me of you!

Hartini, enjoy the fish recipes: the Fish Fingers, 10-Minute Fish and Chips, and Fish Tacos. I have officially dedicated the 10-Minute Fish Burgers to you!

Tania Fraillon, I am so happy you enjoy a balance of both meat eaters' recipes as well as raw vegan foods! Enjoy the dessert recipes, too. I am confident these recipes are tasty enough to make that weight loss easier.

Hazel Pardinas, enjoy the varieties of cooked vegan dishes to make it easier (and more delicious) for you to eat more plants and less meat!

Jill Meendering, for your family who enjoy both raw vegan and meat eaters' dishes! Enjoy the nourishment as well as joyful eating.

Izabela Zawadzki, enjoy the raw vegan dishes, especially the salad jars. I am excited to hear how you enjoy them with your family, friends, and even strangers!

Collette Pasos, the Mason Jar Salads are for you! Enjoy the greens, corn, red onions, seeds, etc., all tossed into a bowl that looks absolutely vibrant and yummy. I think you will love the taco salad, too.

Debbie Firbank of Henley on Klip: I wanted to acknowledge you for nourishing people with fresh food in South Africa! I hope you enjoy the salad recipes in this book.

Rosie Pineda, I hope you enjoy the plant-based dishes that will nourish your absolutely beautiful body from the inside out and have you feeling healed, whole, loved, and fulfilled!

De Luna, I hope my Sides and Sauces recipes have met your expectations. I hope they will continue to excite you throughout the rest of your life as you share these dishes with family and friends! Enjoy.

Y. Holland, enjoy the bowls and meat eaters' dishes! I am loving the bowls these days, such a fun, vibrant, and delicious way to eat.

Sherry O., I am so excited for you to try the smoothie bowls and hear which one is your favorite.

Kim Propp Belcheff, thank you for your review and for being a lover of clean, beautiful, healthy, natural lifestyles.

Brenda Hill, I agree, and The Earth Diet isn't a typical "diet" as we know it—just a natural lifestyle that we can enjoy for the rest of our lives. I am so glad that I included adult beverages in this book; I really hope you enjoy them, especially the Pina Colada.

Trena, I hope you enjoy the sides and sauces.

Heather (Hr352002) you are amazing; thank you for gifting copies of The Earth Diet to your loved ones. I hope you enjoy this book as much as the first, especially the cocktails and the warmer winter foods, like the 10-Minute Soups. I made sure to put plenty of appetizers in this book for you.

Alexis, I hope your dream comes true to start up a wholesome organic vegan fast food chain; it sounds amazing, and you know I would eat there all the time—haha. Enjoy the new raw vegan and cooked vegan recipes in this book.

Glen Stokol, thank you for your list and requesting raw vegan main dishes and cooked vegan main dishes. I really hope you enjoy them and am looking forward to hearing about your favorite one.

Samantha Barrow, thank you for your beautiful blessings. I hope you enjoy the new vegan main dishes.

DeAnna Willman from Levelland, Texas, I am sure you will appreciate how easy it is to make these main veggie meals. Enjoy—they are dedicated to you.

Karen Sacco, the chocolate coconut balls in this book are officially dedicated to you.

Gaby Cuellar, I hope you have fun making the cooked vegan dishes and desserts in this book.

Marie-Lou Levesque, the quick bowl recipes are dedicated to you and your family. I am excited to see your pics of the breakfast bowl with nuts and fresh fruits. Thank you for crowning me Queen of Desserts; I respectfully accept that designation—haha! I am sure you and your 4-year-old will love the new recipes in this book. Thank you.

Ramona Ibbotson, thank you so much. I hope you enjoy the main meals, both the vegan and meat eaters'.

Jayashree Acharia, enjoy the cooked vegan dishes while you are on your happier, healthier, balanced journey!

Bhupi Rajput, the salty gluten-free recipes are dedicated to you. I admire your audacity to convert recipes even if they end up a huge mess—lol. I think you will love the Chickpea Fries, and you can add them to a salad!

Nathalie Thibault, I hope you love the new recipes. I am looking forward to hearing about which ones are your favorites.

Hersh, the raw vegan main meals are dedicated to you. Enjoy all the variations; there is so much you can do with them.

Zahra Atwi, I have included plenty of cooked vegan dishes in here. Thank you for requesting them! Excited to hear which one is your favorite.

Jacqueline Taylor, it's such an honor to hear your positive feedback. The Cashew Oat Raw Cookie Dough is dedicated to you; enjoy that for breakfast, raw or baked! Add some cacao powder for those days when you want more chocolate. The Melt-in-Your-Mouth Chocolate Chip Cookies have become my all-time favorite cookie recipe; I hope you enjoy them as well. I hope to hear about the variations you create, like that Chocolate Mint Breakfast cookie, which sounds so wonderful! Just add a drop or 2 of essential mint oil and then invite me over; we can enjoy them with a cup of tea—hehe! The tea will represent our fire element, for the warming healing benefits for the body. Thank you so much for standing at the mountaintop and for yelling THE EARTH DIET. It's up to us to keep spreading the word.

Mitra Mohaselli and Kay, enjoy the raw vegan main dishes.

Marilyn Baxter-Fuller, the Butternut Squash Ramen is dedicated to you! And please add some cubes of fried eggplant (in olive oil) on top as a variation to make it even more delicious.

Annie Graham-Coleman, thank you for reminding me to include a grocery list. I hope the vegan meals inspire you!

Kris (rgklwarn), enjoy the super-low-carb recipes in the book, especially the salads and smoothie bowls that help reduce blood pressure. Thank you for being an awesome human being, too! Go team!

Olivia Grange, I have dedicated the Vegetable Stir Fry in this book to you. I hope you enjoy all the different variations that can be made from this base.

Deborah, I have dedicated the Chocolate Coconut Acai Smoothie Bowl (which is a variation of the Chocolate Acai Bowl) to you. You can enjoy this for dessert and add your favorite toppings to it.

Natayla Bazz, I have officially dedicated the popular Vegan Sour Cream to you! I hope it impresses you and that you can enjoy it with friends on salads, in tacos, or with crackers and raw vegetables. There's so much you can do with it. I think you will also love the pizzas in this book, the vegan cheese, Bean Burgers, and Acai Bowls. And enjoy the amazing Smoothie Bowl combinations! I don't think we could ever get bored, lol.

Louise D'Amato, I hope you enjoy the abundance of cooked vegan recipes.

Kristin Sciarra, you are so beautiful. I have officially dedicated the Chicken Pad Thai to you! It is a variation of the Vegan Pad Thai, and you can use the organic chicken you have been getting from the farm.

George Lizos, the Cosmopolitan is for you.

The Strawberry Daiquiri is for my sisters, Nadine and Caity.

The Bloody Mary is for you, David Masters and Diane Ray. Diane, just add some cayenne pepper to make it hotter.

The refreshing Mojito is for Courtney Kohout and Jessie Jean. I hope you enjoy it on the beach somewhere amazing.

I am proud to say the Espresso Martini is dedicated to Nadine Gray, Tara Stewart, Shanna Stein, and Lisa Kulakowski.

The Moscow Mule is for you, Colleen Sanford, Diane Ray, and Elicia Thoday. Elicia, yay, Tito's gluten-free party in the USA—haha.

The Mudslide is for you, Shawn Chapman. Cheers, mate!

The beautiful Citrus and Elderflower Cocktail is for you, Giselle Pahlevani!

Finally, I want to thank the people who inspire and empower me with their example: Anita Moorjani, Joel Osteen, Doreen Virtue, Kyle Gray, Tara Stiles, Teal Swan, Deepak Chopra, Oprah Winfrey, Ellen DeGeneres, Eminem, Mehmet Oz, Representative Tim Ryan, Bruce Lipton, Esther Hicks, Cara Delevingne, Suki Waterhouse, Ellie Goulding, Kris Carr, Vani Hari (aka Food Babe), Natalie Jill, Dr. Mike Dow, Mother Teresa, Princess Diana, Gandhi, and the great divine source, God. Thank you, Eckhart Tolle, for reminding me in *The Power of Now*: "I will create no more pain for myself. I will create no more problems. You won't make that choice unless you are truly fed up with suffering, unless you have truly had enough."

Thank you to the sunshine that truly warms my body from the inside out.

Again, thank you to our beautiful, wonderful Earth, for your wisdom and plentiful luscious lands, fruits, and vegetables. Especially thank you for cacao powder!

author photo: © RoxxeIreland

Liana Werner-Gray is a holistic and natural health advocate whose mission is to help people heal with nutrition and lifestyle choices. After being hit with a string of diagnoses, including a golf-ball-sized tumor in her lymphatic system, chronic fatigue, Epstein-Barr Virus, and disordered eating, Liana created an online blog, The Earth Diet, to hold herself accountable for her health. Upon regaining her energy and vitality through embracing a natural lifestyle, Liana wrote the best-selling book *The Earth Diet* and began lecturing and teaching internationally.

Today, as the founder of The Earth Diet, Inc., Liana directs a team of health coaches that helps people all over the world find recipes that work for them. Through her company, she has helped thousands of people improve, and in some cases even entirely heal, conditions such as acne, addictions, cancer, diabetes, depression, heart disease, thyroid issues, obesity, and more. She continues promoting a natural lifestyle through avenues such as her weekly radio show on Hay-HouseRadio.com.

Liana was born and raised in Australia and now resides in New York City.

WEBSITES: LianaWernerGray.com and TheEarthDiet.com

We hope you enjoyed this Hay House book. If you'd like to receive our online catalog featuring additional information on Hay House books and products, or if you'd like to find out more about the Hay Foundation, please contact:

Hay House, Inc., P.O. Box 5100, Carlsbad, CA 92018-5100
(760) 431-7695 or (800) 654-5126
(760) 431-6948 (fax) or (800) 650-5115 (fax)
www.hayhouse.com • www.hayfoundation.org

Published and distributed in Australia by: Hay House Australia Pty. Ltd., 18/36 Ralph St., Alexandria NSW 2015 • Phone: 612-9669-4299 • Fax: 612-9669-4144 • www.hayhouse.com.au

Published and distributed in the United Kingdom by: Hay House UK, Ltd., Astley House, 33 Notting Hill Gate, London W11 3JQ • Phone: 44-20-3675-2450 • Fax: 44-20-3675-2451 • www.hayhouse.co.uk

Published and distributed in the Republic of South Africa by: Hay House SA (Pty), Ltd., P.O. Box 990, Witkoppen 2068 • info@hayhouse.co.za • www.hayhouse.co.za

Published in India by: Hay House Publishers India, Muskaan Complex, Plot No. 3, B-2, Vasant Kunj, New Delhi 110 070 • Phone: 91-11-4176-1620 • Fax: 91-11-4176-1630 • www.hayhouse.co.in

Distributed in Canada by: Raincoast Books, 2440 Viking Way, Richmond, B.C. V6V 1N2 • Phone: 1-800-663-5714 • Fax: 1-800-565-3770 • www.raincoast.com

Take Your Soul on a Vacation

Visit www.HealYourLife.com to regroup, recharge, and reconnect with your own magnificence. Featuring blogs, mind-body-spirit news, and life-changing wisdom from Louise Hay and friends.

Visit www.HealYourLife.com today!